THE RIVER AND THE DOWNS
Kent's Unsung Corner

THE RIVER AND THE DOWNS

Kent's Unsung Corner

by

MICHAEL BALDWIN

LONDON
VICTOR GOLLANCZ LTD
1984

First published in Great Britain 1984
by Victor Gollancz Ltd,
14 Henrietta Street, London WC2E 8QJ

British Library Cataloguing in Publication Data
Baldwin, Michael
The River and the Downs.
1. Kent—Description and travel
I. Title
914.22'304858   DA670.K3

ISBN 0–575–03463–7

Typeset at The Spartan Press Limited, Lymington, Hants
and printed in Great Britain by
St Edmundsbury Press, Bury St Edmunds, Suffolk
Illustrations originated and printed by Thomas Campone, Southampton

for
Liz and Barry

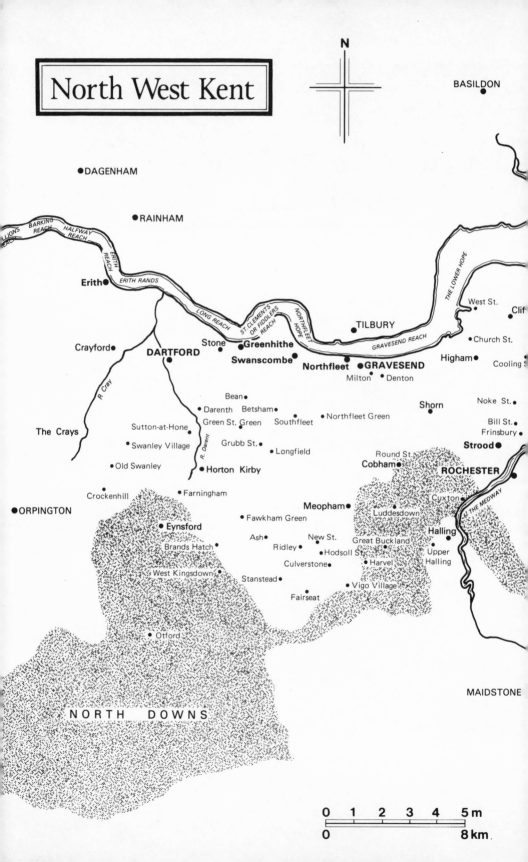

Maplin Sands

SOUTHEND ON SEA

Maursell
Fort

CANVEY

THAMES

YARLET CREEK

Allhallows

St. Mary's Hoo

Grain

ISLE OF GRAIN

ooling

High
Halstow

L. Stoke

Stoke

SHEERNESS

North St.

THE MEDWAY

MINSTER

Warden Point

Queenborough

Hoo

Eastchurch

Warden

pnor

Leysdown

LLINGHAM

ISLE OF SHEPPEY

HATHAM

THE ISLE OF ELMLEY

THE ISLE OF HARTY

THE SWALE

The Ferry Inn

Milton Creek

SITTINGBOURNE

FAVERSHAM

N O R T H   D O W N S

CONTENTS

ILLUSTRATIONS

All photographs by Gillian Beale

CHALK AND WATER

CHILD ON A PADDLE STEAMER

A watermill strapped to a bus
It froths in slowly, big as Crystal Palace,
Docking its name by the upstairs rail.
There is lipstick on its funnel and it smells of beer.

Men with chins blue as buckets
And flags on their forearms stand flexing anchors
All tarry-eyed. Their fingerends
Weave rope from tobacco, splice steam and cloud.

They cough live seagulls, oysters, fish
But tread oh so delicate around
Little whelk-haired women with scented
Brooches and smiles on hatpins.

Then the big mills churn and they all grow busy
With stout and lettuce, while down beyond the Fiddlers
Dwindling with distance in Gravesend Hope
Liners go hull-down on greenwater salad.

NEVER MIND WINTER. Here was where summer was invented, the skies an incredible chemical blue, written on by cranes and funnels and chimneys; the grass in garden and park vivid because grounded on chalk. All down our side of the river there were pits for digging this chalk and factories for burning it, between them making ten-acre fields disappear into hundred-foot holes of sunshining dangerous water.

For mile after mile of childhood, everything was chalk. Here it was gritting the sole, then collapsing dizzy underfoot in scars and drop-ends and quarry-lines. And here it was falling through the air, when the skies were serene and the sun looked witless. Just beyond Northfleet a certain drift of wind would make the black hulls of roofs become cloudy white, and then if you all stood still you could see it turn your friends into cemetery statues. In those long ago magic places the trees did not end in leaves but brandished fists of cement or limped under powdery rigging, so the eye crossed the riverline easy from copsewood to salty barge.

Behind us, away from the river and the pits, were slow-rising hills. These too were scabbed in white, and covered in woods and weeds that only prosper on chalk, straggling and limp in the hollows, rock-edged and black on the scarp, as if it were a world undersea.

Easy to feel submerged, or up to the waist and half-seas under, without slipping once from the washed-over planking of the estuary jetties. At the bottom end of town, every town, at the street foot of half the riverside villages, there was always a point where the brightly painted ships seemed to float overhead, to be upstairs in some higher dimension than the clinker-built houses which rattled from the throb of their engines. It was partly the tilt of those ancient high streets, from Stone right round to Strood and beyond; partly the cliff-sided tallness of the coal-burning liners of the old P. & O. and Orient with their arrogant funnels; but much more the fact that the low ends of towns were always under water-level, weighed down to the gunwale of their riverwalls and seawalls like overloaded lighters and anxiously aware of the Plimsoll line. When the wind sat right on the tide, generally in spring, then the town-ends sank and the whole town knew it. Out on the marshy levels the sheep would panic and be drowned, the cattle be stranded. In 1953 during the big neap, the estuary wall broke in as if Kent had been driven on to a large rock. Between Milton and the Hundreds there were dozens of communities flooded and farms irretrievably ruined.

For a child it was exciting territory, rich in itself and with challenging limits. The river was vast, with a strange soil beyond. As you turned to watch it east it became wide as the sky, and ships appeared out of it first by masthead then by funnel, then by bridge and by topside, and those bridges and those topsides often thronged with yellow faces. "Laskers," someone would spit. "She's a complement of Laskers." Then the vessels would drop anchor, two, three and four in a line, queueing into Tilbury or up to the Pool, waiting for a Pilot and a clean bill of health, and the yellow men and brown men, and strange tattoo'd white men, would gather in the waterfront pubs, having swarmed in by jolly boat or bribed the local watermen to ferry them ashore in their bawleys and their peters and their back-sculling dobles — a child could be in raptures just to listen to such names; only children were hurried past them, tucked up under baskets or bundled into prams. And this was another mystery, for men who came from ships, men of whatever colour, were very friendly to children and more so to their mothers.

Once the yellow men were in, and the promenade unavailable to us, even the Fort Gardens swarming with red-bobbled Frenchmen, there was nothing else to do but take us off for picnics. But even these led straight to magic. Behind us, as I say, the land lifted slowly; but a few pennies' bus ride would take you where it dropped off the end of the world — not a distant drop, but deep enough for childhood; for the lands at the foot of that fall, the lands of the Kentish Weald with their different churches and trees, looked enchanted and indistinct, whether seen through summer haze or a dull autumn mizzle.

Slowly even we townschildren would learn the names of the chalk trees we found ourselves among, and many of us would follow our parents' short social migration to the hill-line and live there for ever; but that would be later, and much would have changed, but not the ancient landscape of river and downs, not the marshes widening between them, not entirely the high streets and churches, and certainly not the chimneys. The Kent riverside still makes its paper and cement and makes it more and more.

All that would take time and growth and a war, and many of our changes are due to the alterations bombs make, for we were both a target and a jettison area. But I started as we all started in a street full of women. It is the women I remember, for I began in an age when men were not domestically important, and women once married did not go to work.

There was a small house whose back wall was the boundary between Gravesend and Northfleet, my grandmother's house. It was built of stock brick like 10,000 others, had a front bedroom that ran the width of it, and two tiny rooms behind that folded round the staircase. The beds were of loose-knobbed brass, and deeper than cloud-filled pits, each with several mattresses of feathers. I would share them according to room either with my grandmother or with one of my two aunts, sinking into infant sleep by myself but waking at dawn to find one or the other of them mysteriously there — no, not quite there, already rising and washing at tiled and marbled washstands, tilting water from kettles and ewers. Playing up and down the road with friends I soon found the others' bedrooms much the same, save they lacked my grandmother and her beautiful daughters.

Downstairs there was the bay-windowed front parlour, narrower than the room above by the width of the passageway; and behind that the living-room kitchen, which was narrower again by the width both of passage and stairs. There was a range out back in the scullery, which also had a built-in copperwash. We called this last the copper, though it was not made of copper but from cemented brick and iron. There was no bathroom, but no one with a copper needed a bath.

The lavatory and the coalhole were both out back, and both back to back with the neighbours' lavatory and coalhole, with which they were connected by airvents. Nan, my grandmother, was rarely stirred to visit the lavatory unless she heard Mrs Beadle, our neighbour the policeman's wife, opening her own back door and slamming her lavatory door to go likewise. It was a code. That way, the ladies could sit and talk through the airvent for an hour at the time uninterrupted by husbands and children. Everyone's house was the same. Everyone's mums and nans and sisters and aunts did the same. A man who went out when he heard one of the neighbouring women go out would be regarded with suspicion; and several did and were. It was, after all, a way to chat to a woman not your own. When I see working girls going to the cloakroom together at discos and parties, I wonder whether the custom didn't have its ritual origin in those old back-to-back terraces that sprang up all over England at the time of the Industrial Revolution. Perhaps not. I once heard my nan reciting while she was in there, and idling closer I noticed Mrs Beadle doing likewise. They were murmuring the prices of soap and soda and sugar. Mrs Beadle the policeman's wife had fallen on hard times since her husband had been pensioned off, and had followed many another lady in opening a small shop, hidden and undeclared and unlicensed behind the lace curtains of her front parlour. My nan and she were merely engaging in a little barter, to cut down the chaffering time in that illicit shop. Now I come to think of it, Mrs B. used to spend much more time there than my nan did, and my nan used to have visitors from up and down the street who would slip out the back the moment they arrived, like ladies incommoded by a long journey. But sometimes my nan would merely chat, I know that, about the weather and such things. Sometimes she merely spoke about the garden.

We had a flint-walled garden, flint because we lived near to chalk and flints grow in pockets in the chalk, can be picked up in garden or field, or dug out richly in Deneholes or Daneholes. Flint-mining began in the Stone Age, but lasted in Kent until the beginning of this century, for flint is one of our early building materials, used by the lowly in past times as a foundation under wood, and by the architects of church and tower as a facing stone between patterns of Kentish Rag.

The garden was hemmed in between an elderberry tree* — another local name for a local growth — and a flint-walled stable where a baker kept his horses. Working people were just beginning to buy cars, but there were no garages for cars. Street sales did not thrive on petrol engines; they still called for horse-drawn vans. There were dozens of small bakeries in town, all making real bread, but only the bigger ones delivered. If they delivered they delivered by horse, and their bread tasted of fields and beasts and leather, like the countryside drying after rain.

There was the smell of those horses, bread-horses, and that tree, the odour of dockleaves and nettles, and the cool breath of flint. People go into raptures about flints, pretending to themselves they're quern-stones or knocking them for fossils; but a flint's best magic is its smell. I've seen old men sort flints by nose before building walls with them. If you can't catch the scent of a flint then you've no sense of history and very little chance with the supernatural. In this bit of country we have both skills, as I was told early, but lockjaw is prevalent as well, growing in our gardens under rusty ground. Tetanus, like arthritis, is related to flint.

I remember my mother complaining of arthritis, by which she meant leg-ache, to an old countryman on our first move to the Downs.

"Arthritus? Not yet you ain't. You might get stiff joins, but if you had arthritus I'd smell it."

"So what does it smell of?"

"Midway between flint and chalk. That's why there's so much of it hereabouts. You go and rub your joins."

He went back to sniffing flints and fitting them into a hole in the

*"Elder" in English, of course.

wall of St John the Baptist Churchyard at Meopham. Part of the church itself was flint, as was St Mildred's at Nurstead and a dozen others about; but this did not interest me so much as my mother's joins. Women, I thought, were made all at once, not cobbled together with joins.

I shall have to write of language later. Clearly we had crossed a language boundary. In those days you could do so simply by moving from one side to the other of the old Dover Road, the A2. South of that line, as Taffy Richards, my much-revered English master, said, they had a dialect. On our side we had a disease. Our main symptoms, more pronounced than those of the South-East London sickness, and at their vilest and most virulent in Swanscombe he averred, were a kind of rising hysterical chew to the voice, culminating in a damnably wet — as distinct from the Surrey dry — glottal stop. It is not a tongue to take much of at the time; so we are shy about it with strangers, and either use Kentish posh — a modern accent brought to its highest pitch of perfection by Edward Heath — or laugh a lot. It's an eager gallopy four-in-hand kind of talk that leads well into laughter, particularly when our syntax runs wild. But then we are as lax with syntax as with sense. Witness myself who started with soil and gardens.

In my grandmother's garden the tilling was full of grouts and a fine shell or shale not unlike coaldust. Some of it was coaldust, no doubt, for we bought cheaply and thus bought dust, though we tried to burn what we bought. Similarly the grouts could sometimes be recognized as tea-leaves or the peel of finely scraped potatoes, for the land itself had little surface. But the soils would have been acid even without all this, in spite of the proximity of chalk and lime. It is alluvial on the lip of the town, for our foundations mix with the river, which once flooded all over hereabouts then ebbed back during Roman times, leaving us first with this bottled tilth, a kind of dried-out methane bog that runs half up the town, and then a kind of stench clay which packs down harder to dig than concrete, and which navvies hereabouts call bullhead. Bullhead is full of unextractable aluminium which festers in the lungs for days and makes the breath smell like a furred kettle; and in my experience of trenching it actually comes to colour the spit — so even on the dried-up marshes or the dip slope of the Downs, both fine places for beef, bullhead is not a term of affection. General Gordon of Khartoum despaired to find it in his garden here, and Pocahontas — sad Indian Princess — lies buried in it, typically so engulfed that the thousands of American visitors who come to pay her their respects each year cannot find her grave. Mercifully, underneath it somewhere, or beside it somewhere, say a street away, is the chalk; and it spreads even more, now the bombs have blown it up in petals.

A road full of the old working class, more rigidly hierarchic in these small Kentish communities than ever in London. Perhaps, indeed, working class is a wrong term, or one that only fits the industrial conurbations. We had labourers truly, but none, now I come to think of it, in our street. I was the first one from Salisbury Road to sink to that. Upon that unskilled band, slender in town and slimmed almost to invisibility in the country, rested a whole aristocracy of tradesmen, by which I mean men with a trade, each subcontracted to for his own labour, and each proud of his place. My grandfather was a cabinet-maker, and thus above the family opposite who were merely carpenters. But that family had chintzes and carriage clocks, took their tea with an indefinable air of superiority which came from being carpenters and not merely joiners like one or two they could name further down.

I dwell in the past because such people do not migrate. They move if their job dies, true; but such jobs do not die easily. They migrate socially, but not far, for their job is their society; and they know that life is a matter of ladders and boxes which must be taken in sequence and treated seriously. If they move up a box or two then they still do not move out of the district. How could they? Their work is here. They buy here; they make here; they sell here. They move up a street or two, opting for one of the taller parts of town. Between the wars, when distances were longer, they sometimes packed up, like my parents, and moved into the country, say a whole three miles. Today, the same people do it less. They have cars. The town has grown bigger, four times bigger, but it is still small; and they know that in less than the few miles my family moved they can have the whole Kentish hinterland at their back door like a garden.

Why are we all so parochial? It is a local rather than a national phenomenon. My grandmother lived in her last house for some 55 years. She moved twice, each move a matter of a few hundred yards, to get there. The move out to the country churchyard, from Salisbury Road to St Mildred's, Nurstead, where she could lie buried beside my mother, was the longest migration she ever made, nearly the longest journey of her life. And so it has been for the shopkeeping classes, including the sea-rich eighteenth- and nineteenth-century ships' chandlers, and for nearly all of our county folk.

Look at the list of patrons, guarantors and subscribers of the original Gravesend to Wrotham Turnpike in 1825, now the A227, the busiest road in North Kent. The names are still prominent among us. The great houses such as Meopham Court, Nurstead Court, Cammer Court are still more or less kept up along its length, and by the same families; the lesser farms and businesses have been amalgamated by marriage, divided again among sons and daughters. Matrimony is the main tide, and the bridal drive the extent of its flood. The plots are preserved in the older churchyards; and in the churches themselves of Meopham, Nurstead, Milton, Wrotham, Snodland and Hoo, just to commence the litany, the memorial tablets stretch down the centuries. In Cobham Church some of these same families trace their more distant scions in the finest brasses in the country. I have been away a long time, but now I return I know all of the faces here; and the occasional unknown face, as in those brasses, is some unguessed-at familiar palimpsest.

I made an earlier return, the fool's return, in 1952. This was to a local T.A. regiment, the oldest volunteer regiment in the country and one which predated every foot regiment in the Line, including the Guards. It was founded by Henry VIII, and among its Battle Honours — the term is used loosely — it can claim the distinction of being the only English regiment to have successfully fought the Royal Navy. It engaged the entire Nore Fleet at the time of the mutiny, and after a brisk cannonade from the fort at Gravesend compelled it to surrender.

The Battery Sergeant Major formed my bit of this regiment very efficiently into threes, called it to attention and gave it to me. When I had dismissed the parade, some half a dozen men were able to step forward and claim kinship with me. Baldwins are everywhere, of course, and not all of them the work of that dirty Flemish Count; but I doubt if there is a Rowe or a Sprigmore in these parts, not to mention a Crittenden, with whom I am not in some way connected.

Most of the inbreeding is honourable and decent, but sometimes I wonder. When we migrated to the village, the old village, there was a good solid farm labourer who lived with his sister, a fey girl noted for her cider and bread-pudding. She was also good with bees, so we could see why he wouldn't let her go.

When she bore his child one or two people murmured — outsiders like ourselves mostly. Questioned, and my mother was a great questioner, he claimed he had married her on a special dispensation and licence from the Archbishop of Canterbury. Canterbury seemed a million miles off in those days. So did the local vicar, for the village was by repute the longest in England, so long that one end of it didn't even reach the War. The village bobby was omniscient, no doubt; but what was there for him in this? Ostracism by one and all if he stuck his nose in, let alone a warrant; and certainly no more cider and bread-pudding.

Is it some sinister chain of consanguinity that keeps us anchored here? Is that what I am suggesting? Hardly. I think it is something I have not yet touched upon; I think it is the riverside tradition.

Half of us have seafaring blood; and a sailor may wander the world by water, but he never stirs far by land, for the sea uses him up. So we are made up of those who sail away and those who await the gift-laden return (when my grandfather was ship's carpenter with the Orient Line the only gift he brought back for my grandmother was his dirty washing). There is less of it now, but in the 1930s it seemed as if half the male population of North Kent was afloat. If a man was not content to plant himself on land he could seek his living on the water, either deepsea or river; it was all one to us for here was the margin between salt-tide and sewer-tide and we treated both callings with equal respect.

So away would go the restless one, like any Saxon warrior in his longboat; but he would always come back here to harbour and to lie, as every sailor says, "in the lee of his own woman". Here he would keep his home and make his family, and here he would come to die; for there are more sailors buried in the green grass of the Downs than ever in the Atlantic.

Here too is my place, somewhere between the river and its hilly backdrop. And this is what I write about.

THE THAMES — DOWNSTREAM BY BOOK
AND BOAT

RED SANDS AND THE MAUNSELL TOWERS

Groaners unreal as a gramophone;
The pulse of ships. I needle the trough
Then ridge up slow. The estuary
Patters its doleful plastic;

I know its tempo, its chomp and tromp.
The marshland straining its evergreens
Sets too much salt (is it
Ice?) on the lip, its waters stiff

As if rowing kale. Lobster pots
Clutter the oar. I shoal
Above ginger gravel while waves
Show me stilted spectres, five in a ring:

The Forts like arthropod giants
Bob closer, skirts up in cloud,
Heads grinning rain. Then the sea
Breaks open on nearly land

Neither Kent nor nothing, neither
Silt from the sun, nor Roman garbage,
But a hegemony of mackerel
Where gulls fish for bombs.

THERE ARE HUNDREDS of books about the Thames, and some of them
have been in and out of print for centuries, renewing themselves much
like the river. With one or two honourable exceptions they are an
affront to the men of Kent and Essex, and therefore to the river itself; for
whether they choose to see it as sewer or salad-bed their authors get so
exhausted punting, sculling, paddling or chuffing past Oxford to
London and noting its locks and bridges that by the time they reach

Greenwich they are content to stagger into the Trafalgar Tavern or Cutty Sark or some such potting shed in S.E.10 and hang up their jockstraps for ever. The buildings are noble all about: locks, lashers and bridges are things of the past, and they fancy they are at the last frontiers of effort and decency.

I have known a book-sailor or two be attracted further — by Gallions Reach, say. What a name. Unfortunately Bugsby's Reach slithers ahead, with Blackwall and Woolwich Reaches on either side, and whoever reads or dreams about Bugsby? To be fair, the north shore gets itself into a mess about here. The Royal Victoria Dock, with its neighbours Royal Albert and King George V, aren't what they were. There are bulldozers where one looks for masts or Far-Eastern funnels; and riverwards, addled on the fierce southern loop between their deaths and entrances, squats modern Silvertown, an architect's nightmare realised in blocks of cheese, its mould changing hue with the weather. It is a year or so since I walked that bit of the north shore and things may be better. An empty dock is the most desolate sight in the world, a sort of wasteland made of water. Woolwich has its fans, though for the purpose of this book I don't need to be one of them. Suffice to say that it enjoys the advantage of nestling against Shooter's Hill, towards which it rises in a way which looks green in most lights. There is an old saw which says that the Kent side of the river is graced by its low hills, and the Essex side by being more than a bowshoot from Kent. The remark needs to be looked at, but I have always taken it in our favour.

It is a pity that the river is falling idle. The estuary can stand it, but not here. Writing of the stream hereabout, Conrad, the greatest of nautical authors, says:

> This stretch of the Thames . . . is to other watersides of river ports what a virgin forest would be to a garden. It is a thing grown up, not made. It recalls a jungle. . . .

The live undergrowth of this jungle is being cleared, the docklands demasted. Gallions Reach is a disappointment, particularly since — again on the north shore — it terminates in a sewage farm and then Barking Creek, where dwells the young lady of limerick fame. The general thrust of her misfortune suggests that the lesser shore may be able to boast the only recorded Thames mermaid.

But I have more or less done with floating on a book. I am reaching the broadening water where my own book begins. I shall need a boat.

The Thames is never easy. It is always colder than it looks, at least by a topcoat; and out in the estuary proper it strikes through heavy clothing to the bone at the very same time your binoculars see landsmen lounging in the sun. Here it can chill you or not, though there is generally a fine stinging breeze which seems to blow up from the East and rattle along the water. There are no opposing hills to form a funnel, and the buildings, less and less at the river's edge, are not high enough or dense enough to conduct it. So the wind must follow the water, and it is wet like water, water perhaps expressed as another element. No sooner does it grab you by the shoulderbone and kidneys than you recognize it for what it is, an icy little draught that has blown all the way from the Caucasus then picked up some spume in the North Sea. On a lucky day, it sets a little by south, in which case there's an occasional grain of comfort from Tashkent. More often I find it by north, and before I have wrapped my mouth in a scarf it has packed both my lungs with Siberian tundra.

The channel is well marked here with port and starboard buoys, and from Tripcock Ness it continues to widen, so by Halfway Reach there is nearly a thousand yards of water at high tide. This is what the maps say, and the river charts confirm it, but things seem different to the eye and to common sense.

The bends are abrupt, and even a powerful launch can snag wide on the tide, and again with the push of the stream. For the old spritsail barges, and even for modern lighters, there is the wind to consider as well; and the same goes for any other boat with enough topside. It is not a stream to take without ballast, even this far inland.

Sailors need to be cautious. Yachts do come this far up, and there are dinghies and other kinds of drop-boards a-plenty, but often only slumming over the shallows or dodging between the mudflats. An old boatman I knew told me that the best rig for these waters is a ketch or a yawl, something with balance. "If you want to float under one stick, buy a cutter not a sloop." He insisted that floating on running water was a whole lot more tricky than dealing with the sea. History supports his view. Barges, whether spritsail, as in the Thames, or gaffed, as elsewhere, always sported a mizzen and thus became yawls or ketches. Long years ago, the bigger little coasters used to progress under a pair of fixed, then balanced, then standing lugs; and did so for at least a thousand years, as soon as the Romans then the Danes stopped rowing.

I am still off Cross Ness, between Barking and Halfway Reaches, and several dangers become apparent at once. There are shallows to starboard, then two miles down to port by Frog Island, and all kinds of ebbs and ripples where the River Ingrebourne washes in from the North Shore. Immediately on the port beam it is shallow again, and three jetties or hard ladings push to where the tide sucks on the outside of the bend. They won't fool a watchful man, but ten-to-one I'm gawping up at the power lines that sag menacing overhead from bank to bank in a single kilometre span. Then behind those jetties there is the severe but interesting face of the Ford Motor Works at Dagenham. There is always some kind of wharfing and winding going on there to take the eye; then the brain starts to turn and I remember going there as a boy, and being shown the sixteen-acre assembly shed, before blocking my throat with soot in the foundry. Milton would have been a better poet for seeing either of those places.

There are riverbirds here, and down at Frog Island (the frogs are nowdays only a rumour, but one that the gulls remember) I have occasionally seen one tustle with what might be a fish.

I was talking of danger. You see how easily the boatman is at risk? Smack ahead of me and plumb opposite the Dagenham distraction a monstrous pier blocks half the river. It is T-shaped, so at certain heights and sets of the water it can become a terminal trap. It fronts a sewage farm and not one that serves the gentler needs of Kent but all South-East London.

According to some reports the Essex sludge that once disfigured the waterline, and the nose between Barking and Rainham Creeks, is now shipped off by scow into the North Sea; and I suppose such measures would be necessary with the stuff from that side of the river. So what is this huge pier? One map, and my own bleared glimpse of a signboard, speak of the G.L.C. main outfall. I shall leave it at that, save to say that outfalls, as well as creeks and the entrances to tidal basins, are a further menace to small craft.

It is always here, or round the next bend, which I will not anticipate, that you meet something big and moving fast. In the high old days of my youth, when the P. & O. and Orient liners used to waddle up nose to tail intermixed with smaller traffic, ships were wont to go at a walk.

Nowadays there is less in their way, and they are less used to stopping. Sooner or later one of them is going to skid up a high street and never float again, merely live to be licensed as a local curiosity. Meanwhile, keep out of their path. They may be coasters or containers, they may be panicking back for more Essex effluent — it is nearly always halfway to dark when they arrive on top of one, screws pulsing insanely and towing a wash like a tidal wave — all I know is they are dangerous.

You may see the pier and the approaching Leviathan, and you may be ready to flirt between the pair of them, then suddenly the shore will disappear, they will disappear and you will disappear. You can see your hand in front on your face perhaps, or at least the instantaneously forming drip on the end of your nose; but unless your nose is magnetic you have not the least idea of where you are. And even if it is and you have, then where are they? Even piers and jetties walk about in conditions like this, and a motor vessel can be anywhere. For the moment it is a noise all around you and accelerating fast.

You are caught in a fret from the Essex marshes. It is a fact of life, and not my invention, that these damps are always from the Essex marshes and the shallow lands beyond them. But why this should be in the 1980s beggars comprehension when you consider that East Ham, Barking, Ilford and Dagenham are built all over them and there is no marsh left except inside the greenhouses of industrious people. There is, to be fair, a little Hornchurch Marsh off the port bow, so called because it is at Dagenham; and this side of Rainham as we leave the reach and ease to starboard round the Power Station and Jenningtree Point on the decent side, there are — again on their side — some silt lagoons and clay pits. Then vistas open out, save we can't see them, and Rainham Marshes, Wennington Marshes and Aveley Marshes lie around in saturated bulk, large enough to manufacture mist and scored by all manner of cuts, dykes, and creeks.

Of course, there has been similar terrain on our side all the way from Woolwich, though backed by little mounds and one or two slopes of substance, but — as every mystery writer knows — it is the Essex marshes that are misty. And this Essex fret, which has been kind enough to hold off until now, can strike you down at Ratcliff or the Lower Pool, in fact anywhere up to the City, where it is called something else. In any event, it doesn't really matter up there. A pleasure-boat skipper once told me that above Greenwich fog presented no problem. If it shut down hard he used to take his boat out of the water and follow a bus.

Clearly the big boat missed us and we dodged the erectile shore, because we've entered Erith Reach. Erith itself is the first community on the landscale proper of this book. It lies due north of the main thrust of the River Cray, and geometry must start somewhere, even when bound by hills and streams.

Indeed, Gallions Reach itself is north of the Crays, though nowhere near the little river's outfall. And I began with Gallions Reach because it is here or just hereafter that the Thames changes its character. It is no longer boxed in; the world stays away from its edge, which is increasingly wet, and there is a sense of surging onward to the sea. Here the old paddle boats used to get their heads down and churn, and the jazz and disco boats know they must turn about, or that small keen wind we noticed before will send the dancers and the couples below. From Halfway Reach onwards — I except Erith Rands but not Erith Reach — the reaches stretch long enough, and their length is exaggerated by the increasing width of the bends, for a dinghy or bawley boat to go hull down, particularly to another one of its ilk or a person sitting on shore. The wind setting up the reach can hump the water by a foot or two; and lower down, at Garrison Point, a strong wind can increase or diminish the levels predicted by the Admiralty Tide Tables by several yards. I have several times fired the Six-Inch Mark 24s from there and found the water shift more potent than in the English Channel. Or sharper than at Dover, where I have also fired.

If we talk of wind, then we need have no more mist. The Erith Reach is a fine stretch of water, and its margins hold much that is good. The Romans must have delighted in the promise of higher ground to the south after so much marsh. Much of their way upstream from Cliffe onwards would have been through a labyrinth of mudbank and sedge; but wherever the mainstream stayed south it ran close to better ground. At Erith the Thames cuts right against the heart of the town, and a town on a bank, as distinct from a margin, is a town with a good heart.

Coming down the Reach, our way, we do not see Erith against high ground. We see it *as* high ground. A little knoll of bricks conceals half of a tiny hill, and the finest theatre in North Kent huddles among them. The High Street has been running beside the water, and now loops up the hill.

Nearer the water, if that's possible, stands the police station, with an

L-shaped jetty beyond it. What most maps fail to show is a long walkway of plank going straight into the tide. Here women parade their dogs, and boys pretend to fish. The water is brisk here; there are no groynes or outfalls, but if there are fish anywhere, this is where they'll be, lodged between pier and planking and nibbling at the bounty of a friendly town.

I was glad of the temporary fret. A mile behind us was an ancient marsh. All marshes are ancient, of course, but some of this one has died. The G.L.C. has stepped in and, mercifully west and north of my remit, has planted Thamesmead. Here where Diplodocus, Brontosaurus and the other huge Jurassic sauropods waddled and waded stand the stiller monsters of concrete. Thamesmead is a bold design, but I am glad it is not ours. There is something oddly blighting about man's attempts to quell the Thames marshes. The result is often ugly and clouded with suicide. I am reminded that from the mud below Belvedere, down past Denton and the hulks, then beyond Sheerness to Thanet was the traditional haunt of the ague, which afflicted labourers and prisoners alike and was known by generations as Kent Fever and then, in more cosmopolitan parlance, Kentish Malaria.

It is about here that we can hear a distant popple of rifle-fire, or, if the wind is right, something nearer and sharper like sticks breaking. The wind will be the clue, because we are midway between two ranges, both on the Essex shore and both pointing towards us, or at least with their targets towards us. Behind us is the Rainham Range, with six targets and a 600-yard firing point, though only on one target. Ahead of us, but not quite looking at us down the muzzle, is the Purfleet Rifle Range, with only five targets, but with firing steps of between one hundred and one thousand yards on numbers One and Two. Purfleet has a barracks at the water's edge, and shallow Tank Hill behind it, so it is some kind of mark. Its chief claim to fame, a silly piece of etymological fooling by the inhabitants of the North Shore, is to pretend that it got its name because the first Queen Elizabeth stood among its quags and wept, "Oh my poor fleet." I was born to resent Her Majesty's fondness for the environs of Tilbury, and it is pub lore among the cognoscenti on our shore that what she in fact cried was, "Oh, my poor feet!"

These are not the only ranges up and down the river, and I shall mention more. An occasional hazard, and we continue to speak of the unsafe tide, is to hear ball ammunition squeal overhead. To hear it, on reflection, is no danger; because everyone knows you don't hear the one that kills you. The detonation of a rifle is a kind of navigational aid, less insistently precise than a bell-buoy or groaner. I was once lost in fog as dense as a sheep with an old back-sculler who should have known better but remained sure that we were still afloat. Suddenly we heard rifle fire, a lovely whack-snap of Lee Enfield that could only have been made by a platoon of men firing looseners at the butts. "Well, at least we now know some of the places we might be at," he said. His enlarged right wrist did a few more twirls with the scull, then he added, "Though how they can see to shoot when we can't even see to hear beats me."

A Trinity House friend of mine speaks of bringing up a Dutchman of some 6,000 tons, setting the helmsman steady on a nightmark, and having a bullet pass slap between them. He says such things happen often, though always from the Essex shore, perhaps because his story is told in a Kentish pub. The Trinity House breed is easily the most benign relative of homo sapiens. Like all watermen it has evolved the distinctive hot, bright or red nose that prevents it from colliding with its fellows in the dark.

We have by now chattered our way out of the Rands and rounded Crayford Ness Beacon, duller but more constant than a good nose. Were we running at night we should be looking towards another mark, Stoneness Lighthouse. That is on the Essex shore, opposite Greenhithe where the river curls abruptly the other way, almost by a quarter of a compass, and goes broadly north-east by Fiddler's Reach.

But that is a long way off, for we have just set ourselves into the beginning of Long Reach.

I shall not mention Slade Green, a little astern of starboard, because it is another denizen of the marsh, but this time with certain landward features to commend it. Old barge skippers will remind me that its Red House used to be a tack point. The wall has blunted some of that, and the choice is between the beacon and the outfall of the Darent River. This is abeam of us, and although not large it will be saluted later as flowing down from all sorts of poetry. A mile or so inland, just about where Dartford Salt Marsh becomes Dartford Fresh Marsh, is its confluence with the Cray. The cheeky descendants of Wat Tyler are rude to its pedigree and make it suffer the indignity of being rechristened Dartford Creek. But that is out of sight, muddled among cement mills and flour mills, and the upward sprawl of Dartford. If

our boat is low — and I am trying to gaze with a lugworm's eye and
not from a masthead — then much of Dartford will be lost behind the
bump of Joyce Green (hospital and settlement, not the Young Lady of
Dartford Creek).

We pass a shed or two, squatting salt-footed, and then come abeam
of Longreach Hospital, known locally and perhaps inexactly as the
Fever Palace. It is an isolation hospital and separated from mankind
the further both by being stuck between marsh and water, right at the
tide's edge, and from having as its nearest neighbour the West Kent
Outfall Works and Sewage Bed. We can see the Works but not the
cess, or not without climbing a mast. There is a clutter of piers and
jetties on the Essex shore to distract us, and the gleam and mod-
ernismo of refinery, and power, and petro-chemical, with the
dramatic, not to say beautiful, cement works standing further back at
West Thurrock. At evening, or in a storm light, this makes a pulsating
picture. There is illumination everywhere: cranes winch and dump by
the water, trains and hopper trucks shuttle slowly up and down like —
I nearly said glowworms till I recalled which bank of the river we were
speaking of. I shall move away from rapture but closer to poetry by
substituting radioactive maggots.

So much for them. We are now running past Stone Marshes, with
Stone Ridge and great chalk scars behind. We can see wounds enough
from the river, and one or two older cement works have soured this
part of the landscape with deposit; but it is the unseen holes which
interest me, the new ones back towards Old Watling Street and now
beyond, which peck off the blind face of Kent like leprosy. I can show
you the unseen holes. Not from a map and by compass. Not from my
local knowledge, because that would be a cheat, since infinite. No, I
can point out the great invisible by signs that are clear to the eye. This
is not merely the statement of a poet, even one who drinks with men
from Trinity House. The truth is that cut chalk bleeds, or that's how I
like to put it, and a low sky or a dusk above a chalk pit has an
unmistakable pink tinge to it.

On the water's edge again, and still on Stone Marshes, is the
considerable megalith of Littlebrook Power Station. It looks well
enough from a little boat, and there's a lading pier to avoid.

We are now directly above Dartford Tunnel, which ploughs a low
groove, partly of chalk, between Dartford and the shallow end of the
ridge. Its construction a dozen years ago marked a thaw in the

relationship between the two shores. It is possible to glimpse the toll booths from the river, and these will be seen to be where they belong, on the Kentish side.

This is still Stone Marshes, a fair way from little Stone, but so named to stop Dartford from becoming greedy. Stone is not much, but it has a double ration of cement works, both potent marks, and some of the rest of it is built of flint, rag and tufa. There is more to it than shows from the water, and it shares some of itself with a miracle called Greenhithe. Here the bank does come down to the tide, so Green Bank or more likely Green Harbour it is.

This is a place to stop at and kick a cobble or two, and I'll suggest so later. If we run aground there meanwhile we'll come to no harm, for it keeps its pubs on the water, and one of them has a pier.

Beyond a glimpse of architectural elegance in its main street and beyond, there are three things to notice from a boat. First there is a huddle of piers and jetties, suggesting its historic importance as a connection between chalk and water. As part of this complex of ancient and modern there is the modern yard and lading, the headquarter harbour, of Thomas Everard and Sons, a Line that trades worldwide, from coasting to deepsea. Coastal work is "navigating by the bannister rail", of course, but you have to be careful not to trip downstairs. My cousin was an officer with Everards' for a time, and he speaks of skippers taking their ships where the charts show no water, and of one who claimed he could steer all round the United Kingdom "by keeping the ship between the beach and the shore". "Between sea and shore" is Romantic Poetry, of course. That captain dealt directly in magic.

The next landmark is H.M.S. *Worcester*, at the other end of the hithe. The *Worcester* was a seamark and afloat, but now she is a long, elegant building ashore above spacious lawns, and her proud subtitle of Thames Nautical College is a little more to the fore. My cousin trained there when she was afloat, and she has had many famous captain-superintendents, of whom Commander Gordon Steele is a prime example. Steele served in the early submarine service, and then in Q ships, before moving to battleships and the fleet action of Jutland. He was by now a regular officer sporting the Oak Leaf — a signal honour, at least in the Navy's eyes, for one whose lineage was *Worcester* and P. & O. — and then the Russian War broke out, and he was on the way to an even more absolute glory. He died two years ago, and I have kept his obituary account of this. *The Times* is a trifle compressed, but it brings a whiff of powder to tiny Greenhithe:

The deeds of conspicuous gallantry and skill which won for Steele the Victoria Cross were performed on August 18th, 1919. Lieutenant Steele (as he then was) was second-in-command of H.M. Coastal Motor Boat No. 88. In the course of the operations against the Bolsheviks it was necessary for the motor boat to enter Kronstadt Harbour. Soon after entering, the Commanding Officer, Lieutenant Dayrell-Reed, R.N., was shot through the head, and in consequence the boat was thrown off course. Immediately Steele became aware of what had happened; he took the wheel and steadied the boat.

After lifting his Commanding Officer away from the steering wheel, he got his boat in a convenient position for launching a torpedo at the Bolshevik battleship *Andrei Pervozanni*. He fired at a range of one hundred yards, and had the satisfaction of seeing his torpedo find its mark. Not content with that, he turned his attention to the battleship *Petropavlovsk* which was overlapped by the *Andrei Pervozanni*, and was partly obscured by smoke coming from the stricken ship.

To get a clear view of the *Petropavlovsk*, he had an extremely difficult manoeuvre to perform, but the evolution was skilfully and successfully carried out, and the *Petropavlovsk* was torpedoed. It became imperative that Steele should make his way from the harbour as quickly as possible if he were to save his boat. He had only just room enough to turn in order to regain the entrance of the harbour, but he managed to do so with success. All this time his motor boat was drawing a heavy and concentrated fire from the line of forts. Nevertheless he passed close to the forts firing his machine guns all the way, and passing out of the harbour he saved his ship. The award to him of the Victoria Cross was notified in the *London Gazette* of November 11, 1919.

After that gallant exploit he returned to more peaceful duties. . . .

Ten years later these were to include taking command of the *Worcester*. *The Times* mentions that he lifted his pen from time to time. I note that three of his publications were on personal religious subjects. This is appropriate to the place, because before we drift ashore, I must point out our third mark, the trees that shroud the remains of Ingress Abbey. There are flint churches quite near, but visible or not these are for later. Ingress Abbey was built with stones from old London Bridge.

Fiddler's or St Clement's Reach it is, and we must hurry on. The shoreline is rich for half a dozen miles now, so all the more reason for coming back by land.

What we are going to see on the south shore, as well as little cliffs, old chalk scars, beacon points, high churches and one more marsh, is the detritus of old and not so old industry. Boatbuilding, tiles and timber are among the most ancient. But the most visible, multiple and dominant factories will be chalk and paper. There are new light industries and industrial estates springing up on once-flooded fields or in renovated wharfage, but cement and paper have dominated this part of the river for a century and been here much longer. And they, more than the outfall of London, have poisoned it.

I do not want to notice much about Swanscombe, Northfleet, Rosherville and Gravesend, because we must come back. Gravesend itself is large and, if the inhabitants of the other places will forgive me, the sandwiching of brick against brick is joining them all together. Our riverside problem is to decide what to lump with Dartford and what with Gravesend, with the slight complication that Gravesend is properly riverside and Dartford is not.

Another point is this. For much of the way, Kent has been secret. Yet once or twice now we can glimpse far inland, even floating on a plank. So the skipper of a tacking ketch, schooner, or earlier brig with boys to send up a mast, let alone the master of a full-rigged ship, could reckon on all kinds of landmarks somewhere round the apex of the Fiddler's and Tilbury Hope. A clipper with a skysail top on its mainmast could see right over the Downs.

Why the Fiddler's? Well, legend has it that St Clement, whose Reach this more properly is, was martyred by being lashed to an anchor and dowsed in the sea. An anchor is a fiddler, and St Clement's device is an anchor. There is a nastier suggestion, with a certain scholarship buried in its roots. Trinity House was in origin the Gild of the Holy Trinity and St Clement, with the saint's anchor for its emblem (the certain scholarship). No boat is allowed up the river

without a Trinity House pilot on board, and skippers loathing the
tariff frequently call them "fiddlers". Enough of that.

Tilbury Hope is narrower than the Fiddler's. Historically the
dredge line is wide about here, because we are close to the turning and
parking and overrunning areas above Tilbury Docks, if I may use land
talk. In fact, the genuine waiting place, the anchorage, is lower in what
I shall be bold enough to christen Gravesend Roads, a widening
stretch of water which starts in my childhood opposite the promenade
and runs right down Gravesend Reach into the glories of the lower
Hope.

We are still above all this, and becoming watchful. I spoke of
pinching shore and a widening dredge. As the tide bates (abates in
English), slackens and turns, so the big ones slew on their chains, and
the little ones follow. You can tell the time by them as if they were
clocks and watches. The thing about time on an ebbing tide is that
there is never enough of it. Fifty little boats that you thought were
fairly moored won't slew at all. They begin to perch higher and higher
on their own image, then almost separate from it. They are no longer
on the water but flat mud, so we need to stay close to the main dredge,
the navigational channel, and there are other and bigger boats with a
claim to it.

The dredger is always at work here, or down in the Lower Hope.
There are all kinds of modern ways to dredge, with modified vacuum
cleaners and power hoses, but these devices are for specialized tasks,
such as inspecting wrecks or clearing outfalls. They are secret and
silent. What a pity they and their divers are so expensive.

The Thames, alas, needs to be cleared by the acre. To do this
requires a powerful motor, the toothiest of gears, and a string of
gigantic beaked buckets on a substantial chain. The beaks are dragged
or dredged through the mud and shingle underwater then up into the
air and back in one continuous motion. At the back of the loop they are
upside down and disgorge their silt on to the heads of waiting
lightermen queueing alongside to take the river bottom away. The
noise is terrible, especially at night. It can be heard for miles inshore
and accounts for nightmarish and nightmaring children and hal-
lucinating adults. The work is more often towards the Essex shore,
and you can judge its effects by looking at the inhabitants of that side
of the river. Over here, from Denton down through the Hundreds,
there are legends of wailing and howling ghosts. I am respectful of

ghosts, and sneer at none of them. Yet I can place my hand on my heart and swear I believe that most of them are a bellyful of the local hops and an earful of the dredger.

Sometimes the chain breaks or a hopper fouls. A miraculous silence breaks out all under the starlight, and in it people make love, bear children and finish their accounts. Then it starts again.

Meanwhile notice the wreck buoys. Quite a few ships have given up and died about here. Along the mud there are little bawleys looking as if they are not going to struggle on top of the next tide, and some dobles that appear to have stayed beneath the last. A wooden boat makes a wholesome corpse, and the foreshore is always littered with wood, not all of it from boats. We have a lot of worm here, though not as much as Sheerness, and that helps break them. An iron boat is another matter altogether: a deathtrap if it sinks in the dredge, and a scabby eyesore if it bottoms out above the low-water line.

The Gauls and the Romans, and before them all the Iberians, would not have paddled up among such flotsam and jetsam, of course. Modern jetsam includes oil and tar barrels, sheet iron, barbed wire, car bodies and metal hatches, all things more or less of our time. Our flotsam is car tyres, plastic bottles, dolls, planking, tarred rope, clothing and "other testimony of summer nights".

Quite a lot of the objects on that list could sink us, and most of the rest would certainly foul a small boat's propeller. Yet the Gauls and Romans would have preferred our river to Cymbeline's. It is deep, has a constant tide, and for most of its way the shoreline is clear, not to say disgustingly self-evident. There is only one place now where a mapless foreigner could lose his direction, and that is at Sheerness. Then the Thames would have lacked a single channel, it would have lost itself in minor tributaries and squandered itself and its passengers' healths and senses in a six- to twenty-mile wide marsh, and for at least a part of the period it would have been closed up at low tide. Indeed, it is possible that the Romans rendered what is now the main stream constantly fordable somewhere between the Hundreds and the North Shore at a point where there are now clear miles of water. More of that later.

I spoke of constant tide. The Thames then would have been little islands. Some places that are town bumps now, Cliffe, Denton, Chalk, Lower Shorne (to designate an area innominate on the map) would have had water behind them. Conversely, much that is now under water would not have been then, as the number of Roman potteries, floors, boatyards discovered in the mud below the tidemark clearly testifies, both this side of the Hallows and round into the Medway. A tideway full of islands and uncovered flats is a terrible place. Leaving aside the fact that the neap and seep of water conspire with the latter to contrive a shifting scenario, even with the mud covered up and only islands to contend with, there would be navigational uncertainty. You can row round one side of an island, steering by the tide, only to be taken aback by the same tide bouncing round the other side. In clear water, tide is not only motion, it is sense and direction. Except for civilization's flotsam we have clear water now.

These thoughts started in Tilbury Hope. In spite of my bias against the other side I shall continue to call it so against breeding and common sense. Many watermen of my acquaintance, and they are bound to be the ones that live on the mariners' shore, call it Northfleet Hope, and so does the Ordnance Survey. Properly a Hope is down the tideway from its object, so Tilbury Hope is as ridiculous as the desire to reach Tilbury itself, but I let it stand in deference to Trinity House. (The Survey as such is not worth a fiddler's reach, because the 1:25000 contradicts the 1:50000, one printing Gravesend Hope, one Lower Hope.)

To our right, behind Swanscombe and Botany Marshes, is Swanscombe itself, seen as a flinty church on a chalky hump. The skull was found hereabout. The hump sags away, and then bucks up again. This is Northfleet, with industry, new piers, old jetties and older wharfage right at the water's edge. The town hump rises slowly, topped by two church towers, one in flint and rag, one in brick; but the scene is overmasted by an enormous chimney belonging to I.P.C.M. who have done something wonderful and futuristic to the riverfront and through tunnels which shine under the near end of the town.

More tall chimneys, though none as tall as this, and everywhere the glow of ancient chalk light. We shall walk this way later. Northfleet is a dusty place with excellent pubs. Meanwhile we have passed a gleaming petrol-storage and lading, and a small concrete lighthouse.

Just ahead, beyond a tangle of jetties and some holdwaters and breakwaters, is another chimney fronted by crumbling terraces. The terraces run endways to the water's edge, though their footings are some 30 feet above the mean. They were built at the beginning of the nineteenth century, and their stucco has taken an awful beating. A year or two ago I almost bought the one on the end. Dickens would have approved, and so would Conrad, though his stories haunt the other side of town.

I mention them as a piece of the river's history. They are at the beginnings of Rosherville, and behind them were Rosherville steps and the spacious landing. This was the site of a famous pleasure garden, accessible to Londoners by means of the early paddle steamers, and by the trains of the North Kent and Chatham Railway Company. Alas, it has gone.

Dickens didn't like Gravesend, perhaps because he spent his honeymoon here; but nineteenth-century London did; and for a time, when it was clean and gracious, it must have been the most elegant place on the river next to Greenwich. We shall come back, of course, but not by water; and by water was how it saw itself.

Beyond Rosherville (not the name to be found on many maps today) there was a foreshore which has slowly been filled in by industry. It wasn't all beauty then. There were ladings, and sheds and timber yards, some kilns and deliberate gougings of chalk. But Victorian England could take a little filth at its feet, and the foreshore was backed by a cliff, partly man-made and partly cut by the river. Along this clifftop ran a broad road protected by planted bushes and wrought iron gilded railings. A row of fine stuccoed houses, with steps and porticoes, ran along the back of the road, facing the river. We can see them today, but there is more to take the attention before the eye reaches them.

Then they made an attractive eyeline, and they were the skyline. No need to lower the gaze, whether from pleasure-boat or royal yacht, and consider the clapboard vista beneath. But even if one did, one need only see places of riverside cheer. Here there were wooden pubs with outside tables for ale, or children sieving and adults boiling freshly caught shrimps. The Gravesend shrimp used to be an immaculate object, sold by the pint or quart for a working man's Sunday tea. It died when Rosherville Gardens died. The name persisted, and perhaps still does, but the shrimp was netted further and further away from Gravesend.

Old Gravesend sprawled in a lump towards the river beyond the end of the Overcliffe. It had some brick or stone, generally flint, lower storeys, but the rest would be clapboard tops. It was a buoyant town, and it detected a gold rush, so it was all shanties. There was nothing unusual in three floors of clapboard, or a front wall of stuccoed brick, and three floors of wood at the back. In general most people built in undisguised clapboard, especially along the river. There is nothing wrong with clapboard: it is one of the traditional Kentish ways of building, so traditional that most of them built in Baltic timber barged up the tideway.

Councils hate clapboards. That is why so much history is vanishing fast. Instead of giving it a good coat of fireproof paint, councils like to stick a match to it and plant tulips. Gravesend Council did a lot of strange things to the postwar riverside; but so, to be fair, did Hitler; and lately sensibility is struggling back.

Tulips or not, you can now see that riverside Gravesend is not just the place where poor Pocohontas died. Ignore the fine gold dome on the steepled tower she lies buried under, itself just a spit from the shore, and fill up your eyes with the town pier and water steps. This and the Royal Terrace pier beyond are not little landings and ladings, but fine walled buildings on stilts, wooden-walled it is true, but the stilts are of iron. They sigh for much more than the *Royal Daffodil*, and she was a boat to sigh for.

Forget the dying Keats at anchor hereabout. He travelled far to write his name in water. Many boats from here have gone further, and their crews sunk further under. In the 1870s and 1880s the Orient Line based itself at Gravesend; and from here in 1887 the *Lusitania* steamed to Melbourne by the Cape in 40 days. The ships from the old Orient Line used to come back till the Germans took to wrecking them.

This was not the notorious *Lusitania*, of course. Though this one did wreck, but in other hands. Once the Orient Line proper was founded, all the newly commissioned ships were named alliteratively: *Orient, Ormuz, Ophir, Omrah, Orontes, Otway, Osterley, Orsova, Otranto, Orvieto, Orama, Ormonde, Omar, Orcades, Oronsay, Orford, Orion* and *Oriana*. Some of these names were used twice and "Orcades" three times, before the recent merger with P. & O. My grandfather sailed as carpenter with the *Orontes, Osterley* and *Orama*, and I remember these exciting floating palaces when I was taken to meet him. They were all between 10,000 and 20,000 tons gross, and the second and third *Orcades* were bigger still. Very striking they were in the offing, with their buff yellow funnels and corn cream hulls with green waterlines. Before then, and before my memory of them, they were black boats, but still with the green waterline; and before 1906 they had black funnels.

As well as the P. & O., other great shipping companies operated from the Thames, used these harbourages, and could be seen off Gravesend: Layland, Atlantic Transport, and White Star being but a few. The great life of the river, and its earlier history, was made up of single ship owners though, the colliers, timber boats, powder barges and for a time the great clippers. Nor must I forget the tugs and service vessels, the jolly boats and pilot cutters, the Port of London authority launches and the police.

Joseph Conrad first saw this stretch of the river in the 1890s. He was coming the other way, and he is worth quoting at length:

Then, on the slight turn of the Lower Hope Reach, clusters of factory chimneys come distinctly into view, tall and slender above the squat ranges of cement works in Grays and Greenhithe. Smoking quietly at the top against the great blaze of a magnificent sunset, they give an industrial character to the scene, speak of work, manufactures, and trade as palm-groves on the coral strands of distant islands speak of the luxuriant grace, beauty and vigour of tropical nature. The houses of Gravesend crowd upon the shore with an effect of confusion as if they had tumbled down haphazard from the top of the hill at the back. The flatness of the Kentish shore ends there. A fleet of steam-tugs lies at anchor in front of the various piers. A conspicuous church spire, the first seen distinctly coming from the sea, has a thoughtful grace, the serenity of a fine form above the chaotic disorder of men's houses. But on the other side, on the flat Essex side, a shapeless and desolate red edifice, a vast pile of bricks with many windows and a slate roof more inaccessible than an Alpine slope, towers over the bend in monstrous ugliness, the tallest, heaviest building for miles around, a thing like an hotel, like a mansion of flats (all to let), exiled into these fields out of a street in West Kensington. Just round the corner, as it were, on a pier defined with stone blocks and wooden piles, a white mast, slender like a stalk of straw and crossed by a yard like a knitting-needle, flying the signals of flag and balloon, watches over a set of heavy dock-gates. Mast-heads and funnel-tops of ships peep above the ranges of corrugated iron roofs. This is the entrance to Tilbury Dock, the most recent of all London docks, the nearest to the sea.

Between the crowded houses of Gravesend and the monstrous red-brick pile on the Essex shore the ship is surrendered fairly to the grasp of the river. That hint of loneliness, that soul of the sea which had accompanied her as far as the Lower Hope Reach, abandons her at the turn of the first bend above. The salt, acrid flavour is gone out of the air, together with a sense of unlimited space opening free beyond the threshold of sandbanks below the Nore. The waters of the sea rush on past Gravesend, tumbling the big mooring buoys laid along the face of the town; but the sea-freedom stops there, surrendering the salt tide to the needs, the artifices, the contrivances of toiling men.

Conrad does usher in a sad fact. With the opening of Tilbury Docks, Gravesend became less of a port. Sailors still visited us, of course, but only because they could not bear to set foot on the other shore.

What I seem to be bemoaning is decline, the decline of industrial Kent, perhaps, and of the river certainly. Let me say at once that there is every sign of recent resurgence, and look back at a few route causes.

The death of the pleasure-boat is part of it. It was inevitable, of course. Inland water is no longer an artery for travellers. The Londoner travels by coach or car, and few roads reach towards the river; and when they do, they stop. They do not follow it down. Gravesend is several miles from an arterial road, and the people who use that road do not know it exists. They are not interested in the watering places of the Thames and Medway, or few of them are. Rivers are an acquired taste, and for the shallow-minded they tend to be at best a second-rate sea. Londoners came to nineteenth-century Gravesend to sit on a man-made beach, look over Lower Hope with its bold hull-down diagonals and fancy they were by the sea. They had bands and fairgrounds and whelks, and it was nearer home than the sea, and more like home than the sea, and the weather even brighter than childhood.

In fact, the decline already threatened before the great years began. Once there were railways, London's river only satisfactorily served the north part of the continent of Europe. And ever since Chaucer's day there have been northern and East Anglian rivals for those routes. Southampton, Bristol and Liverpool were always better placed for the

North Atlantic, and it is interesting to note that P. & O. were based in Southampton until the 1850s. When they moved to London, they still had to pick up the Far-Eastern mail from Southampton, and deliver there on the return journey. London, Gravesend and Tilbury may have seemed psychologically right for the Eastern run, but only to people who overlooked that they steamed towards the rising sun only to double back.

The arguments for the Thames were simply the convenience of delivering to the heart of the metropolis, to use that fine eighteenth-century word, particularly if the cargo was too heavy or finicky to offload and restow.

Once water was no longer the swiftest or strongest carrier, and once the industries needed to expand, or move towards sources of power, then these arguments broke down, and another logic held.

But in fact trade is illogical. The movement of goods originally depended on the energies of men who wished to move them. These men were often slow to move themselves or their families, however. So Liverpool trade was achieved by Liverpudlians, London trade by Londoners. Success was often a matter of geographic accident. Success could be leisurely, and failure only followed as time grew faster.

This anomaly of will and energy and means triumphing in the service of ridiculous causes can best be uncovered by looking at some of the eighteenth- and nineteenth-century barge routes. The example will not be particular to Kent, though Kent holds a lot of unsuspected water.

Baltic timber used to be unloaded at Faversham, reloaded and barged up to London instead of being taken to London direct. Some of the yards at Faversham, Whittle's for example, acted as wholesalers for the entire riverside. With so much timber in use, and so many yards up and down the Thames and Medway, there was no real logic in this, only will.

In the mid-nineteenth century a Maidstone man found himself with too much timber on his hands, or was in need of cash, or simply met a need of someone else's — we don't know — so barged some of it all the way back up the Medway and round to Northfleet. I wonder if the order was repeated? I suspect it might have been. Trade is like that.

The White Star Line made a substantial effort in the Thames in the 1920s. She had been in the Thames for 30 years at an earlier time, but handling cargo rather than passengers. She took her cargo elsewhere, and when she came back for the passenger runs they did not pay. The challenge was not from her rivals as such, and certainly not from other forms of transport. It was from other ports.

Atlantic Transport came back to the Thames in 1922 with two large custom-built ships, *Minnetonka II* and *Minnewaska IV*. They were both about 22,000 tons, yet had accommodation for only 370 passengers. The rest of their bulk was for cargo. The Thames passenger points found it hard to deal with them.

The Thames has done what has to be done. It has served the capital. The capital now has other servants. The survival of shipping along the river depends upon industries independent of London such as paper and cement, or upon the will of innovatory imaginations.

Meanwhile our hands are cleaner than many. We have had a few smugglers, though legend is quicker with their haunts than their deeds or names; but we have not shipped horses and ponies, nor sold slaves. It is true that quite a few men bound for the penal colonies of Australia passed our way; but they were probably far better off there than being chained on our own Kentish hulks. When I come to think of those poor wretches, the Magwitches not at large, I give more credence to the stories of howling ghosts who rattle their chains.

A ferry crosses the river here, the first and the last since Woolwich. It is not the multi-decker thing it used to be, nor does it operate from the old Town pier at the foot of the High Street. It uses the floating landing of an earlier vehicle ferry, a few yards further west. The town pier is now a restaurant; but this at least represents half of its historic function, of providing a leisurely vantage point above busy water. It was never quite a pleasure pier; the pleasure was all around it, in the pubs and slightly more distant gardens; but in the old days, from halfway through the last century until 1939, it was possible to buy whelks, shrimps, crabs and oysters then walk on with a pint of beer from one of the two pubs at this entrance. The beer was frowned at, and in theory forbidden by by-law. The shrimps made a mess. There were winkles too, if you could find an old lady to lend you her hatpin. Latterly, until the pier's closure, we bought chips and sandwiches. They were not an improvement.

The other piers and jetties need not detain us now, though they all have their importance. A couple of hundred yards east stands a church with a belfry, this past broad green banks which were once covered with clapboard pubs and chandlers. The church looks to be built in newish tufa or rag from the limestone edge of the ridge, I don't know which. It is now an Art Centre, and a pretty little harbourage pushes around its back. Between itself and the harbour stands a boarded up house with a bulging wall. It was once a pub with a smugglers' tunnel to the river (take that with what salt you will); but later it became the home of Gordon of Khartoum's Boys' Mission, and then a Seamen's Mission. It is another place to add to my list of nearly homes. The bulge was more forbidding than the price.

Almost beside it is the yacht anchorage beloved of Edward VII and George V, and behind it the elegant frontage of the Royal Clarendon Hotel, now a steak house and pub, but at least decently renovated. In my younger days the bars were the colour of brown Windsor soup and old custard, and the stucco above the main entrance was peeling. We used to go there for dances, hoping to meet girls from the grammar school and convent, but generally finishing up doing sad waltzes with ladies who sported bushy underarms and whose faces were in even more need of renovation than the hotel. Still, royalty used to enjoy the place and sometimes so did we.

Past Gravesend the river will now take a great hump north before reaching the confluence with the Medway at Sheerness and the Isle of Sheppey. In other words, the Medway towns are comparatively close overland; they lie along a short hypotenuse; but to reach them by river is to traverse a tall triangle of awkward estuarial water.

In the eighteenth and nineteenth centuries there was a great traffic between Rochester, Chatham and Gillingham, and even Maidstone, as well as the various inlets of the Swale, and Gravesend, Northfleet, Dartford and, of course, London. Today the trip takes some hours in a fast launch. By sail it could take days and be tedious and uncomfortable. Past Allhallows and Grain there was the added discomfort of the localized "Old Boneless Wind" as it sucked itself over the Medway flats.

The "Boneless Wind" is an East Kent wind, a mariner's wind. The word "Boneless" is an illiterate but effective corruption of "Boreas", the Roman sailor's north wind, and the expression serves to set the teeth on edge quite as much as the reality.

So it is appropriate, as we leave Gravesend's forts and Promenade, that we notice the entrance to the Canal Basin. The swing gates of polluted wood and pecked iron now open on to a yacht and small boat anchorage; and although the canal itself runs away eastward past

gasworks and ancient and modern industry, to thrust its pewter sword
among upturned hulls, under blank bridges, asphalted cross-overs and
all manner of marshy detritus behind the riverwall, it is ultimately blunt
and blind.

What a noble project. It was at first a military one. The Thames
below Gravesend was closed by the cannon of two lines of blockhouses on the Kent and Essex shores. Around the Hundreds and
about Cliffe and Allhallows it was too broad to close effectively, or
even at all. In 1778 the naval dockyards of Deptford and Woolwich
needed to be linked for barge traffic with that of Chatham, so that
stores could be shipped, including powder from the lower Medway.
Plans were drawn, but abandoned. For two thirds of the way from
Gravesend it was a question of peripheral engineering and drainage
of marshland. Then came the chalk ridge that runs from Shorne and
knuckles north to broaden behind the Medway towns. This would
have to be cut. Some of the ridge was thought to be chalk rock. The
project was abandoned.

In May 1800 an engineer called Ralph Dodd received parliamentary
permission for a plan submitted in 1799 to cut a seven-mile-long canal
between East Gravesend and the Medway. It was to be 48 feet wide
and seven feet deep (the sailor's "long fathom").

Work began in 1809; the project, which eventually cost £300,000,
was completed in 1824. It did not comprise Dodd's original "deep
cutting" through the chalk. Instead, as with many a Midland canal,
there was a tunnel. This was two and a half miles long, it was 27 feet in
circumference and had a tow path. Thus it was the most manageable as
well as the longest tunnel in England.

Despite tidal difficulties it worked well, but always at a loss. Its
tariffs were high in order to recover the enormous capital investment,
and these perhaps repelled customers. The shareholders never received a dividend, but in 1844, with typical Victorian enthusiasm,
decided to hybridize their project and twin it with a railway. This they
did, and for a time trains and boats shared the tunnel. Late in 1845 the
canal use was abandoned, and the South-Eastern Railway Company
bought out the Gravesend and Rochester Railway and Canal Company.

Pleasure-boats were early forbidden its use, and foot travellers, who
anyway had to pay a toll, feared the two-and-a-half-mile tunnel. They
left Dickens' mudflats and marshes,

. . . the dark flat wilderness beyond the churchyard, interrupted with dykes, and mounds, and gates with scattered cattle feeding . . .

nd trod into the sallow mouth of the tunnel, through which the wind vas rushing.

Barges were the hoped-for traffic, but consider the toll in 1825. It ost two shillings and sixpence a ton to transport hops or wool, and alf that to take hay and straw. The wage then was round about fifteen hillings a week — as my grandmother said to me even in 1940 when I sked for sixpence: "Your grandfather has to work a long time for ixpence." An empty barge would be charged ten shillings, as much as he skipper paid his mate and certainly more than his boy or deck earner would get. And powder-barges (an important traffic) were aturally forbidden use of a tunnel.

A noble failure. It is there, partly filled in, its tunnel still unctioning. Enthusiasts seek to dredge it open, but one of its fillers is sbestos waste. Indeed, there was a sheet-asbestos industry in those parts between the wars.

So we traverse endless seawall and endless marsh, Denton Marshes, Milton Marshes, Higham Marshes, Cliffe Marshes, Cooling Marshes, St Mary's Marsh, and innumerable little marshes I am too ired to name and you to notice, as well as several marshes that God has left innominate.

Shornemead fort, a mid-nineteenth-century derelict, lies to starboard. There is Dickens' Chalk Church a mile inland, with the clustered cottages and big house of Pip's first dreams. Or was this further on, round by Cliffe and Cooling? Cliffe is a higher block among green cuts, and its great Church, St Helen's, was venerable to Saxons, and to all seafarers since. Then there are the humped fortifications of All Hallows, and its breezy little caravan site beyond strangely brazen sand. In winter, All Hallows needs St Michael and its unnamed saints because it worships the Boneless Wind. We have yawed widely since Cliffe corner, to keep away from flats, and posts, and minor wrecks. But it is high water and we can steal nearer to float above Roman villages unseen but excavated in the silt, Roman pottery, Roman ceramics and burials of Romanized Celts with shrimp tongue and the tides' swill in their mouths. There is a low green ridge all beyond, but it recedes in heat or rain, till the eye bumbles on

distance. This was malaria's home, the Kentish ague. Here at nigh
Grey Ladies walk, sheep cough, Sir John Oldcastle groans aloud, Dic
Turpin's horse gallops in the wind, preparatory to his crossing t
Essex to begin his mad time-slip gallop to York. The boat grounds o
something, lifts forward. Perhaps this is the ancient Roman ford of th
Thames, the street across water, built of wishes, the dung of oxen an
wet stones.

The Boneless Wind freshens. We have slipped everything by, eve
snug Yantlet Creek and little Grain. We are off the Medway, an
putting about for another chapter.

A FEW MILES OF MEDWAY

SOUTH YANTLET CREEK

Water lies into mud and the light hooks under.
Banks soothe down till the wet is flat,

So flat, the rain — first a patter then a peck —
Stands in stalks stands in stumps:
There is grass, stick, rain, always standing rain

Setting here and there into starts of straw,
Sad marsh straw, little stands of wet.

The net, drawing heavy over silt,
Is groaned in slowly, festering the thumbs,
Asking blubber questions.

Tugs the fat of the tide
As tight as a corset,
Squirms, drags in,

Till everything slims
Even rain. No catch,

Not a muscle, not a ripple
Ripe with pith, not an inch,

So the birds — ever here —
Light off with their wish.

THE MEDWAY IS A great river, not the pastoral tributary its name suggests. True, any water in Kent will glide past meadow and orchard, and "little plots run wild", as surely as snakes through salad; but that is the upper stream, an age away from its confluence with the Thames.

To start with the Medway proper is to see it from the gullet as its invaders saw it, or perhaps half a mile beyond its mouth where the

Thames on a blue day is green, but where the Medway breathes out its brown and white, its clay and chalk, and where for tidal minutes the two rivers refuse to mingle their exhalations. The Medway pours itself out into the Nore, into pure saltwater, where the Thames has ceased as a river and is a widening bite at the open sea.

The Thames is eight miles wide here, ten to the silly little creeks below Shoeburyness. The north shore, for all its arrogant place-names — New England Island, Great Wakering, Barling Magna — has nothing to compare with the mouth of the Medway, nor of the Swale.

Its maps tell lies even in Latin. The paltry River Roach dare not spill out into the Thames for fear of competition, but runs away north-east by east to snivel behind Foulness, leaking Thamesward only by Potton and Shelford Creeks, and a dismal piece of water called the Middleway, as slimy as a punctured hernia.

The Medway by comparison cuts North Kent in half, and this takes some doing. It washes between bold shores and harries among hills. It does not dribble into slurry and seabirds. None of its nesses are foul. You need to go up it for fifteen miles, twenty if you swing wide at the bends, before you find a bridge, and that has been there since Roman times, proving, as one would expect in Kent, that the river was prising apart places of resource and importance.

At Garrison Point, the Medway is a mile wide, a full kilometre before low tide grounds you on the flats — not mudflats, if you please — beyond Grain Tower. Until recently, there were guns in the casemates at Garrison Point, and the old Six-Inch Mark Seven could fire at its full range of 21,000 yards anywhere a trifle east of grid north, proof positive that the river parleys direct with the sea. The ancient C.P.2's — the Mark Sevens were allegedly clamped on to C.P.2 mountings well in advance of other types of transplant — actually had their westward stops on Grain Tower. The C.P.2 is undoubtedly a more elderly piece than any that will be reading this, yet in ballistic terms it is a modern gun, firing a screw projectile of forged steel. It thumped it a dozen miles skyward and seaward not by exploding powder or wadding, but by detonating some twenty pounds of cordite. A lob shell, of course, a decent long-lasting gun (none of your newfangled old-fashioned rocketry with flames up the arse like a virgin birth and instant multi-million-pound self-destruct — to think the Duke of Wellington had such rubbish and threw it away!) but its muzzle-velocity was about 1,200 feet a second if you powdered its breech and wrapped it in a clean napkin. Yet the Medway was considered mighty enough in the late nineteenth century, and *wide* enough, to be closed *by the direct fire* of a battery of these. Those were the days when sailors trusted soldiers. The moorings and dockyard were protected by Six Pounder Twins and naval Twelve Pounders, a weapon whose blast is rightly feared by Scotsmen. None of these guns were ever turned on Essex, though the temptation must have been great. The Navy has several times been engaged from hereabouts, but the temptation was even greater.

So here is a river mouth mighty enough to have teeth fitted, and not just a top set. In recent years there were guns on and around the Grain Martello (in case All Hallows craved revenge on Sheerness?), there were quick-firing A.A.3.7's mounted but not used in the seawards firing role behind the western seawall, and I read that there were barbette guns fitted near here in the mid-nineteenth century. Were these merely cannon firing over a wall, I wonder? Or were they trucked or trained to-and-fro in the best barbette fashion, in order to produce a moving target to seamen who would certainly be moving faster? Or was this the celebrated counterbalanced train-loaded barbette gun first proposed in the *Cornhill Magazine* in February 1868, and illustrated again in August of the same year, Moncrieff's Barbette Carriage — a cunning piece designed to shift from side to side and pop up and down like a jack-in-the-box, as sly as a Southend barmaid and almost as top-heavy?

I don't know the truth of this. Perhaps I should mention that the Medway Mouth has been closed by a boom from time to time, again between Garrison Point, Sheerness and the Grain Tower. No one has ever managed to shut it at the appropriate moment, however, neither against Admiral van Tromp (against whom English football clubs still seek vengeance) nor against German minelayers. Booms are like contraceptives, judged only by their failures. The best advertisement for the Medway boom is the one I heard in the Fountain Hotel, Sheerness, namely that North Kent has not been invaded by the French for over two centuries.

Sheerness is a fine place to have at a rivermouth, and certainly not to be underrated as a town to get drunk in. I once shared a room in the Fountain with the Captain of Artillery who invented landward firing with Coast Guns — not a drunken act in itself: he obliterated 2,000 Japanese infantry thereby before they unsportingly threatened to behead him. If they had let him carry on for an hour or two longer we might have been spared all those nasty little motorcars and our balance of payments deficit — and a very brilliant major who would have sunk the *Scharnhorst* in the Straits of Dover if the Navy hadn't stopped him out of sheer envy. The Fountain is not mean with its rooms. We had a room apiece, but it was a foggy night, and this was the only room we could find, and this because the captain knew the way to it. He said it was in Hong Kong. He stood in the corner all night with a pint of beer balanced on his upturned forehead in case either of the other two of us got thirsty. The major got very thirsty. He told us a spider was eating a hole in his head.

I wonder if Pepys slept here? It is a brisk town, full of fine hostelries, each of them more liberal than the last, whichever way you take them. Wherever he slept, he slept well. He himself was a man for an egg-nog, taking more nog than egg, the closer he drew to the Nore. Pepys came here several times to layout the dockyard and improve fortifications, and I shall inspect them in another chapter. Suffice to say that the diarist kept on popping up along the Medway, particularly in the wake of van Tromp, whither the Admiralty sent him to enquire why the boom was not closed. He claims to have built Rochester and Upnor almost single-handed, seeking help only to pinch stone for Upnor Castle. I have looked into this claim, and it has more substance than the one about spiders eating heads, but only just.

But I anticipate. I leapt ahead in embarrassment because I was about to detect little Sheerness telling us a lie about itself.

Sheer Ness. What a boast. Ness means headland, and at first blush it would seem an awful whopper to apply such a lofty Anglo-Saxon label to anything on the Isle of Sheppey, where the only point higher than a sheep on Harty Marshes is a man on a sheep on Harty Marshes.

Then there is Sheer. The tallest cliff hereabouts, as I have already established, is the one between pavement and gutter along from the Fountain Hotel, and it is probably the most vertical too, give or take a pebble.

Am I saying that a Man of Kent would lie? Certainly not. Even though Sheppey is not so much Kent as an offshore island it has not yet drifted as far as Essex. Nor am I saying that the Founding Fathers of Sheerness christened it after a hard night with spiders in the Fountain. Compared with Essex nesses, Sheerness stands high. Garrison Point keeps its feet clear of even a wild sea, and there are places such as Pump

Hill that might tire a nonogenarian to run up, or the churchyard at Eastchurch, that a skeleton would grow quite breathless climbing back into, if it weren't for the pub across the road.

No, Sheerness is a bright place, and it positively glimmers when approached from the water. The town was named long before Milton accidentally transformed Anglo-Saxon "sheer" from its meaning of bright (as once applied to the quality of silk stockings) to its modern connotation of vertical. Blind John had a potent influence on English (his only fault was not to be born in Kent) and when he wrote of God's expulsion of Lucifer, the Light Bearer, from Heaven: *Sheer o'er the fabled battlements he fell*, he mussed up a bit more for us. I forgive him this, but not for trying to withhold "buxom" from barmaids.

Across the river, the Isle of Grain is an unpleasant sight: hundreds of petro-chemical tanks too clinical for the reflex image of putrescence, but a hive of pimples nonetheless. Indeed, hives is what they are — bubbles on the body politic. I hear that the Grain refinery is closing down, and the operation concentrated among the Essex Cities of the Plain instead. I shall not jest on the matter. Even *they* do not deserve this.

Instead, on the Sheppey tack, let us haul down past the Lappel (another sheep-high bump) to West Minster.

Facing us is Queenborough Spit. Queenborough itself is up the Swale. This is the Swale's narrower end — 500 metres from hard to hard according to O.S.178, though it always looks less. Even so, there is nothing on the Essex shore as broad as this; and eastward, beyond Elmley Island and Marshes, and ship-shaped (though hardly ship-shape) Fowley Island which stands among four "deeps", the Swale is a mile wide, though it is sometimes hard to tell mud from water or mist from fleece. The Swale's Eastern Entrance, past Harty Marshes, is wider even than the Medway proper; though it has a narrower dredge. To study it, and its spidering creeks and streams that maunder both north and south, is to understand why this part of Kent bears the signs and sometimes scars of so many ancient industries. The Medway has a concealed delta, infiltrating both Grain and the orchard landscape south of Sheppey. That is why Sittingbourne and Faversham and a whole band of villages and hamlets running towards Rainham-by-Gillingham are exactly where they are, waterside places where no creek is suspected, and seemingly owing nothing to the Medway direct. Ocean boats have been built here, timber stored and seasoned,

explosives manufactured and fine antique papers laid – all in an area
where a coarse map or plain common sense would suggest people's
main concern should be lowland sheep and then apples.

Now we have passed fairly into the Medway, it is worth reminding
ourself that we are in a new situation and on a completely different
tideway. We are not merely, not even nearly, running our senses over
a watery component of the Thames. We are in a different kingdom,
and the sense of difference is emphasized but not falsified by heading
upstream, whereas the Thames was taken coming down.

The size and importance of the lower estuary is already obvious. It is
wide, devious, vigorous and scouring; the activity on its banks, the
oiling, building, lading and mooring, all testify to its greatness. It is
only above Maidstone — no, above Teston — that the Medway flows
past the world in the way the Thames, or rather the Cherwell, does
above Oxford. From Grain and Sheppey to far below the so-called
Medway Towns, the land is a tributary of the tide. What happens
there happens, or once came to happen, because of the river. I can
think of no greater tribute to a waterway than that towns as substantial
as Chatham, Gillingham and Strood, with a city, Rochester, in their
midst, should be known as "the Medway Towns". The cathedral at
Rochester is the Medway's cathedral, grey by the grey water; and the
castle, one of England's greatest, is only one of the Medway's many
castles.

I do not intend us to stray in detail as far as charming East Barming,
East and West Farleigh, or Wateringbury, dunked though it is for me
in the sunshine of eternal childhood (what a place to swim, or just
simply to be!) save to say this, and I hope the river will let me get it said
and forgive me:

The river splits three ways about here, or rather, since water unlike
sparks cannot rise upwards, there is a triple confluence of the River
Beult (itself twinning and partly rejoining the Teise), the River Teise,
and the Medway itself. But the Medway is no longer itself, is it? It
cannot be itself, nor even a tress of itself. It is a split hair. It may stretch
for ever like one of Rapunzel's but I propose to have nothing to do
with it, nor with Yalding, its Lees and its weir, where this pastoral
tragedy occurs.

Not to split hairs any longer, I would notice just this. Surely there is
no river in Europe that gathers such a head out of such fragile
beginnings. From Maidstone to the river mouth is only some 25 miles;

from Maidstone to Rochester only ten. Yet by Rochester it is a mighty river, wide enough to let a Sunderland flying-boat taxi, build water under its hull until it can hydroplane and finally take off, with room for it to gain enough height to lift its payload above substantial banks.

And once round the bend below Upnor, the tideway — and it is nearly all tideway — opens into the broad estuary we now float upon.

The matter is not one of size merely, but character. It is a pity we cannot compress a century's timeslip into ten minutes while we are rounding Sharpness or sliming through Sharpfleet Creek (pronounced Crick in this neck of the tide), or one of the other three creeks below Slaughterhouse Point — you see what a maze we are on.

Because when Medway boats were under sail, they were different boats. There was something a trifle fantastic about the rigs built hereabouts, particularly in the creeks off the Swale. (After all, it was here that they constructed a hull out of concrete, and actually strung up a three-masted barge and sheeted her like a two-topsail barquentine, making a nonsense of anything ever written on the subject.) In general, even the barges built above Maidstone had a sprit, like anything steering out of Greenhithe or Gravesend; but the fishing boats were different, the dobles more stolid with a heavier clinker, and the bawleys – dare I say it? — more elegant, and a trifle more jaunty at the stern.

I'll touch on those boatyards in a later chapter. They were myriads then, because men born by water went by water. As we come back through time we can see slipways turn to skeletons, and others no more than ghosts.

I said a different kingdom, and it is ruled by a different king. At Upnor there is a planted stone which proclaims that the Medway up to here is still under the sway of the Lord Mayor of London and the Port of London Authority. The stone does not lie. It was simply stolen from Yantlet Creek. London once laid claim to the Medway, but never to its fishing. From Garrison Point, right upstream until rod and line take over from the net, it is under the jurisdiction of "The Admiral's Court", an assembly of elected watermen whose "admiral" is now the Mayor of Medway, and whose elected body is called the Jury, with its leader the Chamberlayne. This ruled the lives of the old Medway fishermen, conferring upon a man the right to fish, and deciding where he would fish and for what — which holes and shoots he could work for smelt, whether Bush Hole, Whorne's Place,

Scunch, Parson Gate, Gravel Hole or Stone, all between Rochester and Aylesford; or what business he should have down river with mussels on the oozes (Bishop was good for something), sole in the lower reaches, shrimps, herring, whitebait and lobster. There is a little work still for the Admiral's Court, beyond its occupation with Charity, but most of the fish are gone (gone relatively and in some cases absolutely). I have seen marvellous lobster at Red Sands under the Maunsell Fort, for instance; but that is in the Nore, not the Medway.

Still this is the court that holds sway and not the Lord Mayor of London. Once upon a time it served such famous Medway names as Squeaker Letley, Whistler King, Rocker Wells, Gosh Pocock, Hurricane Pocock, Curly Hill, Bluey Dallas, Scratch and Cully Carter and Seals Seagull. Where too from their number are Deerfoot, Beeswing, Soldier, Bottle and Bear?

The Court also decided where fish should be taken. The Medway had and has its close seasons for everything save the eel. It is probable, however, that a lack of general conservancy, as well as the prevalence of chemical and sewage, killed off the smelt, which were most prized during their breeding season, when they had a special "cucumber" flavour when ripe. A relative of the salmon, this beautiful but aggressive fish, *osmerus eperlanus*, came up the Medway to spawn; and it was then that it was taken, before it could repopulate the seas.

People who live by rivers, but who do not work them, are often slack in their terminology; and doubtless I am one. We know all the answers without having been forced to ask the questions, but here are a few Medway pointers.

The Nore "peter boats", the fishing smacks of the lower Thames Estuary (St Peter, the patron saint of fishermen, is a possible progenitor for the name if not the design) seem to have bred several offspring for narrower waters, in particular the bawley and the doble. The doble is the smaller boat, simple of rig, often running under a single gaff-sail, generally with no topsail above it; though some Medway fishermen did fly a topsail. It was, and is, more normally rowed than sailed, and like many a fishing boat rowed with pinned oars dibbed into holes on the gunwales, rather than slotted between rowlocks. The fisherman needs hands for lines and nets. A good doble-man did not row too much either. His life was worked by the currents and the tides, the eddies at the mouths of the creeks, the trickle above flooded flats, and then by the piston of the open stream.

Whether he fished in the Swale, or here in Saltpan Reach, or worked the holes above Rochester Bridge, it was a hard life, but reasonably lucrative. There were fish to catch, including the famous Medway smelts above Rochester, and there were oysters lower down. "Were" is the word. The tense is past. Cement came to the upper Medway in the mid-nineteenth century — the mucking for sand and gravel was a factor too — and although much of the work has now gone away, the fish and the oysters have gone with it. Not just gone. "Gone under." The Medway oyster used to be much sought after, the Medway smelt — a miniature game-fish — prized beyond compare.

Along at Swanscombe by that other river, they speak contemptuously of the bawley. They call it "a bawley boat". It is a term of comedy, if not contempt, as if every man keeps one in his trouser pocket. That part of the river, and towards Northfleet, saw an early migration from London, though — again because of cement; and it's well known that Swanscombe is where they found the skull, said by some to be enormously old, and by others to be the discarded head-frame of a typical inhabitant.

A bawley is a beautiful boat, and often quite big, big enough not just to stream a net, but in plusher years to rent itself out to a twenty-rod fishing party including their barrel and their individual hampers. It is sloop- or cutter-rigged, and can stand into the wind in ways a doble wouldn't think of. When I say "beautiful" that is what I mean. When a bargeman speaks of beauty, he means barge-beauty; but a bawley *under sail* is an absolute, like the Venus de Milo, Discobolus or the Spitfire. Glimpsed near-to from the "mushes" in South Yantlet Creek a bawley is as fine as many a schooner. There's salt water in my eye.

The bawley was properly a fishing vessel, and its tapered leaf-like lines made it unsuitable for lading. Some bawleys were open, some half-decked — again not the best of boats for those things barges carried, which included hops, bricks and earth for bricks, timber, barrels full and empty, coal, chalk, cement, gunpowder, leather and tanning products (including barrels of "pure", i.e. dog shit which was a much-prized dye in the nineteenth century, as well as various barks), and all manner of fertilizer and manure including sewage: this last would be dredged or emptied from the exits of the London tunnels and cuts, or collected from "night soil contractors". Barges also transported garbage. There was often very little ordering, and presumably not much hygiene, connected with this medley of cargoes, which might be fish offal, bonemeal or guano (at best) one day and dessert apples the next.

Nowadays sailing barges are nearly always for play, but until the First World War they did the main work of the water. Even during my childhood and up until 1948 there would be a good few moored by Conrad's Ship and Lobster at Gravesend, or along the lading at Strood. There were fleet boats, sometimes serving a single calling such as the Blue Circle barges which kept themselves to their owners, Portland Cement, and worked its dead weight cheaply from Halling to London. Another Medway fleet of specialist boats were those of Stewart Bros. and Spencer, of Strood, later British Oil and Cake Mills; and there were Eastwood's "brickies" still working to Lower Halstow and Otterham Quay. Then there were lines that took general lading, but were fleets nonetheless, such as Solly Brice's barges with their blue rails, who took mud, cement, coal, ballast or anything else; Albert Hutson's boats from Maidstone; and the London and Rochester Trading Company, which was 80 boats strong in its heyday just after the First World War, and sported a red bob and white crescent moon to distinguish them on Medway and Thames alike.

Owner bargemen were as common between the wars as owner-drivers of taxis. A barge, particularly a sailing barge, made a simple appeal to industry's pocket. It offered doughty transport of weighty and bulk goods that was not necessarily cost effective if shifted by other means. Coal was a good example, and timber another. Coal was never "black diamonds" when its retail price was a few shillings, a handful of new pence, a sack. Timber was almost too cheap to carry. The trees in those days seemed to produce it free and beg people to take it away. If it weren't in such demand as a building material along the two rivers, as well as for paper-making in what was then the world's industrial centre of the craft, it would not have been worth shifting. Nor would earth for brickmaking. People were making something from nothing, and the price of moving it to where it was wanted had to be kept down to nearly nothing if its application to life was to be worthwhile. This was where the owner-operated barge came in, and was to stay in long after the fleets began to wither. A man, with his wife or son for mate, could earn a decent wage and repay his borrowed capital by moving bulk between the Medway and London, or the Medway and the East Coast. To do so by sail was ideal, when there were enough barges and time was no real object.

Motor power was slow to come to the barge, partly because a steam-barge should have been a self-evident nonsense, weight for weight. When at last the diesel was married to the barge, it quadrupled its speed but put the costs so high that it decimated the trade. Bricks and coal became expensive, and timber suddenly worth its weight made up as armchairs. Strange things began to happen. Once a man fitted a motor into a barge as anything but an auxiliary, he began to realize that the barge was too small for the job. So it was a self-destructive exercise. And then the Arabs realized something that had unfortunately been overlooked by all nineteenth-century merchant adventurers. When you have something that everyone wants, you can charge what you like for it no matter how cheaply you get it. The oil tankers that slime their way into the estuary terminals are in fact outsize motor barges; they are that exactly. The crew are few in number, and they have comparative space and comfort. The skipper generally travels with his wife in a suite of cabins and . . . there are some horrendous mishaps. I bet no spritsail has ever foundered because the captain was having a quarrel with his mate.

As I write, I have before me a barge list as long as a giant's arm. They are nearly all dead now, but consider some of their names and ports of origin round the Kentish rivers: *Afternoon*, Rochester; *Agnes and Constance*, Frindsbury; *Lark*, Greenhithes; *Albert*, Maidstone; *Asphodel*, Deptford; *Annie Byford*, Conyer; *British Lion*, Chatham; *Coot*, Halstow; *Honest Girl*, Upchurch; *Hydrogen*, Rochester; *Henry and Jabez*, Sittingbourne; *Melody*, Rainham; *Plover*, Swanscombe; *Providence*, Milton; *Sir Richard*, Gravesend; *Surrey*, Milton; *Swift*, Northfleet; *Plantagenet*, Erith; *Renown*, Halling; *UVW*, Borstal.

I could go on. The surprise, surely, is in the places a barge could tie up to, but their naming is of historic interest. Men named their barges after beautiful women: *Bessie Hart* (1886) *Alice Watts* (1875), *Astrild* (1889), *Nell Gwyn* (1897); after members of their own family: *Will Everard* (1925); after birds: *Plover* (1898), and in Swanscombe too; *Petrel* (1892); after characters in books: *Sam Weller* (late in 1903); *Trilby*, twice, in Rochester and Sandwich, by two different owners who were keen on du Maurier in 1896; and famous people: *Baden Powell* (1900); *Cecil Rhodes* (1899). There are plenty of fishes and some trees, many which changed names as often as public houses, and on my list the depressing *Cadmus*, the only example of a prison hulk;

but of course books could be written about the hulks moored or grounded beyond Gravesend in the nineteenth century.

Enough of the litany of sonorous names. The salt has chewed them from boards that lie in the boneyard at Gravesend, and on many a flat up many a creek. We have Colemouth Creek on our right (once connecting with Yantlet — as distinct from South Yantlet — Creek in the Thames, and thus offering an evasion of the Boneless Wind), followed by Stoke Ooze. Stoke Ooze is an ooze, the sort of thing you find all too much of in Essex; but it drains itself slowly into East Hoo Creek or fills itself with square miles of water on an east wind. Meanwhile we have rounded Sharp Ness entire (some maps confuse it with Stamgate Spit) and are in Ket Hold Reach. To port, between Bishop Spit and the oyster-coloured slime of Bishop Ooze, lies the water of Half Acre, offering a way either through South Yantlet Creek, and a re-emergence in Pinup Reach, or some nasty moments in Nor Marsh via Bartletts Creek. To enter Bartletts Creek in a mist is not so much like going up a rat's arse as losing yourself in a lugworm's pancreas. One is bound to say that Stoke and Bishop Oozes, whether looking cowpat green or cowpat brown, are not for ordinary eyes in a bleak light. But at sunrise or sunset, when they are being dibbed by gulls and waterbirds, there are acres of wet land and half-dry water as fine as anything in the Camargue. In the Medway, God has let very little slip.

That being said, it should be admitted that Satan took a tumble hereabouts. Not only is the petro-chemical still visible to the north, with all its nasty piers and jetties; but ahead looms Kingsnorth Power Station with Hoo Works at the back, each with a mile or more of jetty serpenting out on either side of First Hoo Creek. Bee Ness Jetty and Oakham Ness Jetty are their given names, if anyone should wish to be acquainted with them.

For miles hereabouts a wise man follows the scour and the dredge. From Upchurch with its convenient steeple it is six miles north to Lower Stoke. There are five and half miles of marshes (called islands) and of oozes (called oozes), wet land or dry water. We must stick to the middle of the half-mile, unless we are floating on a plank. If we run our eyes east and west, between Queenborough and Hoo Salt Marsh then the bump of Lower Upnor, the same thing is true: we are on the same plate of porridge, but with a longer spoon to play with. I wouldn't be anywhere else in the world.

Lower Halstow was just before my trip inside the pancreas, its church tower an excellent mark. Newington, with another tower, is behind, and Hartlip's tower invisible.

So far we have snaked about somewhat, but over broad expanses. But as we turn out of Long Reach — just avoiding the main jetty of Kingsnorth Power Station which runs due south a mile and half beyond its previous manifestation and blocks half the river, we must turn sharply to port into the narrowing Pinup Reach with the old artillery fort on its marshy island beside us, and Hoo Fort and light ahead to starboard.

We turn thus into Gillingham Reach, with all of Gillingham beside us, and the magic of Gillingham Strand. Recently this wonderful foreshore has been "done up". It has been lightly landscaped and cleaned. There are now a boating lake and swimming pool, refreshment rooms and a miniature railway.

When I was a boy we used to come here on our cycles, or by bus from Gravesend, changing near Chatham barracks. What we did was swim. The swimming seemed safer than at Gravesend and along the Thames seawall, for reasons I do not now understand. But I know why it was better, and still is.

There were little offshore islands, bits of which would sink like submarines. They were built of thick Medway mud, plated with marsh turf and painted with sewage, but decent stuff, Kentish and of Kent and the occasional mermaid.

There were boats, and boat skeletons and anchors on these little islands, for us to swim out to, an enormous childhood cross-channel swim, all twenty yards of it.

Back to Gillingham later, and to the Upnors and the rest of Frindsbury Extra that beckons on the opposite shore. Upnor has a castle, set among trees, but starkly visible from the front, and it was here that Pepys came in the wake of the Dutch to build up this castle (with stone taken, alas, from Rochester Keep) and strengthen the defence of Chatham Dockyard.

We shall walk this way in due season. Chatham Naval Dockyard is on our left now, with gates into both Gillingham Reach — there's a nest of little cuts, and yards, and ladings at the far end of Gillingham Strand — and Upnor Reach.

To boat round it we must travel by Short Reach, longer always to my eye than Pinup Reach, which we left on the starboard turn at Hoo Fort.

To the map eye, Chatham Dockyard and Barracks are in Gillingham; they are adjacent to Gillingham and its engulfed little subsidiary of Brompton, while being separated from the main sprawl of Chatham by open ground.

In fact, only a fool tries to separate the three Medway Towns of Gillingham, Chatham and Rochester by pacing about on land or pondering over a map (Strood is clear enough by being across the river). But from where we are, afloat, the identities are sensible, if not entirely obvious. The kinks of the water may pinch the towns together in longitudinal slabs of brick, and river frontage may be at a premium; but the fact remains that there are over five miles of river from the beginning of Gillingham to Rochester Bridge, which is by no means the end of Rochester. So historically there was room for a number of townships to plant themselves here and thrive.

We are now running south in Chatham Reach towards the Sun Pier. The land pinches in, and the water narrows. The river curls northwards abruptly in a tight vee, and takes us into Limehouse Reach at the divide between Chatham and Rochester. Here town and river really embrace. It is suddenly only 200 yards wide, in a canyon of old wharfage and face-lifting office-space. Strood, and the old barge ladings, squeeze us from the right bank, and there is a steepening hill beyond. There was no real height to the skyline, and yet suddenly we are in a little world of swift water, and claustrophobic vistas. We no longer float past Kent. It has got us by the throat.

Strood, and its nearer neighbour Frindsbury Extra, are given to steeples, but they in their turn nestle and are lost against little Strood Hill which is now an all-important hump of old stockbrick and slate, and the occasional new roof.

The apex of Rochester is serene by contrast, yet I doubt if we shall rest our eyes on it yet. The boat itself is turning southerly once more — between Gillingham and here it thrashes about like a sidewinder — and we are confronted by the iron and stone of Rochester's hooped railway bridge, and its road bridge. The railway came in 1844 through that long Strood tunnel that was drilled through chalk for the barges. It was what led our eye from Frindsbury forward to the bridge. The road bridge is almost as old as Kentish time; or rather a bridge upon this site is older than Christian Kent.

Appropriately we are in Bridge Reach, and facing the arches that presented problems to the sailing-barge skippers who had to half-collapse a mast while keeping movement on the boat, sometimes in the teeth of the tide.

Once past the bridge, we see the square Norman Keep of Rochester Castle on our left — gutted, but all the more imposing because of it — and the river walls of its outer defences, with a terraced path in front of them and the cathedral beside.

O.S.178, which by now should take over from an Admiralty Chart, was drawn up by Christians but hardly by warriors. The cathedral is marked, and one of the best-sited Norman castles omitted.

This is Old Rochester, and it is a pleasure to see so much of it preserved, even from the water. We cannot see the excellent High Street from here, nor much at all if we hug the port side; but from the far side of the river, or the bridge, we can see stone buildings, a few stone and lead roofs, and some really excellent slate. Some of these have gone to time and shrapnel, alas; but the impression is good, and Edwin Drood leans in upon us. Dickens lived close to here as a boy, and only a couple of miles up Strood Hill and Gadshill on the other side of the river in the last years of his life. That brief plunge between cliffs of wharfage was a prelude to his proper ambience.

Ahead is the high shelf of the new road bridge, which bisects the anchorage and the old seaplane flight path to bring the M2 across the Medway. This is a windy place, with the air funnelled down the groove between Borstal, Wouldham and Burham on the left, and Cuxton, Halling and Snodland on our right. On this shore the railway — a branch from the old barge tunnel — is an occasional disfiguration, or it is when we can see the scar of its cutting. Wooded hills hang over the Rochester shore, opening back slowly as we approach New Hythe. There are long wooded slopes of extreme beauty angled to our right; but the river edge hereabouts has been gouged for gravel and sliced for chalk. Kilns have defiled the air, and something still needs to be prized from the landscape like old porridge from a dirty plate.

Most of the industry, that executioner of fishes, has died here and left its dereliction: but the river still supports much that is new all the way to Maidstone and beyond. It is interesting to reflect that the old sandpits and the new mills about New Hythe, Ditton and Aylesford are here because of it.

I nearly said that the ruined cement works have a certain Gothic beauty, but the Carmelites by gracious Aylesford Bridge are nearly upon us. We have floated beyond our boundaries, and into another time.

Perhaps I am wrong in my opinion, but it seems to me that the townspeople of the Thames and the Medway have grown a touch too independent of their arterial water. "Arteries" and "arterial" are fine nineteenth-century applications. They present an apt image for commerce during those great years when our two rivers flowed literally to every part of the earth. But an artery also brings blood ripe with the oxygen of life. What is striking about the cultural history of North Kent is that it reflects a landscape deeply in harmony with wave and water. The Downs themselves curl like a wave and are a fossil sea, littered with the calcium of long-dead fishes; the plough turns the fin and the scale. We stand here upon the first face of existence. We had better acknowledge it a little more, or we are likely to become rootless as any migrant on the planet.

THAMESIDE — ONE

KING RAT IN RAT RIVER

At a cold noon, dusk.
The estuary stretched
Its ten million pelts
Skinned year after year
From the Central Rat.
The pelts, when they touched,
Were not stitched: where they did not touch
Was a gap, and under it
Tar or another pelt, tinned sardine
Or sometimes a whole corrugation of iron
Like a wave ridging up to run out.

The pelts, sleek-haired, flat,
Laid on tanker-oil, lead paint, rust
Drooling off from a bridge,
Would, at a pile up of tide
Or a big push of tin
When the crab boats came down,
Rustle a bit,
Showing mud swept under the mat —
Mud and six other bits
The world did not want:
A dead King, the drowned lip of Kent,
The sun craned up on its string,
Wreck-buoys like unpicked hops,
Wet clothes-lines anchoring ships
Whose chains part under the tide
(Salt-bite, snagging a fluke,
Or a dredge-tooth wild in the Lane?)
But mostly the fox-brush pipes,
Steam of oxide, tannin from mills,
The sour-mouthed froth of cement,
A paper-town processing pulp
Down the mud's gullet.

Rat
Though raw, has not died.

His eyes in the deepwater cobbles
shrink
As his mouth grows wider. Entrails
Outlasting their sphincter, stretch.
He still bites the sun by the head
And the moon's fin slims to a scale
As he gnaws out a hole by the keel
Of this mainland's
canting boat.

ERITH STANDS NORTH of a line from the Crays and the Darent Gap, so
Erith is the first town on our shore. It is also the nearest place of character
and substance to the Darent's eventual tribute to the Thames. Next to
Gravesend it is the biggest town on, as distinct from adjacent to, the
Kentish River.

Until this century it was completely separated from other settlements in North Kent by fertile marshland north-west and south-east
along the river frontage, and by the low ridge on which it stood —the
only firm ground so close to the Thames for miles. North-west of the
town even now, off Church Manor Way, there is firmed marsh, with a
pair of sports grounds glimmering with that newly made alluvial look
that distinguishes so many town edges hereabouts; and beyond that
again there is Belevedere Generating Station and a succession of those
distressingly straight marsh parallels: Crabtree Manor Way, Picardy
Manor Way, Norman Road, and then the inevitable industrial estates,
built as only such places can be, on morose eyelines below water level.

We have by now reached Erith Marshes, but these are encroached
upon by Thamesmead, and I promised to have nothing to do with that.
In any event, it is separated from Erith by what is left of the marsh, by
some deep drainage cuts and triple pylon lines, then by Lesnes Abbey
Woods, just as it itself is severed from suburban London by the
Southern Outfall Sewer.

I shall pause by the foundations of Lesnes Abbey. Properly, we
should have nothing to do with it, because its woods give their name to
Abbey Wood, which is a London suburb if anything is. But the Abbey
was grubbed down, just as everything in Kent and much in Erith has
been grubbed down. Wolsey ordered its final decomposition, and some
of its stones were used at the rebuilding of Hall Place; but its first fault

was earlier, and very much in accord with the Kentish character. The Archbishop of Canterbury stripped it of honour in the fifteenth century because its inmates were found chewing meat and sniffing at women.

East of Erith the marshes are nearer, but inland the map suggests not so much a marriage as a communization between this little town and Belvedere, Bexley, Barnhurst, Bexley Heath, Old Bexley, Sidcup and some of the Crays, with Crayford as a kind of kissing companion. Nothing could be further from the truth. Several of these places have characters quite their own, or at least their centres have, and Erith is shut off by its own recognizable boundaries, its relationship with the river, and by certain characteristics which linger from a past age.

It was a port. In the palmy days of excursion by paddle steamer between London and Southend or Margate, or nearer Rosherville, the riverboats occasionally put in to pick up passengers, and sometimes to make a brief stop. Erith pubs were always famous, and an attempt was made in the nineteenth century to make an esplanade running north-west of the town centre from the junction of the High Street and West Street. Indeed, West Street, with its early open vistas of the Thames, shows the potential of the scheme: and there are clean lawns, park benches and flower beds even now. Another focus was provided by the old Erith ferry which ran across to Coldharbour Point in Essex.

The town itself is all of a piece. Theatre, Town Hall, Library, Police Station, Post Office, pack themselves within a few hundred square yards around the quadrant formed by the angled High Street, Pier Road and Walnut Tree Road. The buildings are mostly new, with traces of the nineteenth century rather than much earlier; indeed, the eastern side has been modernized, or rather vandalized in stressed concrete; but when there is any substance in a Kent foundation people tend to hold on to it, so there are some interesting basic lines. For example, the eighteenth-century windmill which stood in open ground half a mile away on the sadly diminished Northumberland Heath had had its fabric incorporated in buildings in little Mill Road. There has been a lot of change hereabouts. Adjacent roads are named after Hengist and Horsa, who pretty certainly never came here.

The Barons did. They came to the Church of St John the Baptist to meet the Commissioners of King John after the signing of the Magna Charta. I wonder what they said.

The Anglo-Saxon word *Earhith* means a gravel harbour. Walleberg states it means a dirt harbour. I won't go into this, save to point out that

Ear (gravel) does not exist by itself in Anglo-Saxon, save as the name of a rune. Nonetheless, Erith stands on a jut of the lower gravel terrace of the Thames basin. Dirt or mud harbours would be common along the Thames; gravel harbours would be rare, because the gravel deposits of the three Ice Ages only rarely reach the river. Therefore a gravel harbour is worth a mention.

Across the river is Coldharbour. *Harbour* in Anglo-Saxon means a shelter, sometimes a kind of corral or laager as it does to the modern field artillerist, though the whole compound may be a corruption of Celtic. There is strong evidence to suggest that the Anglo-Saxons applied the word to the remains of Roman staging posts, the sort of places that elsewhere in Kent are called rat castles. The name appears at three other points on the Thames where its only significance could be to denote the terminal of a ferry crossing. So it seems clear that Erith was a ferry point, if not a port, in Roman times. Great Coldharbour is now a rubbish tip (I shall refrain from remarking upon the appropriateness of its siting in Essex) and an industrial estate; but the case is strengthened by the discovery of Roman bricks on Great Coldharbour Point.

As a riverside port, Erith served London. Until the coming of the railway, vegetable produce and livestock, particularly sheep, would have been barged up, the vegetables from the disappeared orchard land of North Kent, and from the Darent and Cray valleys, and the sheep from the marshes.

Historically, and for hundreds of years until the late seventeenth century, Erith's main export was wood, both building wood and fuel. London lived in uneasy balance with the fuel resources of its hinterland during the Middle Ages. A town of only 40,000 people could not reduce the surrounding woodlands too quickly, but wood was needed for house-frames, furniture, transport, boxes and barrels, as well as for fuel. The fuel problem was solved early by creating copsewood, and by cutting young coppices for brushwood or faggots. Erith was a main faggot lading. It also shipped up hoops for barrels. As Defoe said in 1724, ". . . they make those faggots which the wood-mongers call ostrey-wood, and in particular those small light bavins which are used in taverns in London to light their faggots . . . 'tis incredible what vast quantities of these are lay'd up at Woolwich, Erith and Dartford". He goes on to point out that the increasing use of coal is killing the practice, and it did. The land south of Erith went under the plough long before it went beneath brick and tarmac.

Erith is worth a visit for its long river views up its Reach and its Rands — best seen by walking along the plank jetty to the west of the Police Station in the High Street. Its theatre, the Playhouse, almost next door to the police station, keeps something very close to old-fashioned repertory alive, with contemporary programming and at a professional level. It also tours and has workshops for children.

Manor Road beckons from the town centre, but this stops on nothing. Or rather it terminates in Crayford Marshes. The way to Dartford is via the Crayford Road and its successors, and then along Thames Road. Or we can take the train. It is just two stops.

It was the coming of the railway to North Kent, particularly the most northerly loop, which helped finish Erith as a port. This line down to Dartford past Slade Green is one of the most quirky lines in the world. In its entirety — if, say, we follow this loop from Charing Cross or Cannon Street to the Medway Towns — we cut right across industrial and riverside Kent.

It is surprising how little we see. This is not only because the windows are traditionally filthy. Some of the grime goes back to the day when British Railways took over from Southern Railways, whose North Kent trains were never conspicuously clean. The main reason is that much of the journey is in cuttings driven into the lower terrace and occasional bands of chalk. Sometimes, as near Northfleet, an amazing vista of ancient pit is revealed, with St Botolph's Church looking like a distant gravestone; but generally it is a myopic progress with only the town centres revealed. Dartford is seen at its best from the train, though; and to arrive that way is an antidote to those who pretend nothing good has happened in Dartford since the Peasants' Revolt. There is an imposing mill façade "well seen", as they used to say at the Royal Academy, beyond the millpond formed by damming the River Darent above the race. There were mills here when Domesday was compiled. The present building is connected with the origins of "Daren Flour" and "Daren Bread", a local and for many years superior Hovis. It was invented by the grandfather of the Kent poet Sydney Keyes, who perished, alas, almost as young as Chatterton, but whose verse continues to haunt the memory.

I anticipate. We are not nearly finished with the environs of Erith. Erith and its immediate hinterland stand, as I have said, on each of the three rising Thames basin shelves of gravel. Indeed, the directest way

into it from London and the A2 is to turn north in Bexley at the Black
Prince Junction (what an excellent hostelry for a roadhouse! In the
severe spring of 1968 I ate roast pheasant there and drank Chiroubles,
when I thought there would be no more than chemical beer and a
polystyrene sandwich), turn north and avoiding, till another chapter,
the temptation to look into Hall Place House, go up *Gravel* Hill, cross
the old Watling Street — the Romans had an instinct for well-drained
ground — and behold Erith Road.

South-east of Erith there is no gravel. There is ancient marsh, and
hoary reclamation. To see this at its best we must go to Slade Green,
between Erith and Dartford. We can do this by riding one stop from
either by train; by going past the historic yacht club at Erith and along
the depressing Manor Way, and turning at right angles south through
the new industrial estate. It is light engineering hereabouts, in one-
and two-storey buildings; though gantry cranes suggest pile-drivers
and a sudden contempt for reclaimed marshland.

From Manor Way, the road south is first innominate, and then
called Slade Green Road. This is sweetly residential. Poor Slade Green
only boasts about a dozen roads and a pile of breeze blocks anyway.

Have we been rising? The road begins to plunge at its south end, and
there is a fall of at least half a dozen feet as it joins Wallhouse Road at its
south. All in all it must squander some ten feet, a tremendous altitude
in these parts; but all the little estate round here is on a series of almost
imperceptible bumps, presumably of gravel or chalky knob.

Whatever Slade Green was before the marshland was drained stood
about there, in a triangle between the nineteenth-century station and
station pub, the ancient and partly original tithe barn at Howbury
Grange, and this little residential maze of brick, wide glass, moulded
tile and coloured concrete. Betjeman would have hated it.

In the sixteenth century most of it would have been wet earth and
dry water. We can understand this if we turn east and then by north
along Wallhouse Road. After we leave the sportsground on our left,
we pass an oldish red brick wall, soggy footed on uncertain foundations, and strike across the marsh proper. There is dingy-looking
plant-hire to our right, chain-link and concrete fences everywhere,
with here and there little walls of North Kent's ubiquitous corrugated
iron. Even amid burgeoning wealth, there are glimpses of marshland
frugality: house doors still in their peeling undercoats used as field-
gates, a bicycle-frame plugging a gap. The road is good enough to

hold lorries (I wonder how much brushwood and rubble it is laid upon?), but water trickles in an ill-cleared ditch at either side, then suddenly enlarges into two properly maintained cuts a fathom broad, teeming with spawn. Bullocks yawn and gawp at it across awkward barbed wire, mourning among other things their loss of scenery. There is a pillbox by the ditch, and some more solid blockhouses behind them. Then, a few hundred yards further on, a surface bomb shelter in a landscape that only a fool would spade into because it is built of turf laid on water. We are halted by the gates of an industrial estate, and a turning point for vehicles. At some stage or other the military were here; in any event, the gate-sheds look very like an old orderly room.

Crayford Ness Beacon stands ahead of us, a modern dished signal pylon. The word "ness" is nonsense. The highest thing here is the riverwall, and from the marshland it is a stark scarp above the landscape, quite as impressive as a Mississippi levee. On the far side of the wall, the water will be above us on the flood of the spring tides. Indeed, a mile back in the undulant Slade Green Triangle we are nowhere above the ten-foot contour. Howbury Farm is planted at five feet above mean sea level, and Lower Farm (it of the red wall) stands as its name suggests.

The riverwalls hereabouts were largely built in the seventeenth century, though eastwards there is Saxon and even Roman work. The hinterland was fertile, and needed for coppice and crop. Landowners looked increasingly towards the riverlands, as now, to raise sheep. Even if they had larger plans, the sheep could tread the sog until it dried out. There must have been plenty of scab and maggot, but the intention carried.

The reclamation of land consisted of firstly walling along the river's edge (and walling one's own inland boundaries if neighbours refused to co-operate in keeping out the tide); then in making cuts, and venting them through the wall. The most elaborate river gate in the wall just west of Crayford Ness Beacon is a fine modern example of this. Originally there were hand-operated locks between levels, and sometimes pumps.

Finance was arranged Dutch fashion in the East Anglian manner (hence the expression "Going Dutch"). A man would offer skill and labour to a landowner, and in turn be given half the land he reclaimed. He might "go Dutch" with some of his own workforce as well. It was all in accord with the general Kent tradition of land division.

It is impossible to understand or appreciate the riverside without experiencing at least some of the landscape between here and All Hallows. It is not as kempt as poulder land, and it is consequently even more depressing. It screams aloud, and its waterbirds and waders cry, for order. Instead it shows mostly the detritus of abandoned beginnings and sour imaginings. Yet its character is unmistakable. On a hot day in summer, away from the outfalls, one can stride along the seawall between flat water and flatter land; then lounge among mallows and a hundred different grasses. When rubble has been dumped to give a footing, there is goldenrod and digitalis, and even wild scrub lilac and elder. I have laboured up and down this riverwall, repairing it with turf and with stone. Just after dawn it is possible to pick mushrooms as plump as cabbages, and to dance among and harvest a dewscape of tarry eels. Eels and marsh mushroom, half-boiled and half baked, make the best breakfast in the world, especially eaten hot from a bucket.

Slade Green is an ugly place, and Erith is latterly perhaps only saved by the river. Yet, perhaps because of this, the people who live there are energetic and lively. I can only speak of what interests me, local initiatives in the arts and the liveliness of its schools. I remember Howbury Grange School with particular affection. In an area deprived of focus, this school is the focus, holding concerts, and exhibitions, and writing circles with and on behalf of the people who live near. It also publishes a monthly newspaper, *The Concord*, full of genuine news and views, professionally designed and printed, and with a circulation of 10,000.

Back in Erith proper is the Picardy School, until recently head-mastered by an old (not so old at that) military comrade of mine, Ken Fife, from Kent coast-artillery days. I visited Picardy recently for a book-fair. It wasn't a book-fair really, but a borough-wide celebration of the lively arts, including film and television.

All of this area is under the benevolent aegis of the London Borough of Bexley which, with Bromley, is one of the most lively, at least in literature and the arts.

Dartford is a classic "gap town" built where the Roman Watling Street fords the Darent. It is a natural focus for the industries of that significant little stream, and to a lesser extent the Cray; but it denies itself the river. I mean the real river.

The Darent and the Cray are not rivers. They are persistent streams, like so many in Kent. Historically, they had enough push of water to attract settlement and support industries. By the time they had ceased to urge watermills, Kent had become a landscape of windmills. The windmill, too, has died, but slowly as the sailing barge, and leaving the same social and economic gaps. All things driven by wind and water run cheaply and cleanly.

So Dartford is an historic accident. What isn't? The force of the process can be seen whether one approaches from Crayford and the west, Stone and the east, or just south down the gap. Old Dartford, *the* Dartford, stands hemmed in between little hills, with traces of heath all behind and ineradicable marsh all before. The old A2 (now the A225) bites all about it; and the new A2, the motorway in all but name, takes a bite further south. In my younger days, The Black Prince and Hall Place (the pub so named because the noble warrior was supposed to have bedded the Fair Maid of Kent in Hall Place opposite, and sired Richard II) were the one constant on every variorum of route save the original Watling Street. A dozen or so years ago, the dual carriageway came, Dartford and Crayford were by-passed completely, and the motorist could no longer gaze over the crazy pit-and-river expanses on either side of Stone. Dartford rises up its two hills, appropriately called West and East, on either side of the cheekily misnomered Creek. All around it, save westward, is fine country or the wreckage of it. Darenth Wood, Ladies Wood and Lords Wood south-east, are remnants of the Great Forest reinforced by medieval plantings. South beyond the Dickensian Bull Inn, Sutton House and the Fishery, all is a delight save for the funereal excrescence of stockbrick called Hawley.

Here I have it. We are in a landscape of qualification. Half of the riverside settlements began life as shanty towns. Dartford is inland, but it has the shanty mentality. If it was built yesterday, pull it down. Nineteenth-century hospitals replace substantial earlier foundations. Shop façades have their triennial facelifts. This was fine when stockbrick was used, as in west Dartford, or when good late-eighteenth-century stucco was spared in Highfield Road; but the hub of the town is a bomb-planted carpark, an Arndale Centre in fauvist brick and several bands of stressed concrete. Wat Tyler's (alleged) old pub nestles uneasily among all this, and its current interior decor of windlass and binnacle would have made any thatcher (let alone the Reverend John Ball) extremely uneasy.

No account of historic buildings that I know finds anything of importance still standing in Dartford. Yet Chaucer's pilgrims were here; so was Henry V on his return from Agincourt. The area was disputed by a series of skirmishes in the Civil War, and Fairfax certainly passed through with his troopers. John Wesley preached here frequently, and returned to the area often.

A Dominican nunnery and priory used to stand near Holy Trinity Church. Conceived by Queen Eleanor, wife of Edward I, the institution was eventually founded by Edward III between 1349 and 1361. Queen Elizabeth suppressed it in 1599. A few stones remain from the nunnery, nothing from the priory.

A thoroughly happy piece of demolition was the killing of Dartford's prison, the Bridewell, in 1932. But I have before me a picture of the High Street in 1900 taken just outside the King's Head, which shows Dartford to have been a most elegant place at the turn of the century. Not much of the alteration was effected by World War Two, and none by World War One.

So why do I like the place? Is it for its Norman Church of the Holy Trinity and a few buildings in Bullace Lane? Because it still gives off an air of inner-looking? I remember — and this colours recollection — buying the first of several collections of Robert Graves' poems there when I was a sixth-former, and of walking about the place numb with needles after several trips to West Hill Hospital. I had beer with Wat Tyler only the other day, and found the old rebel still friendly, the bar crowded with local sunlight. I hope the town remains prosperous but does not spread; so Blackdale Farm, Chance Spring Wood and Brickhill are not swallowed up. I hope that Wilmington may remain as a village, Clement Street not be touched, and Birchwood Road suffer no more but become an everlasting shrine of ribbon-led suburbia in honour of Mick Jagger, who next to the revolting peasants must be the town's most famous son. I have a photograph of him somewhere, aged nine, and pulling my beautiful cousin by the scarf or pigtail or nose. That is a genuine example of Dartford manners, tactile but friendly. And if the town diversifies towards light industry, it is worth recording that England's first rolling and slitting mill for iron was built here in the sixteenth century; and that in Victorian times there were powder mills, locomotive and chemical works, the famous flour mills and some breweries. Vickers itself used to stand by the masked lake on the old A2.

THAMESIDE — TWO

THE PORTLAND GIANT

A giant fell down from a distant planet,
A giant with outstretched claw
Who dove wrist-deep in the earth
Impaling his hand or his cockerel's footprint

Up to his elbows in chalk. His scream splayed out
All its fingerends, with fields forced under his nail
Then tore him free.
                Printing these pits
He stumbled under the Downs

Then rose and straddled the Thames
In a cloud of concrete.
                Where he wristed the earth
The dene-holes grew. His unstoppered groans
Blew grit in the stony sky

And dusted the slate of the leaf,
While from vortices in the magnetron
His pain slewed out in a silver slurry

To set bone-hard in its metaphor.

SEGREGATED BY THE lumpish mound of Joyce Green, Dartford avoids
the River. The Tunnel Road carries down and under, but that is
eastward. Dartford has none of it. Yet eastward is where the magical
riverside begins again, beyond the bulk of Littlebrook Power Station,
and the lewd scab of the tunnel's approaches.

The chalk is thinner here, perhaps only 300 feet deep, but it runs
comparatively near to the shore to scar long lengths of railway line
between Dartford and Gravesend. Stone, Swanscombe and Northfleet are all disfigured in some way or other by powdered chalk, close to

the river though they lie. Nothing flowers on chalk, or not until a little soil settles on it, and nothing settles on verticals.

I must not belittle this chalk. Here is where the main cement-making industries of England are sited, so good clean chalk must lie close to the river. Not chalk-rock, perhaps, and not Melbourn Rock, but chalk suitable for all kinds of quality cements and plasters.

Lime has been made all over Kent. There is some evidence, for example, that some of the dene-holes were dug for liming chalk in the eighteenth century; and there were certainly kilns on a variety of inland sites; but English cement-making proper, indeed world cement-making, started on this stretch of river and has come to dominate it.

You cannot live here and like cement, but it is impossible not to be grateful to it. With mass-produced as distinct from hand-laid paper it represents our main economy, and here is their inevitable environment. They both need the Downs, for chalk or glaze or water. They both need the River for transport and supply. Cement has more to hand than paper, and perhaps less world competition, so I suspect it is more secure; but I am in the business of description, not prophecy, so enough of that.

Lime-burning and rough-kilning were here early. So was James Parker, who was in operation in Northfleet in the late eighteenth century and who, in 1796, took out a patent for Roman Cement, the "reducing to powder certain burnt stones or agrillaceous productions called nodules of clay". These nodules or stones were collected from the London Clay cliffs of Sheppey and Whitstable but roasted and ground like coffee beans at Northfleet. The nodules were called septaria by the Romans, but so were ground slates, and so was finished cement. I suspect that experts are less clear about what was really in James Parker's Roman Cement than they pretend to be, but that is by the bye. What interests me is that on his industrialized slab of Northfleet foreshore Parker ground his rock, including soft chalk rock, not only by windmill but by tidemill, a soon-to-be-resurrected force in the alternative landscape. Parker, a shrewd man, sold out quickly to Samuel and Charles Wyatt.

In 1822 and 1823 a James Frost took out a patent for a chalk and clay cement called British cement; and in 1824 Charles Aspdin patented Portland Cement. This was probably not the modern high-temperature cement but a hydraulic lime. Still, the name was there.

Heat and water seem to be everything in cement-making, rather like cooking a bag-pudding. Anyone who has tried, as I have all over the country, to hand-drive a rawplug pike through old plaster knows that after about 80 years the consistency changes towards a very hard "toothlike" density. This is what the mixing and baking process is about. To manufacture a good cement is, in chemico-physical terms, to compress history.

James Frost expanded his operation to Swanscombe in 1825, and a succession of notable pioneers bought him out and moved his ideas into partnership. In 1835 the great Isaac Charles Johnson became manager of this enterprise at the age of twenty-four. He was an influence almost until his death in 1911 when he was a hundred years old. First he made traditional cements and plasters, including those mentioned above, but eventually he by-passed Aspdin's experiments, in spite of a confused trail among burnt bones and copper sulphate, and made "true" modern Portland Cement in Swanscombe in 1845. It is possible that Aspdin's brother beat him by a year or so; but what we have is a picture of men up and down a few miles of riverside locked in an industrial competition as fierce and slyly secretive as anything in Silicon Valley, and much more important to the world in terms of useful knowledge and real-estate measured wealth.

Cement-making surged forward. A consortium, or consortia, including Aspdin took over the Northfleet Creek operations, and diversified their location up and down the area. White and Frost expanded mightily at Swanscombe, until they were running well over a hundred kilns. Kilning, and clinker milling, produce dust, the cemetery sediment I wrote about in my introduction.

In 1874 there was local agitation at the pollution; but so many men were working in cement that the protests died away. It was no good pretending that cement-dust ruined the amenities, because without the cement there would be no amenities.

In 1882 the Wreck Commissioners complained that "Smoke from cement works at Swanscombe hung and drifted on the river so as to create a partial obscurity, and so probably prevented the Master of the ship and the Pilot concerned from seeing the riding lights of boats ahead". The manager, Arthur Glover, asserted that dust and smoke were minimized in his process by leading them over the mixing slurry of wet chalk and clay. This refinement had been patented by the same engineer, Isaac Johnson, who left Swanscombe to set up the first works on the Medway, at Frindsbury; then another at Cliffe; then finally Johnson's Works at Greenhithe in 1877. Legal processes dogged the last venture. There was pollution, visibility and sheer rivalry to contend with. The first two matters were set aside by building the first of the "high chimneys". This one was 300 feet high, and it began the time-honoured custom of freeing the locality of fallout and depositing it instead in a more dispersed state over Essex or the North Downs. The whole landscape from Greenhithe to Northfleet shows signs of historic pollution — white flints in walls, white roofs, and a white scatter on topsoils where chalk is not immediately underfoot. It would be more than I dare say to assert that there is *any* deposit from modern cement-manufacture; but I know of people who left Northfleet quite recently because of it.

In fact it is not a killer, though it makes for dusty roses and all kinds of problems for housewives. Cement smoke actually neutralizes the industrial nitrites and sulphur dioxide in the atmosphere, and to that extent plays its part in halting the spread of "acid rain", which is a killer, at least of fish and vegetation.

In the years I have written about, each charge occupied a kiln for five days; but by the turn of the century cement-making was rendered a continuous process by the introduction of rotary kilns. Unfortunately, this method not only makes more dust by making more cement, it also produces more dust for each ton produced, as the clinker is being continuously ground.

This was first combated by a "vortex", a sort of vacuum-trap in the escape. But the best answer was to use an electrostatic precipitator, which glued the dust downward the way fluff is attracted to a live television screen. Johnson's Works at Greenhithe was the first place in Britain to install one of these, in 1933. Bevan's Works, Northfleet, did not acquire one until the 1950s; and White's Works at Swanscombe and Kent Works at Stone did not have precipitation until the mid-1960s; so "ancient" pollution is not too geriatric a term, and is yet live among us.

Swanscombe has long been a centre of Portland Cement diversification, such as "Snowcrete" and the coloured cement paints, Snowcem and Sandtex.

In 1970 the Thameside was transformed again by the opening at Northfleet of the biggest cement works in Europe, a modernistic maze of tunnels, strobing lights and pure lines that straddles and undercuts the front of the town and is capable of producing three and a half million tonnes a year. This is I.P.C.M. To balance its opening, five of the smaller Blue Circle Group works closed — Cliffe Works, Kent Works at Stone, Johnson's Works at Greenhithe, Bevan's Works at Northfleet and the Metropolitan Works across the Thames at West Thurrock. The death of these has left gaps, skeletons and ghosts for the landscape to endure.

North Kent about here is an anatomy of dead ends. Yesterday I drove about looking for a pub drink. Two roads I have driven recently south of Stone now end on the abyss (do all of these gaps first go before Parliament, or may every tooth be drawn from the gum of the Downs on a single prescription?) and another little country lane that the latest Ordnance Survey and the A.A. London Atlas are both confident about is now no more than a metaphysical concept twining 200 feet above a deep hole, which has incidentally swallowed in its entirety one of the woods my last chapter asked God to let be for the sake of the wider comfort of Dartford.

Hole erection is our talent. The current monster is to the north of the Old Watling Street, the A296, at the little Bean roundabout. It is voracious, and acres big, enlarging and consuming time by the roots. There is a new Ice Age underneath the grass and the grazing bullocks, and all of North Kent will shortly fall into it.

This is the way to see the riverside in miniature, and do it all in a long mile. Take the Bean–Longfield escape off the A2 but turn north past the little nineteenth-century workmen's cottages towards Greenhithe and Stone. The ideal is to take the first turning left and thread round the back of the pits into what becomes Henge Place Road; but to head immediately towards Greenhithe will do almost as well. Either way glimpses ancient and modern pits of chalk and gravel, beautiful unspoiled Downland, shabby buildings and then the strange erosion, renewal and ruin of the foreshore.

If we turn left, little Stone Castle is tucked away on the right, home of current research and development in the local cement industry. The monster that feeds it has already been awesomely visible, a map-square of gouged glimmer, with arc lights showing green around a temporary railway track that curls north-east between Knockhall and Swanscombe. Newly cut chalk is impressive in any light.

Henge Place Road runs past the concrete and wire-link barriers of another pit on the left and a herd of bemused Friesians near the Castle. The pit has a lip of rubble. There is a tendency all about to obscure these places from near view, as if there is something obscene about looking into them. There is a sand and gravel pit similarly concealed on our right before we reach the London Road and the Bull Inn, not *the* Bull Inn, at Horns Cross a mile east of Dartford.

The hill down to Stone and then the River lies over the crossroads. It plunges steeply, past more old gravel pits on the left, so I suspect we have encountered the middle gravel terrace unusually close to the Thames.

More interesting to myself is the drill hall opposite the Bull on the London Road. It is part T.A.V.R., and part Army Careers Information; but for a number of years it has also housed one of the Bomb Disposal Squads of the Ordnance Corps. Traditionally, soldiers — particularly civilian soldiers like myself — think of the Ordnance as a deskbound lot, but their job is by definition to do with the supply of ammunition and explosives and things that go bump in the night. So largely speaking, not quite entirely, it is the Ordnance who defuse all the nasty devices that get left around Northern Ireland and occasionally Southern England.

I used to attend this drill hall at Horns Cross with my battery and troop, at the time of my regiment's metamorphosis from coast to field artillery, when we were denied our own drill hall at Milton. More of that later.

Down Stone Place Road, at the back of which the gravel pit inextricably twins with a chalk pit, is a shop on the corner of Upper Church Hill that used to be a baker's. A painted advert for "Keyes' Daren Bread" dies yearly on the stuccoed side, and may now drown totally in Snowcem or some such. The shop is now a tiny pottery, reaching back nearly 2,000 years in aspiration to some of the Romans' earliest industrial endeavours in these parts.

St Mary's Stone, behind its trimmed flint wall and very odd wooden gate-frame, is well worth a visit. There is Roman tiling in its footing, rag and flint in its building, and that rarest and most beautiful of Kent stones, tufa, in its corner-work. Part of the tower is being repaired (tufa, crudely expressed, is a sort of hybrid between limestone and sandstone so it is friable), and it looks as if tufa is being used for the job. The church is approached by a modern close, very spruce in board or tile and brick. New building about here and along at Greenhithe is tending to use these older Kent facings, and I hope weatherproof them better against the historical disapproval of councils who only have to see a plank house and they demand its demolition.

This little platform of buildings looks broadly across the river, still a few hundred yards away, towards the busy jetties and piers west of Stone Ness. The river may be dead for commerce but its industrial traffic is voluminous, and its many ladings rarely empty.

The railway from Dartford to the Medway crosses ahead, neither in a cutting nor upon an embankment, but right behind an ancient snort-hole. There is an old level crossing beside the hostelry: indeed this is Stone Crossing Halt, not even a proper station, but a kind of whistle-stop in a wilderness. The gate does open, *sometimes*, and one can walk across or drive longways around. If one chooses to wait, with ear cocked for the gate, then the pub is endearingly called Lads of the Village. There can't be many of them.

The long way about is short enough in a car. Retrace up to the drill hall and turn left towards the crossroads by the vast Railway Tavern above Greenhithe. The map says the turn is earlier, down King Edward Road; but King Edward Road has been blocked and rotated through 90 degrees, perhaps so someone can dig a hole under it while it is still dizzy, and it now strikes into Station Road, Greenhithe. This new junction has produced a sort of fenced village green cropped by horses.

There are old pits on the left and a disused school as well as more Portland Cement. Once we have crossed under the railway we pass another pub called The Lamb opposite an active gravel pit with overhead machinery, then enter Ifield Terrace and Charles Street. These really are the old dwellings of the riverside, one better than shanties, because built of brick and cement, and their new owners are being brave with them. Those on the north side of the road are built up underneath, as if the nineteenth-century workgate builder (architect would be too grand a term) hoped for a semi-basement and then realized that the water might lick around the furniture. Their frontage contrasts starkly with a small modern refrigeration factory, just before the north side of Stone Crossing. This faces an emptiness of footing and rubbled hole and elder, approached by two imposing gateways (no gates) in curved concreted recesses. Here stood the disappeared Kent Portland Cement Works, once the life of the place.

Stone Marshes begin to widen but there are trees, a little sewage

works and St Mary's Road straight ahead, with a track on to the
marshes forking right. St Mary's Road has one house of substance,
long and low in old stucco. It was probably the nineteenth-century
factory manager's house, and on a hot day it looks like something out
of Tennessee Williams. The rest of St Mary's Road resembles Charles
Street, only much more so. It has settled itself down among a little
wilderness of fluffy creeper, birches, tall geese, genuine green grass
(sometimes on a rooftop), gulls and pigeons, and presumably the
council will forget it until it sinks out of sight. It is not quite a track,
and it looks full of happy people who have the impudence to grow
flowers. The only building on the north side is called Thames View, as
gaily painted as a doll's cottage. Everywhere else is doubtless better
than nothing to live in, but to visit friends there would be rather like a
prison sentence.

The other branch, towards the marshes, runs between flooded holes
and past gravel, and then a chain linked field in which is marooned an
enormous turbine from the demolished factory. It lies on its side like a
red sausage, as long as a First World War submarine. Then there are
sheds, and low brick buildings, and brick runs that resemble
ammunition stores with hoists fallen into disuse, all owned by Blue
Circle and looking like a film set for the End of the World.

The last time I went there a man in blue overalls walked out of a
sliding door with five slim brown tiles on his head. They were so
heavy they nearly broke his neck. It was as if he had just stepped from a
dream, like so much else on the marshes. As I drove away between
double drainage cuts, the sun came out, once. I saw huge reeds and
three different kinds of sedge, standing moon-high. The landscape
only wants heat to make it feel like the Zambian Copperbelt, which is
nowhere. Then I remembered that Bram Stoker had Count Dracula
cross the river here and walk these marshes to the next station. He had
an exact sense of location.

West of Stone, and those jolly Lads of the Village, the road passes the
intriguing entrance to a rifle and pistol range in a sudden fold of
ground, and then blunders into downland. This is a good way to leave
Stone, especially at sunset with the light refracting more and more
north over mudflat and river and distant chimney. This may be
Dracula's place and the beginnings of his hour, but he seems rather less
credible among wheat and oil-seed rape than he did on the marshes.

Rochester Cathedral

Cooling Castle . . . where Falstaff began

Gravesend fort: Casemate opposite Milton Chantry

Gravesend fort: Bofors Gun and terrace tiered for concert

Upnor Castle...post-Pepys revision

Cottages at Longfield Hill

Country clapboard

Stone . . . . gravel by cement

Pulp lading at Rosherville

Stone Marsh . . . where Dracula came ashore

Left: The River
Darent at South
Darenth

Right: West
Kingsdown by
stormlight

Left:
Nineteenth-
century viaduct
between Horton
Kirby and South
Darenth

Right: Town
clapboard

Bexley's unique church

Old Gravesend . . . one of Conrad's pubs

Our way is east, though, downriver into little Greenhithe. By car this means returning among tethered horses and chicken-mesh streets, almost past the railway pub and into little Station Road again.

Greenhithe is a beautiful waterside village, the sort of place it is good to take a drink in. It is exactly east of Stone, and cheek by jowl; but whereas Stone falls off the chalk and gravel and sprawls among hideous sediment, Greenhithe stays astride the same ridge, and the Thames bites closer, right up against it.

This fact is not immediately clear. Yet just under the railbridge there is a row of nineteenth-century houses and little shops better kept than anything in Stone, which until recently had Johnson's as well as the Kent cement works to contend with.

The road swings abruptly right and becomes the High Street. There is a wall on the outside of the bend, and gates to works, offices, storage tanks and ladings. Opposite there is an imposing double-fronted house occupied by the National Westminster Bank. This is as it should be. One can change up money before darting into the White Hart, free house, which stands on the edge of things.

I suspect the bank is more to do with commercial Greenhithe than with thirst, however; though in a land of cement, thirst is to do with everything. Next to the White Hart is the entrance to Town Wharf, now called The Wharf, headquarters of E. T. Everard and Sons, famous among seagoing men. I mentioned them as we came down river. It is good to see them among eighteenth- and nineteenth-century houses, even if like "Accuba" some of them are pebble-dashed and (dare I report?) Snowcemmed. But next to Accuba, painted bold on a housefront, is the salty sign SHIPS PROVISIONED. Greenhithe has its chandlers; and like anywhere made famous by Melville or Conrad it smells right.

My grandfather, a deepwater man himself, used to speak of "getting a lungful of seagulls". You can do this at Greenhithe. It is quaint and waddles.

The road takes another right-angle, climbing south and away from the river; but a path goes straight on past some fine eighteenth-century houses, and a row of little nineteenth-century workmen's cottages fronted by two old gas-standards. I have seen one glowing, whether with odourless electricity or as a sewer-light I am not sure. Then there is a green turfed bank — Greenhithe means green harbour — and a path past the Greenhithe foreshore.

The kink in the road should not be deserted in a hurry, especially after only a few drinks in the White Hart. For here is the Pier Hotel, now demure behind cobbles and recently painted, facing an old-fashioned post office and stationer's, in case you need to cash more money for your second drink.

There is a well-ordered yard (fine Saxon word) at the back of the Pier Hotel; and, yes, there is a pier, with everything well bulwarked in high concrete to keep the spring tide out of the beer.

I proposed to walk up the hill, or even drive up. The Nautical College and the remains of Ingress Abbey can be seen from the riverside path, but there is a more comprehensive way to visit them, either from the top of the hill or from right round the back. The *Worcester*, the old three-master that used to house part of the college and all of its excitement, has now gone the way of the *Pamir/Arethusa* round at Upnor, so there is less to detain me than formerly.

The hill is called the Avenue. There are trees, several, but they nod in by accident; so it is hard to understand the name.

On its apex at the London Road there is a bizarre sort of gatehouse built of flint and imagination, fronting a driveway that runs back to the left. This used to be the way to both the *Worcester* and the Empire Paper Mills; and it is still the signboarded entrance to the Mills.

To the right there is a hole. I used to take this particular spatial concept to be an old chalkpit, like the one across the road, and I nearly said down the road as well. I expect man has had something to do with this last one — he has certainly at least trimmed the edges of it so that some of the sheds of the Empire Paper Mills may sit neatly on its floor — but the first contains something called Eagle Cliff. Possibly this is the sort of map-making that starts in pubs, for nowdays there aren't even buzzards hereabouts, nor nearer than Shorne and the Hundreds to my knowledge; but it could be that along to the north of the London Road is the lip both of the middle gravel and of the second chalk, turn and turn about. It is possible to trace a line along them, though old maps do not help, save to assure me that the hole *south* of the road *is* a disused pit.

I suspect eighteenth-century chalk- and lime-burners had a hand in all this, though. For a start, chalk was originally "arm-chair" quarried. That is, a level, or open drift, would be cut into the side of a hill. A right-angled triangle would be excavated beneath the slope of the hypotenuse. Cement-making proper was a riverside craft, and this trimming of the tumbled chalk terrace along the river would give the most immediate access to the necessary raw material, so it seems likely that the scarps that run to the north of the London Road from Eagle Cliff, through Swanscombe, Northfleet and as far as the Overcliffe in Gravesend, are all the result of shaving a natural lip in one of the bands of chalk. I have before me a number of nineteenth-century books on the Thames, all of which speak of the "cliffs" at Greenhithe.

Instinct prompts me further, though. North Kent hates its cement-making and its pits, so it shuts them wherever possible behind flint walls. All the old pits are flint-protected. It is quite possible to walk past them, drive past them, or even ride a short horse past them and not know they are there. The advent of the double-decker bus has made us less furtive — and, of course, the new pits are not modest six-acre holes but blights on the landscape as if the moon has fallen.

The London Road rises and falls on either side of The Avenue. About 700 yards further east we can turn down a little lane opposite Knockhall Road and plunge past and then through the Empire Paper Mills. This is a large factory with extensive floorspace — multi-storey to the north and shedded in the undercut to the south — with wharfage and jetties on the riverfront, and a skein of trackways. Beyond its reception point, that is back towards little Greenhithe, are the new reddish buildings of the Nautical College — a school for officers in the mercantile marine — set against the remains of Ingress Abbey. The abbey building, like the church at Warden on Sheppey, is built of stones from Old London Bridge; but as these were rag and granite I suspect that something else must have been used for the intricate traceries of its tower.

To the east of the Empire Paper Mills there is an old pit which has been turfed in to provide a playing field. This setting of grass on the depths of chalk has been undertaken in a number of places between here and Northfleet, and it is both cheaper and more practical than filling the pits, or it is when there is no flooding. One or two pits have been deliberately and tidily used as dumping sites, with earth decently compacted with urban and industrial rubbish; but I suspect no one can be easy about this. Even our little dene-holes are always opening up or caving in. A great cavity occurred quite recently in the Medway Towns, and in what used to be called Crab Apple Hole (or Coal) Field in Coldharbour at the back of Northfleet there were constant attempts made by farmers and council to fill two large dene-holes with brush-wood, soil, refuse, bricks, stones and even chalk; but every spring would bring a fresh sag to the ground, and sometimes an ominous fissure. There is now a housing estate built above it all. By one of the linguistic sleights beloved of our bureaucrats the nearest land is now called Dene Holm Road. It had better be called Dene Hole Road and have done with it; because something is bound to fall in sooner or later. But I digress from pit to patter, if not to prophecy.

Swanscombe comes next. I have never liked Swanscombe, but only because the worst English known to philologists is found here. Nowhere are glottals more glutinous; but this is no one's fault. There was an early nineteenth-century migration from the metropolis, and lazy London collided with cautious Kent. Or perhaps London took over. When a raping party settles, whether Roman or Norman or Viking, it is the women's tongue that prevails (I bet all the early Latins spoke Sabine); but when, as with the Saxons and the Londoners, the invaders bring their own women there is no hope for the local dialect at all. What is evident to the social biologist is amply reinforced by any study of linguistics. Woman talks and man listens.

There is, nonetheless, an old Swanscombe. After all, in 1933 at the back of tiny red-brick Childs Crescent, the Skull was found, a hundred thousand years old if it was a day. There is no pub called the Skull, but down the road there is the Wheatsheaf, an ancient sign, and it pours excellent beer. Swanscombe in general is made up of small turn-of-the-century housing and early council estates. This is a harmonious combination. Of all the places along the Kent coast, Swanscombe is the least violated by disarray.

The parish church stands at the junction of London Road, Galley Hill, Pilgrims Road and the High Street. Like the church at Stone it dresses flint with tufa, dug from the western end of the rag band, presumably at Malling, The church humps above the main bus route between Dartford and Gravesend, and upstages one as it should. But to see it in finer elevation, it should be viewed as a tack mark from the river, or as a general lode from Swanscombe Marshes or Botany Marshes. Dylan Thomas speaks of a church looking like a snail. On a mizzly day, when one's feet are slipping on the alluvial slime, it is exactly like a small-shelled snail crawling along the leaf of Swanscombe Hill against the scud of the clouds.

Ekwall gives the derivation of Swanscombe as being "the CAMP or pasture of the SWAN or swineherd". Perhaps. Some of the early written forms are suited by this, and "combe", meaning a narrow valley, is not much used in Kent, if at all. Swan can also mean a servant, or royal servant, as well as swan. Swans live on all the Thames marshes, and it wasn't too long ago that there were swans at Swanscombe. Swan Field or Vale of The Swan are not improbable.

Before we step down to the marshes, you will let me reveal a fad of mine. I am addicted to ley-lines. One passes from the tumulus at Shorne to St Mary's at Stone. On it, exactly, as well as a number of other interesting sites, are the Roman and Neolithic burials and potteries to the east of Swanscombe, and the Swanscombe skull.

Part of Swanscombe's strangeness, like Dartford's, comes from its separation from the river. It is also remote from its own hinterland, with only the Southfleet Road joining it to the rich downland behind it. Yet Knockhall and Milton Street, its two subsidiary villages, must one day have been connected with Stonewood, Bean and Betsham by direct track. How else can we explain the richness of prehistoric and Roman sites in the area, so many of which seem to take Swanscombe as their focus? The old track south through Swanscombe Park is still there, but chalk workings are already moving in that direction. Indeed, there has been a great loss of roads altogether in this part of Kent, some of it stemming from simple causes, such as the early nineteenth-century turnpike improvement of what is now the A227; but by far the greater part of Swanscombe's recent isolation is to do with its being sand-wiched between marsh and chalk.

Only short Galley Hill and the Lower Road separate its dusty flanks from some of the traditional industries of the river, and it is worth asking what they are.

Boatbuilding for sure. Boats have been built at Erith, Greenhithe, Northfleet, Gravesend and Milton and Denton from time immemo-rial. Not much in the way of big iron ships; but wooden hulls have been laid down in plenty, particularly small boats such as tilts, barges and smacks; then in the nineteenth century a huge variety of pleasure-craft from little skiffs and punts to large river yachts. By "river yacht" I don't mean something unseaworthy, merely something old-fashioned. The modern "hull-boat" is not a natural outcome of this part of the estuary.

The great days of manufacture were in times of wood and sail. So not only were there all manner of shedded subsidiaries here about —

sailmakers, rope-makers, oarmakers: there were all the tributary operations for the wharfage and storage of wood, pitch, resin, varnish and paint. Paint and nails were manufactured along the Thames.

How much local wood was used, and tree products such as resin and tannin, is hard to determine. Bark tannins went in and out of fashion. When they were in fashion variously for boots, harness, gloves and various bits of the leatherwork in whips from seat covers to chapping for the rigs and tackles, some of the bark was imported, not only from the rest of England (which was foreign enough) but from Europe. Mercifully, when importation had reached its peak in the eighteenth century, the value of excrement as a tanning agent, particularly dog excrement called "pure", was rediscovered. Pure became what might be termed a lucrative business.

London pure used to be bought in, rather than gathered locally. It was the sort of trade best managed at a distance; but there have been bark, or bark and soil, tanneries all over Kent for ages. Historically these were in the cattle-country of the Weald — Saxon and medieval tanneries at Plaxtol, for instance, on the feeders of the upper Medway; more recently closer to the Thames. Indeed, wherever cattle came there were skinneries and tanneries, even on the marshes once the salt was drained. These were local trades, current until the late eighteenth century began the sapping processes of specialization. North Kent leather-making was partly for the river, partly from the river, in that bundles of skin or bark, or barrels of pure or lye, were natural barge-borne goods. Kent needed leather anyway, and it manufactured it all over, particularly in the days when horses wore out as much of it as man did.

It is a moot point to discover just how much Kent timber went into Thames (or Swale or Medway) boats. We know that the agents of Henry VIII, as well as of the Admiralty in the time of the Napoleonic Wars, visited woods at Dartford, Meopham and Cobham, and had oaks marked and grubbed, as well as planted for the future. Since the *Victory* was built at Chatham, it would be pleasant to make a connection.

Paper-making began in North Kent, and we see how it goes on. Historically, paper-making is a waterside industry, as is brewing; and although increasingly both beer and paper are made with water from a tap, the finest examples of both were earlier held to be possible only with the aid of the appropriate and trusted stream.

Brewing, if not paper, has largely moved elsewhere; but I will not have Thames water scoffed at, even now. The riverside swarmed with coopers and coopers' yards (Cooper was a highly incidental name in Kent) and into their barrels went not only beer but Thames water from just above Gravesend. As I said elsewhere, it was held to be filthy enough for a long voyage, as filthy water ferments, and alcohol kills germs. You don't hear Kent beer complained of for being "watery".

Northfleet, like Greenhithe, has been derided as a "white town", a "boneyard"; but only by poets of the opposite shore, and no one literary lives there, not since Cymbeline learned to speak Latin. Cement is always blamed, and we confess to a little airblown chalk and gravel hereabouts; there are those who say it is better than snuff and makes for less infectious sneezing.

Northfleet looks white from the river, not now because of cement which is dispersed by taller and taller chimneys, but because like Greenhithe, West Gravesend (and Dover) it has visible chalk cliffs. White is hardly the term. Freshly cut chalk may have a pinkish light about it, a blue light even; but eroded river cliffs, ribbed and groyned by the small growths that sit on them, look distinctly grey.

Northfleet is a grey town, grizzled even; but it has a comforting flavour. There is not much that is very old, and what there is is dispersed: the Leather Bottle and St Botolph's, say, and then some stray cottages on Vale Road; but Northfleet is a spread town anyway. In spite of its recognizable centre from Stonebridge Road to the Hill, it spiders out to the south-east, along London Road, Dover Road, Vale Road, and Springhead Road, all of them recognizable extensions, their directions dictated by old pits. Newer developments are now threatening to cross the railway line to the south as well; and there are some pleasant modern closes overlooking the I.P.C.M.'s sunken road. They may come to fill some of the old pits, but this is a limited hope, because five of them are flooded; the flooded pit nearest to the town centre measuring 600 by 300 yards and waterlogging a fair area of usable space. Other ancient pits have been utilized, for example as a soccer field and tennis courts near to the station, and there are some uneasy looking allotments here about.

A fairly ancient council estate squats above the dry pit near to the Anglican and Catholic parish churches, and I must say its antiquity gives it a vaguely rustic air. Perhaps this is as subjective as my feeling for the allotments. I remember sitting at tea in one of the houses with a bright-faced girl for whom I had just written a sonnet-sequence. Only a fool writes a sonnet-sequence for a girl, and only an imbecile shows it to her. I was sixteen at the time, but that was no excuse. She used to lead me out of the rustic house above the chalkpit and take me for long country walks. Once we reached Knoll Park, not in a straight line, though I used to tread on air in those days. Our relationship foundered on her confusion of the words celandine and concubine. She thought I was making an improper suggestion when I was only pointing out the glories of wealden woodland. Life is full of linguistic confusions, particularly along the Thames. My father told me I wouldn't get very far with girls, or poetry, if I fazed people as to whether I was discussing botany or zoology.

I first got myself drunk in Northfleet, in that lovely clapboard pub on the Hill. There were ships hooting on the river and I hooted back. There's a fine view of the river from outside that pub, especially if you stand on someone's shoulders. I tried all of that.

The Catholic church nearly next door is a bleak affair on the face of it, dark-bricked and as inviting as a crematorium; but it is beautiful inside, clear-headed and simple. I fancy its unprepossessing exterior was a political act. It was one of the earliest of Catholic churches — I don't talk of pre-Anglican days — to be built on a main road, or at least a main thoroughfare, in the teeth of unpleasant laws and by-laws that forbade Catholics the right to worship on high streets. Not all these laws have been repealed, I think, but they have fallen into proper abeyance.

I have begun backwards, at the wrong end of the High Street. Because I started at a pub, I had better confess that there are a number of good pubs coming up Stonebridge Road from Swanscombe, and that the Gravesend and Northfleet Football Club and Ground are there right at the beginning of things. So is the New Northfleet Paper Mills and an entrance to wharfage and petro-chemical storage, just where Botany Marshes lap against the hull of Northfleet. I nearly said Northfleet hill, and the town is uphill from this end, and stays cliff-high at the front until it joins Gravesend.

The front proper, as well as its two lighthouses, its wharves, jetties and overall commitment to I.P.C.M., must be celebrated as the cradle of modern cement- and paper-making, old ceramics, and ancient and modern shipbuilding.

The laying down of hulls, even for tugs, was becoming rare by the outbreak of the Second World War, but this whole riverside was given fresh life, as were boatyards large and small all over Britain, by the need to build landing-barges. These were child's play for firms who had made lighters and towing barges, so a fair number of troop-carrying craft came from along here.

Even more interestingly, the five Maunsell anti-aircraft Forts were built in a yard near the I.P.C.M., before being towed out and planted in the Nore and further out to sea. The three big ones, Shivering Sands Fort, Red Sands Fort and the Nore Fort (all known less poetically by numbers), consisted of five stalked towers in a star shape, each stilted high above the water on four legs and joined by a walkway. From a distance they looked like robots dancing in a ring; and I suppose they were the shallow-water forebears of the oilrig. I spent a night on Red Sands Fort. In those days they mounted 3.7-inch guns and an assortment of Q.F. armament. Nowdays they are idle, save when there is a collision on foggy evenings, in which case skippers have been known to claim not only that they dance about but that they have waltzed right into the middle of the main channel. I wouldn't be at all surprised. They were full of rum when I was with them.

Northfleet High Street did have its clapboard, but not much, and most of it is gone. There is some ugly brick in place of it, sugar-biscuit brick; but I suppose the planners wished to jazz up the general nineteenth-century air of the place, which I must say I find attractive. An old chapel meeting hall and school house are both worth looking at along the river side of the street. They are solid, and built to stay afloat.

Swanscombe, Stone and Greenhithe all belong administratively to Dartford, which calls itself Dartford. Northfleet belongs to Gravesend, which calls itself and its agglomerate Gravesham. This is a pity. Sudden changes of name resulting from invasion, revolution or marriage — all much the same thing — are to be endured if not enjoyed. But changes brought about by bureaucratic philologizing should not be tolerated. Gravesham is an ugly gobful. It pays lip service to Meopham and a few hams else; but it is really so-named because of roots in a supposed Jutish migration. There is no evidence that Gravesend was a Jutish settlement other than the inference, counter to several others, of a place-name migrated from the Low Countries. For administration to be thus arbitrary is bad enough. But when they attempt to colonize Babel, babble must result. (One authority claims that since "end" in Gravesend is a corruption of "ham", anyway, "ham" has been properly reinstated. The trouble with this argument is that, in language, everything is a corruption of something.)

Now I have done apologizing to Northfleet for the etymological buffoonery attendant upon its marriage (or concubinage?) with Gravesend, it is worth noting some other confusions.

In real terms, they have always been somewhat intermingled, in part because of Northfleet's displaced centre of gravity, squeezed eastward as it is between river and pit. Then Gravesend was for a long time its own Education Authority, separate from Kent; and its magnet came to attract widely dispersed filings. It is hard to define school catchment areas according to the boundaries of little towns. There were grammar schools and technical schools and art schools only at Gravesend and Dartford, then in the Medway Towns. These became the poles.

Then, regardless of where the actual parish boundaries and manor boundaries and old urban boundaries ran, there is the question of Perry Street and Rosherville, interesting outriders both. They were in origin separate villages, one centred on church, chapel and shops, the other on the pleasure gardens. They have been pulled towards both Northfleet and Gravesend, before Gravesham swallowed them all. Certainly Rosherville, close to Northfleet and nearly a mile and a half from Gravesend, held separate attractions from Gravesend's promenade in the nineteenth century, and had its own landing-stage and station, both vanished. Perry Street is one of many Pear Streets in Kent. Here Street certainly implies a village or hamlet, and quite possibly a Roman road or tessellated paving. It is near to the Roman settlement of Vagniacae at Springhead and the supposed staging post of Coldharbour. While I am talking of such matters, it is worth remarking that Northfleet's etymology presents us with a problem, as does Southfleet's. If "fleet" does mean a stream, then it is not one connected with an estuary in Southfleet's case. The tiniest of streams seemed to run, often underground, towards the line of flooded pits from Springhead's old watercress beds. The water table is uncannily near the surface here, even at Bradditch which is near to the hundred-foot contour and too big to be a dew pond. The place-name experts do not suggest Anglo-Saxon "flett", a floor, I notice, in spite of Roman remains in both places. Having mixed this brew, I had better add that "fleot", a "creek", gives the requisite long tense *ee* sound: "flett" is short, open *e*. But where *is* the *South* fleot?

Northfleet has some fine schools. My aunt used to teach reception for years at Dover Road Primary, before finishing her days at Gravesend's West Street. I sit on a national committee which constantly seems to award prizes for creative writing to the little primary school at Sheers Green, too. The secondary schools in Colyer Road were places of pride when they were built. Sydney Harker is right to say, in *The Book of Gravesham*, that they were bombed; but the photograph he publishes is not of bombed Colyer Road (now the Springhead School), but of the grammar school, the county school then, and now something much more clever. I expect other people have pointed this out, the only error in the best book in an excellent series. If not, I will ask history to notice on the left the flagpole from which Joe Phillips' trousers were streamed, the workshop building's covered way, from the roof of which George Smith fell and broke the playground; and on the right the door with which somebody — was it Titley? — nearly broke my nose. The ruined roof and walls were afterwards stripped and a Hawker biplane parked on the foundations, for the instruction of the Air Corps, and the wicked delight of small boys who carried it away a piece at the time (yesterday a propeller, today a wing) in their pockets. The gap has now all been rebuilt, I notice, in nearly matching brick. Girls walk on the re-enclosed landings. There were no girls then, only dinner ladies who glided with folded arms and downcast eyes, and Miss Maslin with the permanent blush. Her trigonometry never recovered from the sight of Phillips fighting the rest of her class to regain his trousers. I have digressed and crossed the borough in a stride.

THAMESIDE — THREE

AMY JOHNSON. 1941

Somewhere above the moon
She flew where night had a gap in it,
A whole hundred miles off course
But certain of somewhere.

Alone even in love
In the Wellington's outstretched pulse
She searched geodetic dark
Counting the needles.

One by one they went down
And only the fog came up,
The estuary bubbling steam,
The North Sea upended in cloud.

She glided where things were softest
To a runway under the tide
Still doing her best by the book:
Wheel, flaps, trim.
                    Or just stayed up.

GRAVESEND IS REACHED by following the London Road east from
Northfleet, by swimming as Captain Webb did, floating in a sea-cabin
like the dying Keats, or flying into its once airport like Percival and de
Cierva and Ginger Lacey. Thousands of Londoners came here by
paddle-steamer and train, and before them by "The Longferry".
People from Tilbury escape here any way they can.

Conrad loved the place, Dickens honeymooned here and hated it,
and caught the train from the town station in his Gad's Hill days —
when he did not walk all the way to London — and Austin Freeman
lived here. So did General Gordon, Edward III, and — as a prisoner —
Richard II. James II and George I saw it in contrasting lights, the one

leaving, the other assuming a kingdom. The French burnt the town in 1380, and the Dutch came past at the commencement of Dryden's Year of Marvels. Pocahontas, plague victims and "floaters" — the nameless drowned — lie buried here; but that is not how the place got its name.

The best way to experience the town's unique flavour is undoubtedly to arrive by water. To come from London, is, even now, to see it as a resort town — though this, of course, is no more than the illusion of contrast; but its fine piers make an excellent impression as one moves east; and although the council's determination to supplant clapboard with tulips is bad for history and aesthetics, it does mean that we boast the greenest bank to be seen this side of Greenhithe and Greenwich. This clean eyeline riverwards is continued by the Arts Centre in old St Andrew's Church, the Clarendon Hotel, and then the promenade and Fort Gardens. To come up river is to see Gravesend in a truer, less colourful light, as the first anchorage and port of importance (towns on the Medway will forgive this, because they are not apparent unless one enters that estuary).

To sample the town best by road, I should forget the Northfleet-Overcliffe route. The Victorians' grand design has fallen into disrepair. The road from the Medway Towns, the Rochester Road, is airy, rolling and open. But its departure from Strood is ugly; and although it passes near Shorne and Chalk, and offers tantalizing glimpses of history, it enters East Gravesend through a prolonged estate of nineteen-thirtyish horror, bow-windows hung on ribbons of red-brick or ovaltine-coloured pebbledash. Similarly the East Gravesend exit from the A2/M2 offers the shock of Valley Drive — a beautiful natural fold of ground obliterated by the same ovaltine. When I was a boy this was a picnic place, right under the lip of the old airport, with gaily coloured light aeroplanes hedge-hopping over one's thermos flask. To begin with Valley Drive, then turn into the nasty end of Whitehall Lane is an improving possibility, however. This arrives one at Echo Square through turn-of-the-century housing, and offers the continuance of Parrock Road and Parrock Streeet, looping around the crazy eastern slopes of Windmill Hill.

Most simply, and at its best, Gravesend is approached from the Tollgate turn-off and roundabouts on the A2's junction with the A227, the erstwhile Northumberland Bottom. There is open ground, arable to the left, golf-course to the right; pleasant St John's School and Church — where for a decade none of the marriages were legal owing to a post-Munich deficiency in its registration — and then Woodlands Park and Hotel. The Park has some astonishing iron gates — I forget which King did what to them, but I was there with a flag. And then we are past some pleasant twentieth-century alms-houses, built in part by my grandfather, I think in his capacity as a decorative carpenter rather than as a builder. Then we are into old Gravesend. If anything looks bad, the river is before us, though there is no convenient bridge at midnight.

For choice I would turn off at Springhead and follow Hall Road, Earl Road, Perry Street and Pelham Road. Hall Road flanks a modern estate (I have said before that part of antique Kent looks as if it was built for chickens. Gravesend's modern estates are much more cheerful and seem intended for rabbits), but there are communal lawns all before, and then the new technical college, sports centre and branch library, and a beautiful piece of wall almost as elegant as the old Wombwell Hall boundary that it in part replaces. This last was an elegant piece of flint and brick which once collided with my father while he was driving a stationary furniture van in a cross wind, doing absolutely no damage to itself whatever. Its collision with the council was a much more drastic affair.

Earl Road is nasty, though not cheap. At least it has the grace to run downhill and enter Perry Street curling past the flint wall of the old church, and then the unredeemable shock of my family's emporium which is almost grotesque enough to be a protected building; but my childhood and most of my father's love and aspirations are bound up in it, as well as his brothers' and sisters', so for me it is as beyond criticism as either of Liverpool's horrible but magnificent cathedrals.

Perry Street is intact in spite of its modern petrol station. You recognize it for what it is, a seventeenth-century village whose fields have been smothered in nineteenth-century stockbrick and wrought iron. Lord Beaverbrook took the iron and shot it at Germans who dropped some of it back very adjacently; but stockbrick was never so good as in the late nineteenth century, and it rises between gristly flint boundaries under thin slate in a way that brings tears to my eyes. I have written two books about this quarter of a mile.

After Perry Street comes Pelham Road, at the junction with the

Dover Road running back to Northfleet, and the Old Road, whose name has recently replaced Dover Road along a part of its length. Old Road holds the old town cemetery, with an imposing gate-house. Pelham Road is worth persevering with. The interesting building of the former girls' county school and then grammar school are off it to the right, set back behind imposing town houses. Opposite, beyond the nineteenth-century shops and the pub, is a row of grotesque follies — large houses conceived as fairy castles complete with turret and tower. When I was in a pushchair I used to long to live in one of those quite as ardently as the young Dickens coveted Gad's Hill Place. Mine was the loftier ambition.

This way into town takes one past the art college and a high statue of Queen Victoria, looking florid even in stone. Her cheeks bulge like bosoms (if the phrase is possible) and everything else matches. The building behind her is now called the Victoria Centre, an adult institute and very lively art centre. It was the town's first public secondary school, housing the beginnings of the grammar schools, and then the technical school.

Gravesend's history has to be dug for. It is not easily stumbled over. St George's Church near the River and Town Pier is a largely eighteenth-century building on older foundations. It nestles among the fast vanishing remnants of "shanty" Gravesend, the town that partially vaporized in the Great Fire of 1727; and somewhere in its tiny yard Pocahontas the Indian Princess lies buried. Her story is well known, in a variety of versions; and whether she died of fever, homesickness or a broken heart is not really relevant to all of the concepts she has come to symbolize: hands across the waves, love between nations, human compassion, female initiative, fecundity. All kinds of American whites claim to be her descendants, in spite of their reluctance to admit to being remotely "Indian". She was, after all, a princess — whatever that means — and both of the Englishmen she married were gentlemen adventurers too wild to be in the Mayflower tradition, which indeed they preceded. The fact that she had an Indian husband as well is a taboo subject, save among feminists, who make much of her. No one can find her grave, and she lies somewhere in silt. There is a memorial to her, raised by American subscription, and the gold ball on the tower is the brightest object in town.

A few yards to the east is the High Street, stuffed with pubs, curry houses (testimony of a later and other Indian visitation) and the early nineteenth-century market building. Gravesend had a weekly market for many hundreds of years, before it was enclosed in this rather imposing building.

STREETS AND VILLAGES

HORN CENTRE

Grass inflects an acre of wormed earth,
A bird supports the day;
Girls assisting at a harvest's birth
Are turning hay;
And placid cows
That give the daisies suck
Make hornbeamed shadows rise,
Until I look
Into the windy rhythm of the hills
Tossed by the girls with haysweet thighs
For treetops full of tempests,
Great beasts with tumbled tails,
To shrug aside my season
And lurch me through the gales.

EAST OF GRAVESEND the land lumps northward, and the landscale becomes complicated. A river is a margin; and there is always a Euclidean component in the brain to suggest that margins should be straight. To the south, the chalk hills, to the north the water. What could be simpler than that? Go to the Hoo Hundreds and find out. The river is tricksy at its end, and the hills wriggle. Nor is every ridge entirely chalk.

East of Gravesend and Riverview Park, the corn and then the ancient woods run up to Thong, Upper Ifield, and Shorne. These are on a shallow but steepening ridge, separated like Higham from the river. Everything to the north is in some way dominated by watery levels: the land ebbs gently downward into a damp crust. To the south, the terrain is tight, secretive and select: one's first footstep beyond the ridge is almost in another world.

Between this world and the river, there are a clutch of old farms, which were once demesnes or *domaines* in the Anglo-Norman tradition.

West Court and East Court Manor come first, one tucked between Chalk and Denton, with its fields largely overbuilt; the other now part of the cluster of buildings on the broken little lane north of Chalk Church. Then, further east, are Green Farm, Queen's Farm and King's Farm. These last lie close to the edge of the marsh, but a little above it. Any last damp in their lower fields was drained after the canal cut was made in the 1820s.

As its name suggests, Higham is on elevated ground, aloof from the river. Its boldest front is on Gad's Hill, though its centre is a half-mile north of Dickens' house on the Gravesend road. Dickens' near neighbour, the Falstaff, is a gracious pub, with a dovecote. Dovecotes always suggest elegant living. The remainder of Higham is decorated in Kentish sand, a melancholy of botched brick and windy ambition.

Nonetheless, Higham is an intriguing place, worth pottering about in. Its original hamlets were Upshire, Chequers Street, Gore Green, Church Street and Lillechurch, as well as Gad's Hill. Some of these lie towards the marshes, the defunct Higham-East Tilbury ferry, and possibly the Roman causeway over the Thames. Higham was supposed to have land in Essex during the early Middle Ages, though the evidence is manuscript gloss rather than map.

In 1151, during "the Anarchy", King Stephen founded a Bene-dictine Nunnery at Lilliechurch (later Lillechurch), his youngest daughter Princess Mary being the Prioress. Within a generation, this was moved to Church Street, and the old church of St Mary's became the Priory Church. I have written of Church Street elsewhere as an odd, magic place where ley-lines cross. It is certainly atmospheric with its cinder roads, scummy ponds and a pub that is like a stage set for Ghost Town. The churchyard and church, with its wooden steeple and fine carved door, are curiously uplifting, though. There are a pair of cottages hard by that look as if they have been thatched with muddy sheep.

Dickens walked hereabout, pursuing his brainstorm. Church Street is a wet place, though there were faggot-ways underfoot. He probably turned earlier, past Gore Green and Little Oakleigh, or even went longways about by Mockbeggar and Lee Green. Or stilted across the rolling land between Hillyfield, Twogates and Lillechurch Farm. His destination, drawing him like a mesmer, was the strange landscape about Great Chattenden Woods, then Cooling Street, Cooling and Cliffe. He visited Cooling Court and the Castle often. I doubt if he was interested in their ghosts. His own haunted him enough. Cooling Court, and the cannonade-scarred castle remains — it is reported that only one shot struck the Gate Tower, and even that from an apocryphal cannon – are the most beautiful of places when they lie under Kent sunshine. When the clouds blow from Essex, they are each as melancholy as a rheumy waterbutt.

Cliffe is unique. It pretends to be near the river, but it isn't. It stands on a hardcore of chunky soil surrounded by old, dry pits, an immense acreage of flooded pits, and then marsh. Either its northbound end-stopped roads ran further into the marsh, or the water came nearer before the centuries-old wall was built. Yet in Roman times the Thames there was probably as narrow as its present deepwater line. There may have been all manner of blind tributaries feeding landwards from Blyth Sands and Egypt and St Mary's Bay. Indeed, there are creeks and streams rather than cuts feeding that way even now.

Cliffe's Anglo-Saxon eminence, its later fire, and always fine church have already been celebrated. Its architecture, all on a square ground-plan, is part brick and part Kentish cottage, with a few rows of clapboard and some plaster. In spite of the nineteenth-century intrusion of cement, at the village's south-western corner, change has been slow to come here. This is to its good. I fancy some of its approaches are Roman, or even older. Otherwise, Cliffe's dreams are for the dreamer. As a schoolboy I was friends with its excellent bakery. One Sunday I walked round its two unflooded quarries with a sergeant from each of the World Wars. The younger one said the place reminded him of a shattered Italian village. The older said it was exactly like the brickfields at Givenchy.

Cooling is almost nothing, Bromhey Farm and Eastborough Farm being outposts of God against the Northern Devil of Salt. Of Swigs-hole, Decoy, Clinch Street and Newlands I cannot really speak. Clinch Street is obviously a decayed village. I once got stuck in a mud puddle north of Swigshole. All of that part of Halstow Marshes reeked of sewage or methane, possibly both, since one so quickly gives rise to the other. This is a place for *ignis fatuus,* but the breeze is often too strong for real marsh light. The waters hereabout have interesting names, Salt Fleet, Buckland Fleet and Decoy Fleet. The seawall — reached across mush pasture, sunken peat and good luck — is probably Roman in origin, though there is Dutch work subsequently.

These are Halstow's Marshes. High Halstow itself is on a rib of firm ground, where the pasturage is lush; it has its "street" and the Old Red Dog Inn, and outsider hamlets at Church Street and Charnel Street. Then there is little Fenn Street, on the road to Allhallows and St Mary Hoo.

Due north there is a wooded hill, about a kilometre square. This is Northward (pronounced Norrard) Hill, once famous for its falcons and more latterly buzzards. It is now a nature reserve and bird sanctuary. In a straight but wet line beyond sits Shade House, squatting between salt "fleets" and best reached by an erratic path from Cooling. Tradition has it that Shade House was a great place for smugglers who landed their contraband at Egypt Bay. Contraband was certainly landed between Cliffe and Allhallows, but, as I say elsewhere, it probably did not amount to much. Still, the local "customers" and their excise men were few and far between, so rumour may be more reliable than history.

Little St Mary Hoo has its own piece of slyness, and one I prefer. A one-time rector of its Church of St Mary, one Robert Burt, was the clergyman who secretly, illicitly, and perhaps treasonably, married Maria Fitzherbert to the Prince Regent, later George IV, in 1785 at Twickenham, where he was vicar. He then prudently retreated here to one of the remotest parishes in the South of England and died. His son took the living, went for 57 years without preaching a sermon, kept the women and men segregated in church and their children in order by hiring a bully with a good stout stick.

Stoke and Lower Stoke — with deliciously named Cuckold's Green hard by — hold no memories for me, save as the spider at the centre of the little web of lanes that catch Allhallows. I remember hot bicycle rides, when even the low contours of the ridge seemed too steep, and a long under-age drink of cider sitting outside the pub there, no bad recollection at that. William Hogarth had a damnable experience at Stoke in 1732, however.

He was getting himself pleasantly drunk in Covent Garden with four companions, when they all decided to rape Kent. A day or two later they arrived at the Nag's Head in Lower Stoke, and were cramped by wet beds and devoured by gnats. The next morning they promptly took boat to Sheerness, which in those plague- and ague-infested days of summer must have seemed like the fire after the frying pan. Hogarth's journal of the trip is surprisingly pleased with things in Kent, except for the midnight watch at the Nag's Head.

Allhallows or the Isle of Grain are the choice beyond Stoke, surrounded by the historic farm settlements which are so much a feature of the Hundreds: Coomb, Barnstreet, Brickhouse, Dagenham, and Avery Farms — most of which have been here (with some change of name) for a very long time. A shallow ridge runs north-east here, so the settlement is much older than on the marshes. Binney Farm, scene of a seventeenth-century murder, is where the ridge dies in the Allhallows Marsh towards Yantlet Creek.

I used to swim at Allhallows, or rather its beach, which is a mile to the north of where the village sits on its 60-foot-high knoll. This area is at Avery Farm, once a village in its own right, with a famous smugglers' inn. Behind the beach there is now a caravan and camping park, with beach huts — not quite such a Coney Island of the soul as Leysdown-on-Sea on Sheppey, but depressing save for addicts of impoverished gaiety. Still, the swimming is good, and on a warm day in early spring there are no people. Malcolm Scroep, one of my more bizarre characters, loves and then murders a girl there. The old fort and the eleventh-century church are worth a visit, but history seems a little dead hereabouts. Allhallows means All Saints, of course. They were probably invoked in turn against Kentish Fever and the Boneless Wind.

The Isle of Grain is a heavy depression. Low land glints with metal hives of petro-chemical. Grain village is remote from this, but cannot escape because everything is so flat and open. Wind, full of discontent from Essex or the Frisians, invades the eyes and ears — indeed there is a windmill, the highest thing for miles, at Rosecourt Barn. The Hoo Peninsula used to boast more than its fair share of windmills as well as gibbets. The mills like spinning crucifixes terrified the dwellers of the sallows with their mad creakings. It is said that their prosperity depended upon prayer, but that the millers had no time for church. I have mentioned the pirate owls. Another saw says that a mill at Halstow was wrecked because giant seabirds tried to mate with it.

Halstow placates the gods with its bird sanctuary. Grain, alas, is its own sacrifice to Moloch. Save for floods, it was last a genuine island in 1823, when the Yantlet and Colemarsh Creeks were redredged where they had fouled at the roadbridge on what is now the A228 causeway. In fact, I have read of barge skippers quanting, sailing or towing up much later than this.

Queen Victoria, bless her, liked Grain. It was private, an amenity it shares with the North Pole; so it was a good place for the Royal Yacht to pick her up and set her down. She even allowed its jetty to become known as Port Victoria. Indeed, in 1899 the Royal Corinthian Yacht Club built a large clubhouse there.

Grain is now a microcosm of the Hoo peninsula at large. The population look like frontiers folk in early American photographs, but they have the wit and resilience of the frontier to go with it. In spite of the corrugated-iron, zinc, asbestos and chain-link, things have probably not changed overmuch since the seventeenth century. Like Thanet, the Hundreds preserve Old Kent in thick aspic.

ROADS AND LOST ROADS

CHALK QUARRY IN THE WROTHAM ESCARPMENT

This moonbite is clean
As Grandmother's set
From the steradent:

Drilled-out clunch,
Caps of Melbourn Rock
Bridged by Middle Chalk —

A boggart's grin
Or candles in a pumpkin
Under permed scrub-oak

To frighten the pilgrim.
Maps don't notice
The path blown crooked

Where blackthorns grow
Their dogfeathered hornwood
Nor tell what street

The sarsens walked in.
Today the weather
Sits snug in the tooth

So I open flints
With a steel hammer
Till the sky spins.

I HAVE ALREADY hinted at loss. The river changed substantially during
the centuries since Roman times, first from the banking of the marshes,
then the locking of the upper streams and confluents, then the
deepening of the dredge. But the roads by the river, to the river, and

across the river, changed even more; and there is no change without loss.

The oldest road, or track supplanted by road, is the Pilgrim's or North Kent Way. This is an ancient, possibly prehistoric trackway, taking its direction from the line of the Downs and running from Winchester or Salisbury Plain towards Canterbury.

In general this contours the foot of the main scarp of the Downs, but not always at a level which keeps it disentangled from the slope. It enters our own area at Otford to the west, and we at once encounter difficulty with it. The beautiful upper road from Otford to Wrotham, the one that avoids Kemsing then disappears only at Blacksole Field near Wrotham itself, is for much of its length called Pilgrim's Way. Across the last little stretch, almost at the confluence of the A20 and M20, it continues as track, not all of it old.

But is the narrow road we have just followed in fact laid on the old track? From near the tumulus above Otford Mount there is another track at the top of the scarp. This runs for about four miles before joining, or being made to join, the other route about half a mile south-east of Drane Farm. There are signs that it might have once continued to run along the north of the slope across the fields between the large inverted vee of road that opens below Terry's Lodge.

I won't continue with this detective work. West, near Guildford, for instance, I have walked two distinct tracks, one above, one at the foot of the scarp. Before Vigo Village was built in the strip of ancient forest north-east of Wrotham, a clear track continued the line from Terry's Lodge. I remember it as a small boy; then when it had been tarmacadamed by the army. East just a little, continuations of both tracks may be traced within, and at the foot of, Whitehorse Woods. I know them both. Later, both swing north with the opening of the Downs at the Medway Gap. A track comes south on the far side of the river. The inference is that the traces are lost among the sprawl of the Medway Towns. I wonder if this is the entire story.

The best thing to do with the Pilgrim's Way is to walk it, not ask questions about it, save to wonder whether it once held straight when the road turns away from its obvious intentions. It is a magic route south of the Downs, and a furrow of high enchantment through the remains of the forest to the north, though the last is a bit more of a tangle. We can be pretty sure that no serious pilgrims trod it: it was certainly made by pre-Christian, probably pre-Celtic feet. In our own area it does seem to link all kinds of early settlements — those related to the tumulus at Otford Mount, for example, "Fairseat Castle", the Coldrun Stones and Kit's Coty. But these last two dolmens are probably the remains of entrances to burial chambers in long barrows. There is no certainty about the rest. One would expect settlements as well as roads along features so clear-cut as the Downs. The sites are commanding, secret, and appropriate to the worship of celestial objects.

It could be that the Medway was unfordable, or unfordable in flood, below the present site of Rochester Bridge. Or simply that pre-Roman Rochester was immensely important. But what about the traveller who wished to keep east? There is a footpath leaving the "ancient track" in Crookhorn Wood below Upper Halling, just where the double pylon lines crink across the road south of Lad's Farm (indeed, the road from this point is laid upon the track). This all happens on a narrow spur of land. Beneath, is the little road through Paddlesworth. This also runs back to join the trackway to the west of Crookhorn Wood. More important is the view across the river. Three churches at Burham, Burham Court, Snodland, all stand in a dead straight line across the Medway. One slightly nearer, also in Snodland, is only 50 metres off the same line. Ley-liners will know what to think.

Chaucer's pilgrim route lies to the north and is almost totally lost. It is not ancient, less old than Christianity, of course; and not necessarily older than the martyrdom of Becket and his holy fleas.

I want to talk about "the old straight track" in a moment. If you bear with me, you will at least ask yourself whether the Romans were the first to see the value of the unswerving line of march, and whether some of the Roman Roads in some cases followed and obscured earlier tracks no less "dodman true" than their own.

That is not my purpose for the minute. The Watling Street, *our* Watling Street, the one from London via Deptford, Bexley, Crayford, Dartford, Springhead, Rochester Bridge, Canterbury and Dover runs almost ruler-straight between Greenwich and Rochester even now. It is not always the same as the A2 — the Sidcup and Dartford bypasses have seen to that; nor does the A2 run exact upon it when it follows its line. The recent widening, coupled with the extension of the dual carriageway, has done its damage; but an ancient road can still be found just 50 yards south of it in Ashenbank Wood above Cobham, secret among rhododendron bushes and military ruins, and then beside the golf-course in Cobham Park. I have walked and cycled along this, and am quite ready to believe that Chaucer rode exactly here. Two miles east, the 1:50,000 O.S. Series One shows a Roman Road running from the roundabout by the Tollgate Motel towards the old site of Vagniacae, along the foot of the field below the World War Two anti-aircraft camps and emplacements. I cannot see the ghost of a legion or the glimmer of a line, merely heavy plough.

I suspect what older maps in part confirm — that there were parallel road systems often a few yards apart. This prompts me to wonder whether the conquering Saxons ever walked much on Roman roads, at least when they were paved. Without getting into the "street" debate again, I am reminded of their wonder at "magic-swords" — old Roman swords, forged unlike their own in tempered steel. (*Beowulf's* "ancestral weapon") — and their refusal to live in Roman houses because they were *entena-geweorc*: the work of giants. Beowulf himself trod his way on paving, but that was in the eighth century, and he was a hero. I wonder if the Roman roads were walked on much in the fifth century, except by spectres?

Certainly the Roman routes out of Gravesend have all disappeared, all except the one from the ferry to Rochester Bridge; and for a road to disappear, it must not only lead from nothing to nowhere, but have lost its memory as a boundary. Until the coming of enclosures, I swear men and women travelled by the shortest line.

Eighteenth-century enclosures did even more damage to the roads in North Kent than did the digging of pits. When the Wrotham turnpike road was proposed in 1824 the existing way down south from the Thames was as crooked as the cracks in a jigsaw: the tracks and the roads followed the edges of fields or were blocked by parks and estates.

The opening of the turnpike caused some of the web to disappear. It is interesting to trace the old route, but the task is not easy, and so typical of elsewhere in Kent that it is scarcely worth discussing in detail. The most interesting section is the one that runs at the back of Nash Street, and once included the detour of Nash Street itself, then ran through Nurstead Park close to Nurstead Court, at this point only an overgrown path but in a place of beauty. There is a denehole, a dewpond, a medieval hall and a fine wall of flint all in this confine. Indeed, another lost road runs past the dene-hole, again now a path.

Once the path must have led straight ahead from St Mildred's, but the railway dug a trench across the next field in 1864, so it died the death. Now all things go by the once-toll road and the bridge. The railway, its station and the resultant Railway Tavern were responsible for all this part of Meopham and caused a new focus of roads. Meopham and Culverstone are villages on the turnpike, both ancient places, but the road and then the railway have changed their shape.

A private railway company joined Gravesend to Strood in 1847, the company that built the canal. Gravesend was linked to London in 1849 and the company taken over by the South-Eastern Railway. I have spoken of the more southern route via Bromley, Swanley and Meopham driving east to the Medway Towns in the 1850s and 1860s. This too was the work of the South-Eastern Railway; but east of the Medway a new company had arisen, the old East Kent, slowly to link up but not always join hands.

The building of the canal must have seemed a mighty project. Certainly, it was a staggering loss when it closed so soon; but our two lateral railways run often below ground in tunnels and cuttings, some of them through chalk and some chalk rock. You could flood a mile east of South Darenth, and then the straight mile by Longfield and have a waterway wider than the Thames and Medway Canal and between five and ten times as deep. The railways did not come easily.

A branch was begun between Swanley and Otford in 1862, and from Otford to the Medway and Maidstone by 1874. Meanwhile the East Kent Company had linked Rochester to Faversham in 1858, and driven north towards Sheppey in 1860. In spite of disasters with the bridge across the Swale the whole area was encircled by main lines and traversed by branch lines by 1882, including the Hundreds.

So the modern pattern has emerged: three stripes of railway, two arterial roads, all systems in parallel, and working east from London.

The first north-to-south turnpike is part of the same progression, but later than the other roads. This is because it was less necessary. The natural ways to the Thames were through the Cray and Darent Gap to Dartford in the west, and the Medway Gap to the east. In the middle of this inescapable frame there were innumerable little north-tilted re-entrants, traversing the folds in the chalk. Most of them had a road, and a track before that. So we may have some classic ford-towns and bridge-towns in the neighbourhood; but we have an infinity of gap villages. The process goes on, along the Downs Road, Northfleet, for example, which has become an autonomous centre of thousands. Or the miles of buildings squeezed like toothpaste but not so tasty along the B260 from Hartley and New Barn, now linking fingers, past Longfield, Grubb Street, and Green Street Green to Lane End. At Longfield in the 1930s this slurry of pebbledash was much photo-graphed. It appeared in school textbooks as the vilest example of ribbon development. But it was not merely a case of buildings sprawling along a road. They were being guided along a valley, the tops of whose hills are now being trepanned for chalk.

There were ferries at Higham or Cliffe and East Tilbury, Jenning-tree Point and Rainham, Erith and Coldharbour Point, Purfleet and Long Reach, West Thurrock and Greenhithe, Grays and Swans-combe, Tilbury Fort and Gravesend. Some of these were prehistoric. The Romans, anxious in kilts, were always in a hurry to cross to south of the Thames and seek Coldharbour. Some of the roads that served these ferries have now declined or disappeared, for example those at Higham, and on Swanscombe Marshes and Dartford Saltmarsh at Long Reach.

Then there was the Essex to Kent ford from East Tilbury towards Rainham. In 2000 BC the land here was 36 feet above present levels, and the river non-tidal at this point. It is hard to know exactly at which point in Kent the crossing was made. The road has disappeared. So too has the alleged Roman causeway. One thing is certain. Turpin did not ford the Thames before riding off to York for his celebrated alibi (they hanged him not from disbelief, but because he had an uncaring family who would not bail him out): he took the Higham Ferry. Where are the pathways gone?

I daresay we can find them. I am obsessed with the relevance of ley-lines in this part of Kent, the invisible tracks. This is a game you can play by yourself and grow quite mad. You need good maps, say the new O.S. 1:25,000 series, at 2.5 inches to the mile, and a pencil and ruler. You can amaze yourself at how many ancient sites lie exactly on a straight line, often by the dozen; old burial places, mounds, circle plantings, known ancient crossroads, churches. Churches generally replace previous, often pagan places of worship, so some latitude is allowed with these.

For example, on O.S. TQ 66/77, the tower of the Saxon Church of St Helen at Cliffe aligns within a very fine tolerance with the steeple of the church at ancient Church Street by the ruins of the Benedictine

Priory, and then exactly with the tower at Shorne. The line extends south through places of significance on the next map.

We know that the ford, and possibly the Roman causeway, must have come south-south-east from somewhere near Coalhouse Point at East Tilbury, on the low spur that supports Coalhouse Battery and Fort. There is a line from the western crossroads in Higham that passes through the site of ancient church, Bronze Age and Roman burial, then Roman remains on Higham Saltings. I suggest the crossing was here. Other Roman finds support this theory. For what it is worth a Roman track and boundary runs back from the creek that exits at this point towards Barrow Hill and Church Street, itself served by another Roman road from Higham.

These are not the strongest ley-lines. Even so, the odds against them being accidental are enormous. I do not believe that leys were laid out to guide gods from the air, or spacecraft as some have contended, but to make direct footsteps for man and woman on the ground, sometimes before they had horses. Some leys are plain to view. Some leave little traces. Some, like other lost roads, can only be traced from a map.

GAP, RE-ENTRANT AND ANCIENT FOREST

ROOKS IN STATION WOOD

Rooks' nests, clodding the trees;
Rooks on clout-ended feathers
In knots of space
              while with Ace's gun
We centred the clods, squirting up eggs
Or knocked down chicks with our thousandth stone:

Yet the rooks still last, hooking up decibels
From crates of glass, old blades and bits,
Or our punched-out teeth under Station Wood.

Here I beat Ace for his gun, in a storm of rooks.
Here Wally beat Ace, and a ripeness later
With his best hand belted to his back
Out punched me for twenty-seven rounds
              while the rooks still swung
In the shrinking brightness of my head.
I heard them cough as I smoked dry creeper
              and still they sung
As I set all their sticks on fire:
              they were great in tongue
But all came back at the talking time of day
To roost on black. I saw one swallow a spark
But take no harm to its linen lung. . . .

Just a rooky cough
When we lifted Toby clean out drawers
For communal delight
Among tribal squarking;
              so what was sung
When I lay by Molly with a wet finger
And heed no caws, having cause enough?

THERE IS A fine walk southward from Eynsford Station. The road and
then track past Lower Austin Lodge and Upper Austin Lodge moves up

a gentle north-dipping re-entrant. The land lacks real height on either side, but all of the ridges are crowned and made steeper by old woods. To keep on south from the head of the valley is to enter this woodland. It only clears on the scarp slope of the Downs above Kemsing. Ahead, across the roofs of Kemsing, Seal and the eastern edge of Sevenoaks, is the tree-dominated skyline of the Wealden Forest. I don't generally walk that way. I turn left for the little pub at Romney Street or right for the ample delights of Samuel Palmer's Shoreham.

Either way involves traversing or overlooking the parallel re-entrants of Knatts Valley and the River Darent.

When a landscape is all skyline the trees seem more plentiful than they are. This piece of Kent is populous; it lies on the borders of Greater London; yet there is plenty of woodland to get lost in, not for days as in Ontario but for a time-wasting half an hour: woods knee-deep in uncleared mould, tripwired by fallen brush, top-branch and bramble. There are nettles, too, barbarous in damp places, ready to slow down reconnaissance. Near David Street, along the edge of Happy Valley, the case is similar. So it is behind Luddesdown; and where Vigo Village now stands the woods were recently a maze of old growth. A little east in Whitehorse Woods this dense tangle still renews itself, and it stretches above the trackway up to and beyond the Medway.

Somewhere towards the river the forest stopped, interrupted by heath or marsh, but even in the Middle Ages the Wealden Forest was not kept at bay by the scarp of the Downs. It spread a long way north, possibly as far as the Old Watling Street, approximately the line of the A2.

The two prehistoric trackways followed the scarp, simply because of its prominence, which made it less accessible to trees, and always presented a contour for the traveller to follow through overgrown or muddied places.

Once I grasped the size of the original forest, I saw how important its otherwise trivial northern re-entrants were. Before the blazing of "the old straight tracks", the dodman marks of tower and steeple, there were only the pathways through the complex woods. These woods were slowly cleared by the early Saxon farmers, then consumed in the fires of an expanding London, but the path between clearing and clearing had to feel its way along the folds of the land, following the two north-flowing streams of the Cray and Darent, the potent gap of the Medway, or the crest or hollow of each re-entrant.

If we forget the more obvious roads by the rivers, not many of those old routes remain in their entirety. The way through West Kingsdown, Fawkham Green, and Betsham is one. It led to Northfleet and the supposed "Coldharbour" but died in the lime-pits and then the cement quarries of the industrial riverside. Another one, more intact, runs from Blacksole Field (and presumably Wrotham), Stansted, then direct for Longfield, missing both New Ash Green and Ridley; then forks left for New Barn and Northfleet via Roman Springhead, or right towards Gravesend, towards which it loses most of its identity among the eighteenth-century enclosures. An alternative, dictated entirely by terrain, runs between both these forks, and probably always did, along the Downs Road. Similar re-entrant routes and ridgeways can be traced running northwards from Trottiscliffe and Birling to Foxendown, or Luddesdown, Cobham and Shorne. The more easterly route is clearly seeking Higham and the old ferry or causeway to Essex. I have spoken of "Lost Roads" already. These ridge and re-entrant routes are not lost; they pass close to most of the major villages on the Downs, and explain why they are there. To the west, say south of a line between Dartford and Gravesend, land is less tightly folded and the tree-clearing is more thorough, and obviously took place early. Consequently settlement has been more random. East, between the A227 and the Medway, the valleys are more tortuous, and in consequence there is still 50 per cent timber. The important towns and villages are south of the scarp, in the Medway Gap, or on the Cobham or Shorne Ridge. All between, there are 70 map squares of not very much. This is what makes Priestwood, Foxendown, Coomb Hill, Great Buckland, Boughurst Street, Henley Street, Luddesdown and even Harvel, David Street and Upper and Lower Bush so very exciting.

I was walking from Trottiscliffe once, up through Whitehorse, Crookhorn, Horseholders and Red Woods — five miles of continuous forest. It was a bright summer's day. I had a good map and compass to keep me away from the roads. Then a strange thing happened. Somewhere between Horseholders Wood and Red Wood the leaf light changed from auburn to rook. I began to walk among younger trees but in a black place. I found myself in a series of naved alleyways of branches, corridors, on the ground-plan of an intricate cross of Lorraine. The coppins were bent over and arched at the top, then racked together with ashpoles and hazel-splints, each about a foot apart. It was like standing inside a geodetic aeroplane fuselage. It was a mausoleum for dead birds.

There were thousands of them, tens of thousands. They were not game birds. There were putrescent magpies and mildewed crows, little hedge birds no bigger than the wind's feather, and enormous gas-bloated corpses as big as farm poultry. Here, perhaps, was the last resting place of the dodo, a long-barrow consecrated to the religion of the gun.

Big woods, wild woods, mad woods. I have never found the place since. I was not tracking a re-entrant.

In theory I can discard the Cray Gap, as Greater London has now swallowed it. The Cray is an unbeautiful river, except for occasional glimpses of its more serene past. The valley that guides it is not always clear, and lies shallowly beneath ill-considered high-rises at St Paul's and St Mary Cray, and the industrial-cum-commercial sprawl along the A224 which leads past carpet and furniture warehouses, then a contraceptive factory, to Orpington, where my friend Adrian Henri is quite clear the world will end.

Yet just south of Crayford, beautiful Plantagenet Hall Place stands in its abbreviated but well-trimmed garden; and although Foot's Cray offers not much more than an ancient church, and St Paul's Cray is now councilled over in red-brick and ruler-roaded ruin, Scadbury Park and Manor struggles to keep its grass blades free of the developers, and at its corner stands Kemnal Manor School, a listed building, though only according to the philosophy that says that the worst excesses of the 1920s and 1930s, like pylons and pressure gas holders, should be held up to delight our children. Kemnal has a bit of the Bauhaus about it, with its metal frames, stacked glass and curved windows. Its exact style is that of the London Rubber Company just down the road, but it is full of fine people.

Diagonally south across the road and hidden from view is a substantial flooding of the Cray where the river has been artificially widened to drive watermills. There is a large paper factory in place now, though not water-driven. The Crays were early in the history of English paper-making.

The mill ends appropriately against a pub on little Ruxley (Rough Field) Lane. Behind Ruxley, and the Cray Gap in general, Kent begins to look rural. This is partly "green belt", but the change is dramatic.

St Mary Cray, with its fine old church framed by a nineteenth-century railway viaduct, just manages to preserve its original village atmosphere, not least in the apparently uninflected genitive of its name. This is a perfectly grammatical piece of fossilized Anglo-Saxon, like Lady Day which offers a similar case. Old English weak feminine nouns took a possessive singular in — *an*, which shortened to a Chaucerian *e*, then dropped off altogether. "Two foot six" is a similar though unrelated piece of uncouth but correct grammar, shortly to be buried by metrication.

Not yet. Just a step or two east of St Mary Cray is the anapaestic countryside of Crockenhill, Hockenden and Kevingtown. Kevingtown has its eighteenth-century manor house, Kevington, now a school. This really does back upon rural acres.

Recently I completed a book of pastoral poems, *King Horn*, about my other home in South-Western France, which incidentally swarms with viperine and colubrine snakes, including the aggressive back-fanged Montpelier Serpent. Then followed the usual anxious quest for a publisher.

I drove into Kevington Manor on a sunny spring day last year and was halted by the debris of the eighteenth-century garden wall which a pair of workmen were shortening to make safe. Suddenly, in suburban Kent, one of them had his hands full of snakes. He had uncovered a little hive of them in the old brickwork, and they were now vanishing through his fingers and feet in astonishing haste.

He kept one as I stopped the car beside him, and I found another. It was a spell from the magic world, "a toe from the old life", as potent as anything in Jim Corbett. I knew that good things would happen that day. When I got home it was to hear that my book had been accepted.

Swanley, Hextable and Wilmington are not much today, being built upon when bricks were easy; but each of them had something to look at, and the Birchwood Road ends on Heath Side, a few acres of primitive Kent. Wonderful to the west is Joyden's Wood where I used to walk with the uncle who died in a small-boat crossing of the South Atlantic. The wood is now half-consumed by an estate, and Stonehill Green, Puddledock and Hook Green will go under the turf and tarmacadam soon.

Swanley is a blight, its nineteenth-century workmen's cottages (as elegant as any in Kent) largely subsumed by modern pebbledash, renovated pubs looking as uneasy as transvestites, and a restless resiting of roads. Swanley Village is a different matter, though its vistas, like Clement Street's, are scarred by the M25. Holts Farm, centuries old and held up by a tree, can still just ignore such encroachments. My beautiful aunt and cousin live there, as for a time did the seafarer.

To the north this now cuts across the Darent near Sutton Place, and with the railway at Farningham Road, the widening of the A20 and A225 and the recent construction of the M20, does what it can to further mar the land about Darenth, South Darenth, Sutton-at-Hone and Horton Kirby. These are all early settlements along the River Darent — at millraces, dam and bridge points — which are a trifle overmastered by later crafts or industries and the proximity to greedy London. They are nearly always at their best when closest to the little river, whose charm is indestructible though it is nowhere as wide as a single lane of motorway.

At Darenth the church is mid-Saxon, with some Roman pottery incorporated and interesting Norman additions, perhaps from poor King Stephen's time. Upstream, beneath one of the river pools, are Roman foundations and tessellations — indeed, some of the very best Roman remains in England are to be found along the Darent.

Slightly further upriver, at Sutton-at-Hone, there are the remains of a preceptory of the Hospitallers. St John's retains an early flint chapel and a complexity of later building culminating in elegant Georgian work.

The Darent, like the Cray, cradled early water-driven paper mills; its bed-filtered water was ideal for hand-made papers long before anyone thought of rolling and squeeze-drying woodpulp. There are mills at South Darenth and sizeable "floods", or millponds, up to Horton Kirby. Indeed, there is a pub saying that "from Darenth's steeple to Horton's tower the fields are all water". They certainly are if one's head is all beer. I once flew low about here in a Tiger Moth, and the slim Darent certainly swells into a big acreage of dark mill water, like a python that has swallowed a deer. I say "pub-saying" rather than "folk-saying" because although Horton Kirby's church is old, its tower is new.

All of these places have their messy modern end, messy not because modern but because of the jumble caused by Kent land-prices, but there is good flint and weatherboard about Horton, and at Farningham across the A20.

Farningham must not be confused with Farningham Road Station, which is two miles away and lost in a draughty field where men loiter and women walk past in a hurry. Farningham itself is just as near to Eynsford Station, on the other branch from Swanley and not in Eynsford village either.

These two are properly villages of the river, not of the road or railroad, though the riverpath that has slowly shifted over to become the A225 is one of the oldest in Kent, possibly older even than the Watling Street.

Farningham's bridge, main street and Mill House are an elegant sight, particularly over a full glass on a pub Sunday when Morris Dancers sometimes visit. There is more than one pub, and the river bifurcates as well, to make a mill cut. Below the bridge is an unusual screen, a kind of gapped wall across the water, looking like the rather fanciful supports of an earlier bridge. In fact this was built to protect the ford from water-wear — suggesting that there was an "underwater bridge" that needed the attention of dumped stone and rubble from time to time. The church has been "done up", but not offensively, and it contains a fifteenth-century font. Roman finds are everywhere about here, and there has recently been yet another one. Eynsford's Norman castle is tumbledown, and looks as if built in flint. I search my memory for Kentish rag, and guess there must have been stone trimmings and possibly facings as flint is never longstanding by itself, since it offers too many jugs to the weather.

Eynsford is a pretty village. Unfortunately it seems to be the centre of a motorbike and leather jacket culture. This is perhaps because Death Hill (now sensibly renamed) rose above Farningham Roundabout on the A20, and provided a twisty "murder mile" on which to achieve the there-and-back including once round the roundabout "clock ton", which is faster than a real "ton" for several self-evident reasons.

Eynsford's Norman church and bridge used to be beloved of watercolourists, and a certain amount of furtive painting goes on along the riverbank even now. I nearly bought a seventeenth-century cottage hard by the bridge's celebrated hump, but decided that the leather jackets or the painters would be too noisy in the pub. The church is to be looked into, after a drink, for its Norman doorway and apsidal sanctuary.

A wise man approaches Eynsford from Crockenhill, to glimpse the rolling corn and orchard land that London has been recently refused permission to destroy. This means crossing the little humped bridge, and this is a congested place, so instead of turning left for the bridge it is an excellent idea to turn right and cool the mind at Lullingstone.

You can keep the castle, partly because it is not that old. There is a touch too much grace and favour about it, as if it was architected and gardened by generations of limp-wristed teadrinkers. Of course its pedigree stretches further than English tea and includes one of Henry VIII's champions who once broke fourteen lances in a tournament, but I know what I mean. I mean, always, to prefer the Roman villa at Lullingstone, which is housed under plastic and has murals dating to the first century. A whole culture is there, some ten generations of Latin good manners presented in a fashion that proves the Romans did more than build roads or groove stone. To see their great walls is always to understand why the occupying Saxons thought they had moved into a land of giants. To visit Lullingstone is also to grasp how the Saxons were convinced their forebears were magicians.

There is something slim about the light all around here. In summer it is corn light, orchard light. It always glows with the calm given off by woods contained by cattle and plough. The river cries aloud to be followed, to Otford if I like, which has unspoiled places, but at least to the Pilgrims' trackway. This brings me to Shoreham, overrated as a village to look at, but not as a village to be in, because it epitomizes miracles.

The first of these is that it stays in Kent, whereas gracious Downe and only recently spoiled Chelsfield have been engulfed by London. We lose Charles Darwin but continue with Samuel Palmer, a painter who renovated Kentish landscape just as the Industrial Revolution did its best to destroy it.

Samuel Palmer lived in Water House, and started a tradition of capturing the Darent Valley on canvas, save he was not an ensnarer but an enchanter. Dunstead Priory and Filston Hall are worth a visit in their separate directions, but it is really the country, with its green secret lanes, and, yes, its lush re-entrants and wooded rides, that should call one. Palmer country. Re-entrant is a clod-hopping word, but it is more exact than valley. We want the old Celtic word coombe to describe hereabouts. It is all little green cwms (to be totally Welsh about it). Such a land can be too green, and it is best seen in later summer or autumn. In any event, it was in the September of 1825 that Palmer brought his friend William Blake here, and the visions mixed.

On their first evening in Shoreham they went ghost-hunting by lantern light. On his second day, Blake was, not unusually, psychic and told the assembled company that he could see Palmer on the other side of the door. They assured him Palmer had gone to London. At that moment Palmer opened the door, his carriage having broken down at Lullingstone on the outward journey.

Lord Dunsany, another dreamer, hales from here. His reputation, like Palmer's in the nineteenth century, has sunk lower than it need, so low that I have not mentioned him among my authors; yet as novelist and playwright he was far from negligible, and as scholar-soldier in the first rank. Even his poems may come back and eat us all.

VILLAGES AND STREETS

TREES

One in St Margaret's
Being cut by my barrel-bellied friend who was jovial
About cutting trees, so he cut it,
A firm-footed beech, by fingers, toes, thumbs
And several good thwacks in the heart;
Soon after was admitted to hospital
To lose several branches himself —
I remember that one, and an elm with the beetle.

Then there was Beauty's garden
The week when the Beast was it died —
No, the Beast lived on; I mean the Prince
Or the King, the man kissing wine, pissing stars
And now bundled under the tall buds of Spring —
And Beauty growing tearful
Could not stand her forest where the Miracle had chased her,
Each Beauty, each Beast, in their four-footed maze,
So gave me a saw and an axe
And bad me chop it down.
The plums came first, and after the greengages,
Then five little nuts. As I chopped
Beauty watched me, as she did so
Growing older, growing ugly,
But ah! What of me?

There was one full of birds, not their bodies, their voices:
I chopped down birds a hundred feet high,
I chopped down the sun, I chopped down the Spring
Like a butcher with a chicken
I chopped as she bad me from each branch in heaven
Little fruit little nuts
                    from God in my season
Then walked home weeping with my legs in my hand.

DIGRESSION BEGAN AT Romney Street. I shall return to Romney Street very soon, perhaps tomorrow, to bite a dog. For the minute my mind is in, and beyond Knatts Valley.

What a splendid place on a map (splendid as from *splendidus*, Latin for "poured out", "tumbled in rich profusion"): Knatts Valley, in apposition and without the apostrophe, is tight, twisting and set with a mixture of wild trees and scrub, rather like groundsel under sprouts. It was, if you remember, one of my model re-entrants, with a road in its furrow and woods — High Castle, Woodlands, Knockmill and Hollywood — at or very near its top.

It is also full of campers' Kent, which may or may not be camp Kent. I have noticed the syndrome before, but not come to grips with it. It is a sickness of mind more than pocket. It says that bungalows are better than houses, because nearer to the ground; and chalets better than bungalows because closer to everything else. Caravans, huts and tents are better again, because closer to God. Knatts Valley is rich (if this is poverty look at Lower Stone, parts of Denton, the gypsy camps along the A2 and A20) but it is straining at a camel, or do I mean the eye of a needle? The camel and the needle have left, and this perky little settlement remains, not unlike a Belgian campsite. Even as the ink dries, decent philistine builders are getting to grips with it, making it more like a Belgian campsite than ever.

I have told you where its road leads, to West Kingsdown, Hartley and New Barn. There are digressions to New Ash Green and Istead Rise, but these are even more depressing. There are also digressions to Fawkham Green, Green Street Green (the younger), Grubb Street, Betsham and Southfleet. Our roads permit an occasional kindness, to keep the traveller's razor from his own throat; but the first list is of the populous places, the ones that grin from signposts and lie pink on the map.

To go to them is to realize how brave is Knatts Valley. That is merely the soul's last frontier; the rest are clones of Doomsville. I keep the frontier image. It is not good bewailing the aesthetics of a bandit town, while failing to notice the mesas and buttes, the cactus and sage at sunset, let alone the man who waters your horse. People have done some amazing things to Kent, but Kent is amazing and they remain amazing people.

West Kingsdown lies along and about the old A20, in the lozenge of land between this and the new length of the M20 running towards the

Swanley interchange. West Kingsdown's principal architectural style
is garage and pump, but there are gracious woods behind it, then
parklands and orchards all around Kingsdown House. It is here,
among apples and football boots, that Kingsdown's interesting little
Norman church nestles like a cat hiding its ears.

Also at Kingsdown is Brands Hatch. The racing circuit, steep and
intricate as the local landscape, is best glimpsed from the M20, though
its entrance is "up top" on the A20 at the summit of erstwhile Death
Hill. I remember Brands Hatch when it was a grass track for
motorbikes. It still retains the character if not the surface. You can hear
its cars ten miles away if the wind is right (or wrong). All the great
postwar drivers have raced here, because it is a grand prix circuit.

Talking of things that go round, or once did, I should mention
Kingsdown's windmill. It stands close to the crossover of the two
main roads. There were many mills about here a century back. This
one is now a stilted rarity.

Impossible to pass over cheerful little Fawkham Green, which until
recently gave its name to the distant railway station which is now
Longfield. It is only a few years ago, with the abolition of third-class
tickets, that Longfield was allowed to exist in one place. Truly, it does
travel ruinously along its westwards valley for several miles, its
architecture linked and repetitive as any railway train and much more
cramped. However, I anticipate.

Fawkham Green is not very much, a grass patch at one end, its fine
old church of St Mary at the other, and a few assorted houses served by
its pub, the Rising Sun. Everything is relatively delightful — rolling,
bosky and rural. You can gaze at its chickens a long, long time,
without discovering one with a significant neurosis.

Fawkham Manor and Court Lodge can still glimpse an occasional
tree. South Ash Manor is only partially engulfed; but at New Ash
Green everything is terrible. A bold plan, a historic site, have
somehow got lost in the execution. *King Lear* has become a B-feature
movie. Contrasted with Vigo Village — not my most favourite place,
either — it seems to fail through lack of focus and, more than that,
trees. Who was the architect who said, "For three people take one
house, six windows, and seven trees."? New Ash Green has the
houses, the windows and the people. Vigo Village has the trees.
On Sundays New Ash Green swarms with people, all of them with
nowhere to go. Yet it is socially lively. I once gave a lift to a woman

who had moved there with her family three years previously and she said that it was the first place in which they had all found true happiness. She lived on the eastern side, closest to those woods. Red bricks rustled in the wind.

Longfield does have its old hamlet close to its church, and at each end of it even along the hideous B260 there are glimpses of what might have been. The little railway cottages to the east are worth a visit, in spite of the rubbish dump, and so is the pert little green at Longfield Hill, with nearby Nurstead Hill Farm. One of the best short road walks in North Kent — I mean of those that actually progress from place to place — goes from Longfield Hill, past Nurstead Church to Sole Street. To take the cross-country route between Nurstead Court and Ifield Church is to compound delight as well as retrace derelict eighteenth-century roads. To skirt anti-clockwise about Nurstead Park by the dryfooted lanes is not bad either. One can go towards Jeskyns Court and Cobham or direct to Gravesend. Three fields before nature gives out there are fine panoramas of the new industries on the river.

Hartley used to be a flattened-out Knatts Valley, dignified by possessing a country club and the Hartley Players. It is said, on good evidence, that Daniel Defoe lived briefly in a cottage near the Black Lion and wrote *Robinson Crusoe* there. I have not included him in "Literary Kent", but on dubious grounds. I once probed the matter in the pub rather than in the library and was told that old clipped ears actually lived in the Black Lion. I apologize to all, and it is not much, of old Hartley.

New Barn used to be a muddy walk. I remember a house or two of substance, but served by cinders, on the old track towards the Downs Road. There were also one or two red-neck wooden bungalows, full of genteel dogs.

There is now a huge development, some of it on unmade unadopted roads, and not all of it bad. This litotes is not meant to damn with faint praise. Some builders have sited their houses around closes and squares, good for borrowing wives and sugar; others have been palatial and kept trees. The site is better, because more contoured, than New Ash Green. It has not plundered the landscape as savagely as the otherwise satisfactory estate near Meopham Station.

The Downs Road has become an unmitigated disaster. Istead Rise was never much, but at least it had a bushy valley behind it. Since the war the whole landscape has been filled in by little roofs and variorum walls, meanly, tightly, and without apparent thought to join the ribbon

development which was already threatening to turn Downs Road into
a little Longfield. One or two flint farmhouses remain, but other
things have gone down or gone under. There used to be a pumping
station at the Nash Street end of the valley. This had a graceful
chimney of variegated Flettons, in harmony with the height of the
landscape and even more with the beech clump on the cheeky Nash
Bank. I had quite thought that beeches, chimney and valley in turn
framing the distant I.P.C.M. towers would form the jacket of this
book. Alas, the chimney has been felled. Still, the Downs Road is full
of beautiful women. My father's youngest sister lives on the farm at
the far end. She can look out towards Bradditch across land under
plough. To the south there is the avenue of trees near Hazells, which
still stands alone.

There is little joy for the visitor to most of these places. They sprawl in
suburban clusters between the scarp and the end of the dip; their size
robs them of their intended rural dignity. None of them has an urban
centre. Some of them have engulfed a hamlet or ballooned from the
corner of a village. The worst of them are based upon a cowpat.
Cowpats are inevitable, towns very necessary. Anything between the
two needs to grow up slowly, around church, shop, craft or farm.

On this basis, Stansted, Fairseat and Hodsoll Street are to be
tolerated, and Ridley and Southfleet to be encouraged. St Margaret's,
Green Street Green, Grubb Street and Betsham should be marked like
Fairseat, say New Barn double plus.

I hope that my every chapter is a hymn in praise of people. People
cannot always dress themselves in appropriate places. Everyone wants
to live in a palace beside a disinfected village pond overlooking a
village green with cricketers. There should be a pub licensed solely to
serve oneself and a close friend.

Hodsoll Street cannot quite achieve this. The Green Man is a fine
pub, though, and there are some excellent walks to every point of the
compass, some by lane, some by footpath, some by simple right of
way. One goes by Haven Manor and lets one sniff at New Ash Green
from the safety of the Anchor and Hope. My favourite skirts the
woods towards Ridley Church and arrives at nothing. The farm
beside the old towered church is ideal for contemplation. Across the
road there is an ancient well, roofed in 1810, and called Bowdler's
Well. Wells are magic and rare out here.

I should just say that since this is not a comprehensive guide book, still less a map and compass, my indolent strolls are not given in detail; nor do I mention every possibility, not by a long chalk. What one needs is the appropriate Green Ordnance Survey Sheet and — for quite a lot of North Kent — the paper guides published by the Meopham Publications Committee. Meresborough Books go further afield.

Meopham has made many mistakes, but remains curiously intact. It is a sprawling, linear village, formed by the amalgamation of its "street", roughly at its centre opposite the very old George Inn, and some half-dozen greens north and south. There has been ribbon development, inevitable when the ground plan is a continuous line, and some of it — between Cammer Corner and the Longfield Road, for example — was obnoxious in the 1930s, but time mellows and improves it. In fact, each blotch of newness in the village is softened by something old. The station end is its own little village, with new and nineteenth-century shopfronts, a couple of gracious mid-nineteenth-century houses, an elegant piece of white clapboard, pebbledash, assorted brick, stucco, and some seventeenth-century cottages. If this pot-pourri is not to everybody's taste, then the eyes can be cooled on the fields and the ash copse towards Nurstead, or made cheerful at Hook Green, surrounded by odd vintage houses, with a farm and barn at its apex which feeds little Melliker Lane, itself terminating on a gutted archers' yew (yew disembowelled for bowmaking but very much alive, archers dead before either of our old churches were considered).

Up the village, that is higher up the hill, there are the old cottages round the church, the street itself, and then a large school, all of this before the main village green charms with trees, pubs, motionless windmill and even stiller cricketers. Wit has it that when anything mighty happens on the cricket field the mill will clap its paddles (localese for "vanes" or "sails"). In fact wit tells a lie. The Cricketers' pub, famous throughout Kent for its welcome — save for moments when mine host dons flannel and pad — has a famous front window, the sort that exponents of the mighty hit to leg gaze at longingly, rather as bulls eye the muletta. A century ago the publican — not, I think, the current sportsman — offered five guineas to any batsman who could send leather with willow through this enticing window. None succeeded. Buses have been wrecked, morris dancers affrighted, lovers surprised among the elms, and a gentleman once met an unfortunate fate in the even more distant but equally enticing public lavatory.

The pub stayed intact until last year when a lad with keen eye and heroic intention confetti'd the glass. Inflation was mentioned, both when it came to dare and repair, and publican and player were both the richer by an award of £50.

The Green is a famous place. It had a clink at one end, stocks, and a wheelwright's and coopers' workshops. A forge is alleged, but I believe this was lower down. Apparently the village lock-up and stocks did a brisk trade in vagrants and long-staff men, for earlier landlords of the Cricketers' Inn used to be paid to keep them fed.

Cobham is a brisk walk through Sole Street. Sole Street has Cammer Court and some fine old cottages at one end, home of artists, admirals, explorers and gardeners. (The gardening tradition is strong hereabouts. John Tradescant, King Charles' famous landscaper and botanist, lived at Meopham and bequeathed us *Tradescantia*, a weed that I could do without.) Further on, there is a "street" that grows better with acquaintance, a railway pub that rivals Meopham's for enthusiasm, and the Yeoman's House, the Great Hall of which is worth visiting. There are several tiny ponds in Sole Street, whose name means "Pond Street" rather than Lonely or Single Street.

There are "Streets" all over these pages. They litter the signposts and maps, and suggest we are not very inventive with place-names. In fact, "Street" has a local meaning, though the word itself is foreign, having swum across the River from Essex, where it was first recorded among the East Saxons. There they meant a road, or a piece of road, or even, as *Beowulf* has it, a stretch of paving, possibly a Roman Road, or just conceivably a Roman floor. This side of the River we are Jutish about the fringes, so "Street" means a hamlet or cluster of houses. There may be a road among them, to be sure, but not a road that goes anywhere, or not in the beginning, for no one raised in our bit of Kent needs to go anywhere. The meaning and its stationary associations are well illustrated by Round Street next to Sole Street.

Sometimes the street becomes a village. Sole Street is now a village. Meopham Street became Meopham, and the original Meopham Street is now called The Street. Everyone knows that if

you say "going up the street" you mean something quite different
from "going up the road": you mean that you are going to the centre
of your community, where the pubs and the shop are.

Cobham is not quite all that it is cracked up to be, but comes close to
it. At five in the morning in summer, when no one is about but
Charles Dickens' ghost, it is very near to perfection. The Leather
Bottle is a fifteenth-century pub, with a stone at its corner that may be
a Saxon scratch stone, a Celtic ley stone, or a chunk of sarson or some
other megalith. It is now full of Pickwick. The Darnley Arms, built
800 years ago, and the Ship both have their associations. Here is an odd
one. Researching a novel recently, I discovered that young Cecil
Schott, son of the artist that Fanny Cornforth left Rossetti for, came
here a century ago and sold watercolours and sketches in the Darnley
Arms in exchange for beer. The pub is an "arms", named after the
family that sprung from Cooling, built the Castle there and then
Cobham Court, and by marriage and good behaviour became earls.
Cricket was first played in their park in the eighteenth century, and
Dickens — a family friend — walked here a few hours before his
death. The Ship is supposed to be framed with ship's timbers.

I have mentioned in another chapter the church's fine brasses, and
its celebrated "College", firstly a dynamo of prayer, then for centuries
after the Reformation an almshouse. It is still occupied, as is the old
stone house nearby. There is a wealden cottage in the High Street, and
a fine oast just behind. Round the corner from the war memorial there
is an isolated hop-garden which is a place of special charm. Ahead,
along the bridleway that starts the park, there is the Darnley
mausoleum. This woodland walk, past Lodge Farm, can be followed
all the way through old timber to Strood.

"Owlets" is a large house on the way back to Sole Street. It was
built in 1684, and was owned latterly by Sir Herbert Baker, as was the
much older Yeoman's House at Sole Street. My parents told me that
"Owletts" had Dickensian connections. It did not, save that he must
certainly have gazed upon it, as must Mr Pickwick. One of
Wellington's Peninsula generals of cavalry lived here, though; and it is
a fine place to visit.

Cobham fields are for roaming, particularly to the south and east
where the land folds and woods thicken. There are tumuli to the
north, though, and a vanished village at Battle Street, site of a Saxon
battle, on a disappeared Romano-Saxon settlement. This has been

followed into oblivion by a separate Dark-Ages village, but it leaves its name.

The bold striker can make for Shorne and its Ridgeway, again with fine old church, mill site, and atmospheric lanes and cottages among much that is modern. Shorne via Strood would be a kibing march for any but my oldest friend and mountain companion, the poet and painter Michael Purser. He would trot it in an hour. I have gone to Cobham from Shorne, but never the other way, and I insist my route is south and then easy by the Cobhambury Valley. Even as I write this pronouncement, I am reminded that the novelist Tony Weeks-Pearson used to live at Rookery Farm, opposite "Owletts" and *run* to the Medway Towns and back by any permutation of these routes. That was in his salad days, but the leafmould must have clung like porridge; and if he stuck — no pun intended — to the brisk roads, then he would have the returning torment of Strood Hill.

I am soft. I have left the Sarsens and the War Memorial and I am running *down* Cobhambury Hill, ideally with a bicycle which is still in the back of the car I am driving. If I am driving, then I'll drink to Sir Wellesley, the Duke of Wellington, at Henley Street. If not I am already on the more easterly fork for Shoulder of Mutton Shaw (the railway arch is a tiny hoop of beauty) and on past flinty Warren House towards Lower or Upper Bush, sites of ancient manorial farms, and then the Dean Farm (not Dene Manor) that has such a fine tilted hop garden growing green beer. Everything is good here until Cuxton or Halling, according to route. Both these latter places have their tiny splendours, and the Medway can never be quite subdued.

It was in Cuxton that the church was built crooked:

> He that would see a church miswent
> Let him crawl to Cuxton in Kent.

And it was in this church that Margaret Coosens was for a century kept pickled (*post mortem*) in a glass cupboard. Possibly she went off colour, but it is more likely the humourlessness of the Victorians that caused them to unstopper her and bury her outside in a dull coffin.

Why do I come here, save to tell this story? Lime, cement, then greedy smelt fishermen ruined the river here, did they not? I come to make crooked amends. Halling had a palace, dwelt in by bishops, and it actually grew wine-making vines between warm walls in this juicy valley. Bishop Gundulf began all this (he was the Ian Botham of architecture) but at this moment I do not give you a fig for him. I am gazing at the brass in the church beside the pulpit. It is too beautiful for a poet to describe it for you, and too painful. You must look for yourself. It tells of the woe that comes from love in marriage. It is known as the Lambarde Brass, and remembers the beautiful Sylvester Lambarde. Her second husband was the celebrated Kentish historian William Lambarde, who wrote everything down in the sixteenth century, giving us hop and grape, church and manor in exact and comprehensive detail. I have not honoured him in "Literary Kent", because, honourable man that he was, he invented nothing. How much I have invented is for you to determine. I punish myself only for the "streets", footpaths and saltings I have left out.

DIP SLOPE AND SCARP

NETSUK REAFFIRMS

He sat in his father's house, resting from women,
Some say his father the spider, some say the giant,
But he lived in the web of whose groin, resting from women
So many hard years out, recutting a tooth,
·Not needing his mother's cave, the preCopernican comfort
But seeking the force, say suckling a star from the spine,
          the long line of seminal hope,
Like a ship needs its chain in the storm

And needing it just like the spider hangs, not from its mother,
But from its own loin, from its bowel

And needing his father's house just like the spider
Suckles on bits of itself and at last is a giant.

WE ARRIVED IN our village in 1940, and my Father immediately paced the garden muttering about Canterbury hoes, bagging hooks and chat potatoes. He was soon arguing with the neighbour concerning Rhode Island cockerels and pullets, day-olds, and sex-links; hinting wildly that we'd be trimming back bines, pinching out tomatoes and harvesting our punnets in no time. I wondered how he knew. Then he bought seed catalogues and bombarded us with Aran Banners, Red Springs, Permains and Cox's. It was impossible, like starting life again. The plumber called in to fix our first burst pipes and I grew happy with a language I had learned in my previous kingdom: water-hammer, lagging and female sockets. My mother joined in with the plumber then. My mother and tough aunt always seemed happiest with plumbers, painters and wall-scrapers. We all spoke about female sockets for ages. Then about ball-cocks and Cox's.

My father hated to see me growing knowledgeable so he counter-

attacked with cooch-grass, bellbine, and wire-worm, then threw
Karlswood Poultry Spice into my eyes.

I think I grew hysterical with linguistic frustration. Or perhaps it
was my brother or the cat.

There seemed to be two cultures in our few miles of living. There
was the water and the land, and they had their separate languages. I
now know that the true inhabitant of North Kent, whether he is from
Culverstone, Cliffe or Conyer, has something of all of them. He sits
among his cabbages, or turns his black furrow, and even while he is
clearing flint and prickle from tine or coulter, the old Boneless Wind
sets in from the river, bringing the imperious hooting of ships making
starboard, and beyond and below a babble then a babel of foreign
voices, as if Old Boneless had turned Boanerges himself with the Gift
of Tongues.

The true Kent dweller, whether Jute, Angle, Saxon, Norman or
Romanized Celt is arrogant, parochial and insular; but his is the
paradox of polyglot parochialism, and of an almost continental
insularity. Richard Church first remarked on this, but he gave the
wrong reason and pleaded for our erstwhile continental connections.
He was wrong. We are immobile, fixed, Sphinx-like, and with
something of that same inscrutable self-amused superiority; but we
have learned continental manners in that people are always passing
through. Planted on our patch for generations we have had to face the
blades of strangers, chaffer with them, outwit them, succour them,
send them on their way, marry with them, learn from them, and
above all teach them.

We certainly know it all. A rooted man is his own man, and the Men
of Kent and the Kentish Men chose to inherit their own parcel of
poverty and not see every second son and daughter driven forth. At
Swanscombe in 1066 they demanded of William I that they retain the
Saxon tradition of spreading possessions among a family and not
confining inheritance to the oldest son. A woman learns wisdom from
her own cow, and a man reads God's entrails in the belly of his own
sheep.

I did not quite realize any of this until I moved on to Downland. I
was, properly, of the River, born beside water among generations of
people who had lived either on or from the water, or done something
of both. But I also lived among the newer industries of the waterside,
with their own loyalties and jargons: timbering, paper-making,

powder-making, cement-manufacture, heavy engineering, brewing, tiling, plastics, chain-link, asbestos, metal-box, wholesale milling and baking. Because to a child's eye they all so resembled shipbuilding, and because they squatted above and beside and were dependent upon water, I soon thought I understood them.

Nonetheless, when I voyaged across the A2 at the age of nine, country speech hit me like a bucket of slops. The main dialect points were not confined to Kent, as I say. It is just that I had never heard them on the lips of the river. Where in Gravesend does a person use southern "be" instead of "am", "are", "is"? Or "were" throughout the past tense? In Gravesend, as in South London, "you was" is a hideous possibility, only flimsily legitimate in even the most distant dialect. My father tells me that when he was young, Old Perry Street was full of such verbs. Possibly. It was on the edge of the fields. But it was also on the edge of industrial Northfleet, and it might have been stuffed up with the general London confusion, a complexity vaster than this.

I also heard "a-doing", "a-going" and many another historic verbal noun, governed by the fossilized preposition and used instead of the modern present participle which is so lazily descended from it.

My father speaks of Perry Street being full of Dickensian characters. The marshes, the canal, Rochester, Gadshill, the Hundreds, and especially Cobham — my next village — is all Dickens country, of course; but I don't have my father's (or Alan Major's) high regard for Dickens' accuracy with language. I have long contended that people and their speech printed themselves on his brain during only one exposure while he worked in the blacking factory. Kent only left him its places and, above all, its atmosphere. He is accurate about the speech of Perry Street (*pace* my father) and the Medway Towns (*pace* Alan Major) because he is accurate about the speech of London. I am reminded too of Raymond Chandler's famous letter to Eric Partridge: "Dialect is something invented by writers at their desks."

There is a shanty land on the Downs. The Downs themselves are a shanty. The difference is that out here man and God have used less clapboard.

Nothing shows this attitude more quickly than inn signs. Ale was traditionally advertised by two or three interlocking hoops set on a pole — a kind of land-travellers' astrolabe, and one or two coaching inns used to show this until recently: The Tollgate above Northumberland Bottom, the Dartford Bull, The Prince of Orange, The Bull at Rochester, and The Leather Bottle at Cobham are examples, but none of the hoops were old; nor are two of the pubs that ancient.

The hoop is not as old as the bush, the bright-green clump on a stake which recalls Yol and Yggdrasil, and must be related to the so-called Christmas Tree. We have as many Bull and Bushes as anyone else, and it is a venerable sign. We have Upper Bush as a place-name near Halling and Bush as old among us as Dodman Deadman as a surname and older as a mark of fertility. How Ale got in I don't know, save it comes from the magic grain renowned among Jutish farmers, and linked with the fertility burials in Jutland itself. I am reminded that pubs like gallows grow by crossroads, and that their callings must have been close both at the Wrotham end of the turnpike and a mile away at Wrotham Heath, at either end of what used to be called Gallows Hill.

Shanty mentality? Well, pubs change their names as well as their pictures. Once our pubs had swinging signs in the air, or even a faceboard, they could be changed *mutatis mutandis* as often as tarts' phone numbers, and were.

Wellington, Nelson, and the battles of the Peninsular War became honoured among us, the latter only when not too damnably foreign. Vigo would do — the old "Vigo" pub now has a modern urbanization named after it, a newer shanty; though there was ale on tap in the pub long before the battle of Vigo Bay.

Some of our holy places became pubs. I think of Milton Chantry that became a pub that gave its name to a fort, a metamorphosis entirely to our credit. But what of pubs that went the other way, like bent clergymen renouncing their cloth? General Gordon's Boys' mission, afterwards a seamen's mission, occupied the site of a seventeenth-century pub, a smuggler's pub so-called with "secret" passage and cellar, all hard by the St Andrew's blockhouse. Come to think of it, St Andrew's is no longer a church but an art-centre not always manifesting continuous erection.

Why are there not more tollgates? The pub at the pike on Dover Castle Hill was called The Dover Castle and is now a private house — I'd rather sleep in a pub than a church; there's less to funnel down Damnation. The Tollgate Inn on the old turnpike road (not so old at all) was once called The Northumberland, hence Northumberland

Bottom. I saw the farmhouse, which was the tollhouse and possibly the pub, burn down. It stood in the muddy hole of the old new crossroads before the newer new crossroads created a crater. After a rushing of winds, and the redesignation of the new old tollgate as a motel, God turned Northumberland Bottom into a petrol station. There is nothing that is more shanty-like than a petrol station, unless it is a new piece of dual-carriageway which will swallow houses and ancient tracks then itself drop into a hole; but I will not be distracted. I once ate Sunday lunch there in pre-motel days and got a flake of glass in my throat, robbing me of speech for a week.

Nowadays we refurbish our pubs on a national basis. That is, there are firms who can take hold of a pub, and in a weekend make it look like an Old English Pub that resembles every bar in North America or soon the Costa Brava. I wish they would visit the pub by the green pond at Church Street, a proper shanty built of clapboard and old catarrh. All the pubs snuggling along the front at Gravesend and Strood used to be clapboard. It dulls the noise of a glass being emptied or a pocket cut. Nowadays, there is only the Three Daws, beauteous in everything save a juke-box.

Pubs can maintain their shantyville essence while proceeding with decorum. At Ryarsh there is The Duke of Wellington, an unoriginal lie, because it was certainly something else before. Nonetheless, it has its Wellesley Cottages next door, named after the hero before he was elevated to attend the Concert of Europe and reinstate kings. It has achieved a metamorphosis of fabric as well as name by building a snug. It has kept the face-lifters at bay, but simply stripped the plaster from an old frame wall. I wonder if the rubble was all horse-hair and dawb, very common around here?

FORTIFIED PLACES

PRACTICE SEAWARDS AT GARRISON POINT
2pdr sub-calibre tube

Casemates fill with our frost.

We sprawl down thick upon straw
Spread thin on the midwinter solstice

Then wake to cocoa and rum
With dawn on the north horizon,
The targets like steam through mist.
The storm comes up with the tide,
Grates its keel overhead, then capsizes.
The sky sits under the cliff.

We fire —
Not the old Mark Seven
But subs from the two-pounder tube
Too slim and too swift to hear.

We fire —
And young seabirds squark
Like smoke from the front of the gun,
Then white out the rest of the air
So reload, in a turret of seabirds,
Ramming the breech with seabirds,
Our purpose these wittering seabirds,
Our aim the renewal of seabirds,
The squarking of snow-white seabirds,

And then the shrill flocks of snow.

KENT HAS ALWAYS been fortified. In 1940, after Dunkirk, a captain and sergeant-major of infantry knocked on our door and gently asked my mother if she would mind moving the compost heap from the south-facing corner of our front hedge. They took away her agreement and a cup of tea and left us some empty sandbags in return. Our windows, like everyone else's, were criss-crossed with sticky paper; we had a dugout in our garden, a barrage balloon at the lane end behind us, and every other night the little station green beyond our neighbours' houses was visited by an appalling anti-aircraft gun that shocked with its recoil and made a noise like teeth splitting.

Pillboxes appeared along the Downs, on the marshes, on banks above bridges or railway cuttings, or in arbitrary corners of bird-blitzed lanes. In our tenth and eleventh years we captured nearly all of them, throwing Molotov cocktails genuinely aflame or knocking out their eyes with catapults.

There's no need to classify every warlike locality in our bit of Kent, though I'll mention them all. They fall into three categories: defended homes or communities (the most honourable, natural and ancient in concept); fastnesses from which aggressive people could issue, perpetrate nasty acts, and to which they could return with impunity — I think of the robber barons of Scadbury by the Crays; and then the offensive forts by the river, from Upnor on the Medway round to the North Kent blockhouses and later artillery forts. Our one city castle in Rochester is on an altogether higher level, an emblem of feudal and royal authority; though in practice it combines the other three functions.

The artillery fort and blockhouse, the "land ship", is a modern concept. The ideal is denial at a distance. This had to wait for gunpowder for its germination, and impact explosives for its finest flowering. In the early days of such forts, although the Thames forts had their successes (in particular against the Royal Navy after the Nore mutiny), fortunes were likely to ebb and flow. A dirt parapet might be more secure than floating wood, but a late eighteenth-century ship of the line could fire with much greater frequency and sometimes weight, so the temptation for land gunners to keep their heads down would be considerable. Successes afloat went wider than the exploits of Captain Hornblower.

Henry VIII was the first British Commander-in-Chief to sense the value of emplaced cannon as a way of protecting harbours and closing rivers. There are many near perfect Tudor Forts in the South of England — I think of Walmer and Deal and St Mawes which I have visited, and Pendennis which I have lived in for a time; but these are all outside our area. Yet it was in North Kent, by the heart of his kingdom, that his work was begun.

In Gravesend, as at Tilbury, he ordered the building of blockhouses and the raising of volunteer regiments to man them. We have this on the authority of Lambarde, writing in 1576:

> King Henry . . . raised a platform at Gravesend, one other at Mylton, and two others over against them on Essex side, to command the River in those places, at such time as he fortified other Coastes of his Realme.

Hereafter confusion. In Gravesend, there are remnants of three blockhouses and a fort. Gravesend's New Tavern Fort, to the north of the present Fort Gardens at the back of the promenade, dates only from 1778, and was rebuilt in the 1860s; so we can forget about that. But the other sites are in Milton Chantry, then west by St Andrew's Church and to the east beyond the gates of the Gravesend and Medway Canal.

The blockhouse by the canal probably is the only site that can be said to be near Milton. Milton Chantry (the cause of the confusion?) and the St Andrew's site are close to the centre of Gravesend.

My own bet is that works were begun at Milton Chantry and St Andrew's. Milton Chantry is the oldest building in Gravesend, and was a religious foundation subsidiary to the Church of Saints Peter and Paul at Milton proper, a whole mile away. The chapel of Milton Chantry was founded in 1832 by Aymer de Valence, Earl of Pembroke. It fell into disuse after the Reformation, and even became an inn — hence the name of the fort. Its walls are three foot thick, clunch faced by flint: this really is traditional Kent architecture, and there is not much around along the Thames.

These were cannon-firing fortifications, close to the waterline and with a narrow traverse. It looks as if their line of fire would have faced directly into the Tilbury blockhouses.

The range is only short, but against a moving target it would have needed to be point-blank, even allowing for the usual coast-artillery off-lay from the bow-waterline of the target.

To crossfire directly into the opposite fortifications seems more risky than it would have been in fact. The cannon might well have fired rubble, or stone passed roughly through a governor. Even with a moulded iron ball its muzzle-velocity would have been in the low hundreds of feet a second.

It is true that Henry's cannons could lob their projectiles a mile or so, but only on a high trajectory close to the upper register. Such a register would involve ranging procedures and be no good against a moving target; and it would occasion a very sloppy depth of zone. Nelson encouraged his gunners to aim short and "skip" their projectiles to solve these problems; but his guns fired a cast not a moulded ball and had a substantially higher velocity. If Henry's shots missed they perhaps skipped once, but then they sank before damaging Tilbury.

I have spoken of forts replacing the blockhouses. Tilbury Fort was constructed at the end of the seventeenth century and, like Gravesend, remodelled in the 1860s.

Tilbury Fort is built to an elaborate ground-plan close to the river, and its design includes a moat. From Gravesend its low shape can be seen exactly midway between Tilbury town landing-stage and the huge new power station. Its batteries are on either side of a shallow vee, so its most natural lanes of fire would be to either side of its twin at Gravesend, which was similarly modelled.

Henry's castles, with their low, layered Tudor-rose design were elaborate forebears of those forts. Although they were clad in stone, their smooth rounded facings had some of the impermeableness of a martello. Their moats were often fronted with a substantial glacis, lowering their lines, strengthening them and blending them into the landscape.

The river forts, certainly those at Gravesend, Shorne and Cliff, *were* the landscape. You can see very little of Tilbury Fort from Gravesend or vice-versa; and from a boat prying up the Lower Hope, Shornemead and Cliffe would be almost indistinguishable from the riverwall. So would Coalhouse Battery and Coalhouse Fort.

All of these forts consisted of cannon, then more modern pieces, firing through embrasures at the top of a scarp. Even the Six-Inch Mark Sevens at Garrison Point, Sheerness, fired through casemates. The raked shields of the old Mark Seven, each of them as solid as a castle, made them admirably suited to this. There were latterly more casemates than guns; I know; I slept in a straw-lined casemate at Sheerness during a snowstorm, and very windy it was. Time had buckled the shields on the gunports; and we lay in the kind of draught that can only gust through doors of iron.

Even modernized, Gravesend Fort was armed with muzzle-loading guns. The invention of the screw-locking breech was long past; but it was still not deemed appropriate for heavier artillery, especially when aimed against ships with a slow rate of closure. The guns of Gravesend and the Tilbury batteries would have each managed about a round a minute; whereas the Mark Sevens at Garrison Point, and the Mark 24s at Warden Point were capable of seven rounds a minute even at long range when the gun had to be wound up to coarse elevation after reloading. Number Six performs this menial task on the Mark 24, winding it up and down with a kind of washing-mangle handle for speed. I started off my artillery life that way. At gunfire, at autosight ranges, the modern Mark 24's rate was given in the Coast Artillery Handbook as fifteen rounds in two minutes. Most competitive artillerists reckoned on eight rounds a minute. This may not sound much until one puts a stop watch on it. We are talkng about modern heavy artillery which can lob a hundred-weight of projectile 27,000 yards. Of course, rocketry does better; but it is hideously expensive, even without its guidance systems. Each rocket is as ridiculous as a virgin birth, a monstrous piece of self-destruction. It will soon become as expensive to sink a ship as build one.

Shornemead and Cliffe Forts are melancholy places, reached across flat, wet lands. The Cliffe Fort stands beyond a vast acreage of floodpans — square miles of them, literally, when they are full. Gravesend is reached by a track that skirts a very nasty drainage cut. I used to wade in it as a child, and I suspect it accommodates somebody's sewage. It is where methane was invented by my friends' silted footsteps; and will o' the wisps are not uncommon along here. To garrison these places must have seemed like being sentenced to the hulks, which were moored very near.

A landfort strikes fear into the opposing ship because of its invisibility; even a Second World War destroyer could outgun it, but the land's vast bulk is sullen and alien when seen from a hostile vessel. Afloat, by comparison, is like drifting motionless in a tin bath. All of the shoreline's intention is aimed at oneself. It is difficult to see just where it is firing from. Its salvoes take long seconds, a minute even, to reach one; and the land is unsinkable.

Where the river fort is disadvantaged is by its lack of altitude above the mean water level. To a modern artillerist it is much more agreeable to be invisible on a clifftop than invisible on a beach. This is because the range-finding equipment depends upon similar triangles in the vertical plane. No matter how meticulous the graticuling of a depression range-finder or depression position finder, or how generously distorted the scale, there can be no doubt that it is much more comforting to operate from a mean base of 500 rather than fifteen feet. For this reason, when the ack-ack 3.7s were used in the coast role to protect estuaries, they were sometimes ranged by means of their stroboscopic aerial predictors. These might have had a base line of only five feet, but they operated by means of actual rather than similar triangulation; and in the horizontal plane, so they were not at the mercy of the tide, which is predictable, or of the wind pressure about the humping of the water, which is not.

In the mid-nineteenth century, when most of these forts were built or refurbished, range-finding over water was conducted in the following ways: by qualified guess, by estimation according to landmark or seamark (a feasible process in a river, but very difficult seawards or in a broad estuary); by correction from observed fall of shot, and by the "fortress system". The fortress system, modified and fed through sophisticated equipment, today a computer, is still the ideal.

A fort, or its observation points, can occupy a frontage of hundreds of feet or hundreds of yards. Bearings from its two extremes can give very satisfactory triangulation on an artillery board, or observable plot on a coast artillery table, which is a kind of manual computer. The early limits to this scheme were simply those of the mouth-aided megaphone; and then of radio or telephone. A fixed landline between Warden Point and Garrison Point, for example, gave the Garrison Commander at Sheppey an operational base line of some fifteen kilometres.

Coast forts, as distinct from castles, may be said to be modern — "modern" as in "modern English" anyway. To the fortifications of this sort already mentioned must be added Slough Fort at Allhallows, an old, modified tower flanked by batteries; the mid-nineteenth-century martello at Grain, rearmed during World War Two, a bleak place marooned by the tide across flats, with half the Medway Estuary as its moat; Hoo Fort and Darnet Fort on mud islands in the Medway; and then the blockhouse ruins to the west of Gillingham Strand.

Upnor Castle predates these; it was built to close the Medway and protect Chatham Dockyard. Despite good intentions it was never properly provisioned, and de Ruyter found its armaments im-

poverished in the raid of 1667. He silenced its fire in a long cannonade —
or rather it shot itself to a standstill. Later, the defenders of Upnor
counter-attacked with a battery of field cannon. I like Upnor, and enjoy
its castle. It nestles among trees which look much more important than
it does itself. Still, it was built at the express command of Elizabeth I,
surrendered to Cromwell in 1642, was captured during the uprising of
Kent Royalists in 1648, and retaken by Sir Thomas Fairfax.

There are the remains of other fortifications around the Medway
above Rochester, at Wouldham and on the edge of Wouldham
Marshes, for example; but not much is known about them; and the
chance is they were fortified dwellings rather than part of a concerted
plan to close the Medway to any enemy. For what it is worth, they are
sited in the general area of the river where anyone using the pre-Roman
trackway might hope to cross it; so there would always have been a fair
number of travellers hereabouts.

As well as ordering the building of Upnor Castle, Elizabeth I
strengthened Queenborough Castle on Sheppey and initiated the
construction of a fort across the Swale at Swaleness. I can't find any
remains of this. Indeed, it is planted in a place susceptible to water.
Right opposite Queenborough, however, the flood wall is prominent
between West Point and the creek behind Deadman's Island. It forms a
partially enclosed space, and may represent the remains of a Swale
battery.

Queenborough Castle was built on Sheppey by Edward III,
supposedly for the defence of the Swale and Medway. I doubt this, but
the site is surrounded on three sides by water, and is in an excellent
defence position. Edward himself spent time here, and the village —
formerly Bynnie — was renamed Queenborough after his Queen,
Philippa of Hainault. It was attacked in 1450 by Jack Cade's army,
supported by the men of Sheppey; but held by 22 men. It was totally
destroyed during the Civil War. Nothing remains today, apart from its
mound, which is near the railway station. Charles II apparently had
visions of rebuilding it, but revised his ideas in favour of Garrison Point.

There are the remains of a number of other fortifications along the
Swale, including Sayes Court across the saltmarsh towards Harty
Marshes from the Ferry Inn, and pillboxes near Kingsferry Bridge.

I must mention, as earthworks on the Swale, Castle Rough, Tonge
Castle and Bayford Castle. They are not modern forts, but the
earthwork remains of motte and bailey castles. They seem to have been

built in early medieval times to defend Milton Creek, if not the Swale itself. They claim to be older, or to occupy older sites. There has been good excavation at Tonge and Castle Rough, and much research. It is not really conclusive either way, in spite of persuasive argument for conservative estimates.

I first went to Castle Rough as a student, years ago, because it was where the first Danish invasion of Alfred's England is supposed to have wintered. About a year later, having read in Lagamon the legend concerning Hengist the Jute and the Thong, I went to Tonge, where it is all supposed to have happened. Hengist, according to the *Anglo-Saxon Chronicle* and Lagamon, helped Vortigern against the Picts, and won the hand of Vortigern's daughter and as much land as he could encompass with a bullock's, ox's or horse's hide (his name, like Horsa's, means horse). He took a sharp knife and sliced the hide into a sort of continuous bootlace or thong and with it encompassed many acres. Some say he fenced off Thanet. Others, more modestly, that he took Thong or Tong. Both are areas of Jutish settlement.

I didn't know that the castles were so close when I came here. I remember the *Chronicle* pretty well, firstly because I studied it; secondly because the Danes are mentioned as having gone up as far as Milton, and I first seized on this as meaning Milton-next-Gravesend and not Milton Royal or Milton Regis.

Since Castle Bayard — now Bayard Court — is nearest to Milton it seems likely that this was the Danes' defended locality, while Alfred fortified Castle Rough (too near the Swale?) or, indeed, Tong. Memory prompts me that the Danes had two camps, *wudu setl*, and *waeter setl*, one in a wood and one by water. They are all by woods, and were all by water; so it is possible that all of these camps, and the mounts across the Swale on Harty Marshes, were connected with this Danish invasion. Whether Hengist and his blood-brother Horse were here is another, but even more exciting matter. This south side of the Swale is a strange landscape, full of many a tricky ditch and whingeing thicket.

Now for the two surviving castles of the area: Rochester and Cooling. They both still live among people, so occur in other chapters where they can speak for themselves.

REGIMENTS AND FLEETS

WARSTOCK

Sergeant Major Farthing, bullish Major Batten
And the Adjutant Captain whose name I forget
Had a three-roomed hut among the Fusiliers
Where they kept steel pens and War Department pencils
And a library of buff Army paper
With instructions to marshal a regiment of dreams.

I was in that Regiment. I was a dream
Noted in pencil on buff Army paper
First by Mister Farthing, then by Major Batten
Then filed away in triplicate, each triplicate in triplicate
By the Adjutant Captain whose name I forget,
Three times a soldier and three times three a thief:

Most of my poems and several of my novels
Were written on paper stolen from them then,
A library of buff Army paper
With the War Department Crest
And a regimental heading
As I ground my way onward through a hutful of pencils
(I prefer to write with pens but they counted their pens)

Keats never wrote with your pencil, Major Batten,
Sharpened by Sergeant Major Farthing
And chewed by the Adjutant in ways I'll not forget;
Shakespeare wrote with feathers, never with a pen:

Yet when I feel sad, when the novel won't obey me
When the biographic ghosts won't come and surrender
Or the poems' little syllables leap into line,
I think of you then, with your paper and your pencils,
Sergeant Major Farthing, bluff Major Batten
And the Adjutant Captain whose name I forget.

IN MEDIEVAL TIMES the men of Nurstead marched off in armour with those of many another parish to do their annual garrison duty at Dover Castle. Rochester was similarly manned, calling upon the Hundreds of the Hoo peninsula and the Medway villages. Both castles were stiffened by professional men-at-arms, but they were locally employed; and there were many other places about the county held not by but for the Crown. Defence followed the feudal code which had been in part imposed, in part merely imported from France. Families owed allegiance to their lord. The lord was loyal to the Crown. But in Saxon days, national defence was even more simple; a man took his bow and his sword and went to serve his King wherever the fyrd was assembled. The axemen of Kent were victorious in Northumberland with Harold just a few weeks before he was slain in their midst above Hastings.

I mention all this with some temerity, but it is true. The Navy claims to be the Senior Service, but on doctored evidence. England raised national armies in the service of its king long before any king raised a fleet. There were military appointments under kings both Saxon and Norman before the dynasties of either sought to fight afloat. So in spite of the dockyards of Chatham and Sheerness, the Navy will fill its place in these pages, and its place comes later, ahead of the two great county regiments, but behind much else.

Our county regiments include the Third of Foot, but even that comes post-Navy. What comes before is a military hydra, with us but not always so named since the beginning of the Anglo-Norman Army. Its heads in order of visible seniority are Royal Engineers — Artillery — Ordnance. The history of these is hopelessly intertwined and linked with Kent and particularly the Medway Towns and Woolwich since the earliest days. The Royal Engineers and the Royal Artillery are now separate arms — two of the four arms of the Army; and while the Ordnance Corps is not an arm it has a sibling, the Royal Army Service Corps, and a child of necessity, the Royal Electrical and Mechanical Engineers. So I begin with this all-important family, with R.E. and R.A. the parental initials, R.A.O.C. their unacknowledged child, and R.A.S.C. and R.E.M.E. the grandchildren or what you will. Of course, none of these initials existed before there was a Navy, but then the initials R.N. are only recent. What is clear is that most of their functions and some of their titles did so exist, and in Kent.

Bishop Gundulf who improved Rochester Castle and laid out the foundations of the Norman Rochester Cathedral, enjoyed the title of King's Engineer. It was he who built the White Tower in the Tower of London, too; and his life exemplifies the duality of many a subsequent member of the Royal Engineers, who not only supervised siege trains and built castles, mines and trenches, but also participated in the design or building of religious and secular architecture for peace. Gundulf gives his name to a bridging pool at Upnor; and appropriately it is his cathedral at Rochester which is the Royal Engineers' garrison church, and sanctuary to their colours and roll of honour.

At the beginning of the nineteenth century a school of military engineering (it has enjoyed various titles) was established on the Medway by a Captain of Engineers who had been with Wellington in the Peninsula; and it was men from this school who designed the Victoria and Albert Museum and the Albert Hall, who helped with the stress calculations for the Crystal Palace, completed the National Ordnance Survey, and then various International Surveys (Everest, after whom the mountain was named, was trained at Chatham) as well as refurbishing the Thames forts, raising sunken hulks from the Thames at Gravesend (the Engineers had invented their own diving bell by 1836) and mapping, bridging and fortifying all over the world.

The Artillery are closely related to the Engineers; and Artillery Officers, like Engineers, tended to train at Woolwich.

When Henry VIII called on his King's Engineer to fortify the Thames, a number of volunteer regiments of artillerists were established to man them. The New Tavern Blockhouse and 415 Coast Regiment R.A. (T.A.) had their origins at this time, though of course Gunners and Sappers had travelled together in siege trains since before Agincourt (Shakespeare's Captain Fluellen was one of the breed, I seem to remember). Since Henry VIII's decree, there have been Coast Artillery units about Kent for generations, generally volunteers. Each of the forts of the Thames and Medway (and it is a long list) was manned by these units.

I wrote of the presence of the Ordnance Corps in our midst whilst mentioning the Drill Hall at Stone. In a sense, the Ordnance Corps is as old as the Engineers and the Artillery, as already acknowledged — though surprisingly their gun- and ammunition-ferrying function was done by civilians, or by civilians commanded by soldiers, until the end of the Peninsular Campaign. The Ordnance at Stone are a

Pocahontas . . . strong above damp foundations

Left: When the eye seeks the river

Right: St Mary Cray
... church and
railway arch

The Medway at low water

Farningham . . . the ancient flotsam screen

Strood . . . waters just above the Roman bridge

Rotary kiln like an abandoned cannon

Nineteenth-century muzzle-loader in Gravesend's surviving fort

Farningham Mill in Spring sunshine

Bexley's mill on the River Cray

Northfleet...dawn tinged with concrete

Royal Terrace Pier...Gravesend's nineteenth-century riverside

The enlarging moon-crater south of Swanscombe

bomb-disposal unit. This is a task they share with the Engineers; but whereas the Engineers tend to dig up bombs from the two wars, it is largely the Ordnance who look after the nasty little devices left by the I.R.A. This is because the Ordnance are, by definition, weapons experts. The Engineers, among other things, are explosives experts.

To Wellington, unlike the French, the Weapon Train and the Food Train were of equal importance, even if the former was more so. So the R.A.S.C.—the Service Corps—deserve mention in these pages. As an old Coast Artillerist I remember the boat units of the R.A.S.C. with enormous affection. They used variously to visit and base themselves at Sheerness and Dover to tow our targets and provide us with spotter boats. The Navy always declined to undertake this service. We had beaten them too often.

I served in 415 Coast Regiment at Gravesend and Sheerness. It was an ancient foundation and had, as was proper, batteries north of the river as well as on our side, though the northerners were a lesser breed. After the abolition of Coast Artillery in the 1950s (a Navy-induced nonsense, in spite of their own failures in the Straits during 1939–1945), we were separated into an A.G.R.A. or Army Group Royal Artillery to the north—well in accord with Essex pomp and indolence—and 263 Light Regiment to the south. I have written about this exhilarating time in *In Step With a Goat*, and see no reason to do so again.

Later 263 was swallowed by a local Royal Engineer unit. I declined to have anything to do with this new state of affairs. Perhaps I should have read my military history more carefully. After all, the Engineers and ourselves carry the same blazon, being twins: *Quo Fas et Gloria Ducut*. The ending of 415 signalled the ending of a unit older than the Guards, and of Britain's least costly form of defence.

That being said, it is difficult to live between these two rivers and not salute the Navy and the Mercantile Marine. There are the two great dockyards of Sheerness and Chatham, and their attendant barracks. It is a tragedy for our economy that one is dead and the other dying. On both rivers, men o' war have been built, refitted, laid-up, engaged or sunk. To stay with the positive, H.M.S. *Victory* was built at Chatham; the *Bellepheron* and *Shandon* across the river, and a host of other hulls in Nelson's battle fleet.

Officers and men of the mercantile marine have been trained on the *Worcester* and the *Arethusa*, and their attendant institutions, and at the Sea School at the town end of Gravesend's promenade. Erith,

Greenhithe, Dartford, and most of the towns small and large of the Medway and Swale are or were ports. There are or were industrial ladings at Dartford, Stone, Swanscombe, Northfleet, East Gravesend and Denton, on the north tip of the Hoo Peninsula and long jetties snaking over the flats east of Grain, and about the creeks north of Upnor. Ships feed us and have defended us. Before roads were either sound or safe, most came by boat; and it was boats that carried our goods to London. For almost two centuries, our cheapest entertainment was afloat or reached by water. In the early mid-century it was cheaper to travel to Rosherville by water from London, than to go from Gravesend pier out to Wrotham — a third of the distance — by the daily bus on the new turnpike.

Chatham Dockyard was a sixteenth-century foundation, handy to Kentish hardwoods, the gun foundries of the Medway and the powder makers of the Swale. It was only a day's ride from the capital, and by the end of the century employed a regular building force of some 50 shipwrights, with many ancillary workers. Throughout their history the Royal Dockyards have been flexible with labour; Chatham sometimes simply took on casual labour from among its subcontractors, used sailors, or "borrowed" workers from the royal yards of Deptford, Woolwich, and latterly and more conveniently Sheerness.

By the eighteenth century it was the largest industrial employer in Kent, and later into the nineteenth it was building ships of the line, steam-sailboats, iron-clad hulls, and then modern all-metal boats. Latterly the Naval Dockyards became places for arming, armouring, refitting and experiment; and Chatham kept abreast of these developments.

Sheerness was founded in 1667, as part of the King's displeasure at Admirals de Ruyter, van Ghent and van Tromp. Fine boats were built here, but as we have noticed earlier, the Roman worm was always a problem for wooden boats in this part of the Medway.

Worm or not, there has been a Nore Fleet, a Nore Squadron or a Nore Command for a very long time. The Navy has not forgotten the damnable Dutchmen (on whom it was revenged) and has well guarded the London Approaches against ships and the air. The Nore Anchorage is a terribly exposed place to be, full of sleet when other skies are moonlit or blue; but it is more sheltered and surer beneath the fluke than anywhere off the Kent Roads or Shoeburyness.

★

Numbers and dates are a nuisance, but the Buffs were the Third of Foot, founded in 1665, a most glorious county regiment before the Somme spelt out too great a concentration of sorrow for neighbourhood enlistment. Even so, they continued to recruit well locally. Nearer to home were the Queen's Own Royal West Kents, the old 50th and 97th of Foot, first amalgamated countywide to form the Queen's Own Buffs, and then with the two Surrey regiments so popular with Londoners, to form the Queen's, this being the senior title of the West Surreys, belonging to the Second of Foot, founded in 1661.

I once visited the East Surrey's Mess, "the Footballers", and drank enough there to make me permanently shortsighted. Our own county regiments were all over the place as terriers until the huge amalgamation, and it was impossible to move without colliding with them.

There was a time too when it was difficult to move about Gravesend without meeting an Inniskilling. They were a long way from home, but managed a most peaceable occupation of the barracks, some of them were tall for Irishmen but distinguishable from the trees in Milton Road by means of the feathers in their caps. They have now become the Royal Irish Rangers.

The "Arms" and some of the historic corps rooted in the neighbourhood have complex histories; and recently the local line regiments' traditions have been complicated, but not weakened, by amalgamation. Yet I started not with badges and blazons but with long-bow and stave, with the Nurstead volunteers; and the volunteer tradition keeps on intruding in Kent. It was highly evident during the Napoleonic Wars and World War One; and after the beginning of World War Two it became a glorious contagion.

The Isle of Grain refineries set up their own anti-aircraft volunteers in the mid-1930s, and nearly all of the big employers — Chatham Dockyard, Short Bros, Bowaters, I.P.C.M., for example — either followed suit or entered into very close arrangements with their local territorial units.

So it comes as no surprise that the Home Guard, "Dad's Army", the L.D.V., was almost entirely a Kent invention. Its forebear, the Stay Behind and Reconnaissance Units, certainly were.

A speech by Anthony Eden on 14 May 1940 asked for volunteers for the L.D.V. By then, a number of Kent units were already in being on an ad hoc basis.

A few months later Winston Churchill insisted that the Local Defence Volunteers should be renamed the Home Guard. They were to be affiliated with local regular regiments, and supplied and equipped through the territorial network.

Initially this meant that most of the Home Guard were infantry; and this was reasonable, since it was assumed that their enemy would be parachutists and airborne troops. So those east of the Medway wore the badge of the Buffs, and those who were Kentish were badged as the Queen's Own Royal West Kents. There were 28 battalions in Kent. In our own area, their battalion numbers and names were as follows: 9 Faversham, 11 Maidstone, 12 Chatham, 13 Rochester, 14 Hoo, 15 Cobham, 16 Gravesend, 17 Northfleet, 18 Dartford, 19 Farningham, 56 Erith, 57 Sidcup. There were also 30 Sheppey, 31 Dockyard, 33 Short Bros, and a few initial artillery formations. Of the battalions that bordered us, some were manned from among us: 20 Sevenoaks, 24 Malling, 51 Bromley, 52 Farnborough, 53 Orpington, 55 Beckenham. 54 Chiselhurst deserves special mention, because very early in their life they invaded us in an exercise, only to be machine-gunned from the air by a Dornier. They returned the fire with their Lee Enfield rifles and brought it down.

Special units in our area — and throughout the country — were 25 G.P.O., 26 Kent Bus, 27 Kent Electric, and 28 Southern Railway. Again there was the rapid progress towards hybridization that so distinguishes Kent Arms. In Europe, railways had been used as fast roads by the tanks, motorbikes and half-tracks of the German Panzers. The Railway Battalion very quickly armed itself with 75mm and other artillery anti-tank guns.

By 1942, Gravesend Home Guard were manning five-inch naval guns at Shornmead Fort; the Sheerness Battalion was manning several seawards batteries, as well as retaining an infantry capability, and there was an increasing number of anti-aircraft formations (though surprisingly the first of these, the Isle of Grain Battery, had been subsumed by the local T.A.). The most interesting of these were the two rocket-armed "Z" batteries of the Medway towns: 101 at Gillingham, and 102 at Lodge Hill, Rochester. The Short Bros unit had also taken on an ack-ack role in defence of its seaplane anchorage at Rochester and its aerodrome and factory at Pobjoys.

Ultimately the Home Guard received some sophisticated weaponry; but its early image was not helped by stories of training with shotguns, sticks and Molotov cocktails. (The men of Nurstead would have understood, and Hitler took the Home Guard very seriously from the start.) Once the .300 Springfield, Remington and Eddystone rifles had come and gone, and the whole guard was armed with standard .303 short or long Lee Enfields, things were easier, the supply of ammunition chief among them.

That being said, the Home Guard did continue to receive a considerable amount of antiquated or experimental weaponry that was never entirely suitable for the Regular Army. The Thompsons and Stens were all right (though there were some unfortunate domestic accidents with the latter); but a serious student of weapons of war can hardly gain much joy from a list that includes the Northover Projector, the 29mm Spigot Mortar or Blacker Bombard, the Smith Gun — a lunatic artillery piece that was shaped like an old-fashioned squirrel trap and fired on its side with a muzzle velocity of 350 feet a second — and the Fougasse. I notice from my photographs that the Northfleet men had the Fougasse flamethrower, and the poor lads of Gravesend the Smith gun. They had pits to practise in. Otherwise there might have been a reluctance to give them weapons which could have ignited the world.

All weapons are deadly when used with determination. Kent had 60,000 Home Guards under disciplined arms. That is ten infantry divisions, and the greater part of them lived and trained in our populous northern wedge. I have spoken of 20 battalions. It is worth remembering that these were often the old-fashioned "big" battalions of over a thousand men. At one point, some companies had over a thousand men. The Dockyard Battalion was bigger than a brigade of infantry. By midway through the war, every man who worked in Chatham Dockyard had to enlist in 31 Battalion.

The numbers seem impersonal, Russian or American; but each battalion was primarily a Kentish place-name, and all those places felt a great sense of corporate loss when the Home Guard stood down. Surprisingly it was re-formed from 1952 until 1958 to meet a new emergency, and in much the same formations. As I glance down the regimental lists, I am surprised by how many people I know, men of my father's age mostly, but some almost a generation younger.

Something of the same tradition of do-it-yourself, of private enterprise in the national service brought the Kent Battle of Britain airfields into being, at least in our area — and this feeling of spontaneity was enhanced by the many auxiliary squadrons which flew from them. Though, as far as wartime Kent was concerned, all wings with roundels on them were more than welcome, as was any light-blue uniform.

There were seven operational airfields in North Kent, and of these Manston was far to the east of our area. Three more of them, Biggin Hill, West Malling and Detling, were peripheral. Still, their planes were frequently overhead, making those little ripping noises as if the sky was tearing which we soon learnt was cannon or machine-gun fire. I only felt really certain of the current Gravesend squadrons; but even this certainty was childish. Gravesend was a subsidiary airfield, and frequently hosted other units, notably from Biggin Hill. Squadrons were shuffled about, and all planes landed where they could to refuel in an emergency.

Military flying began in our part of the world at Eastchurch on the Isle of Sheppey. The lush green site of this famous old grass flying field is now an open prison, but you can still hear propellers in the wind there.

In 1910 Eastchurch was leased to the Royal Aero Club, and Brabazon, Sopwith and Rolls all flew there. In 1911 naval flyers trained on Sheppey, and in 1914 a Royal Naval Air Service Flight was stationed there; for it fell to the Navy to defend us against Zeppelins and Bothas. The R.F.C. were in France.

Later R.F.C. squadrons were formed for home defence, flying Sopwith Camels and B.E. 2cs. One of these was based at Ash Green; another at Grove Park, between us and London.

It is easy to time-gaze past the blitz and poo-poo these early air-raids. A single bomb dropped from a Botha on 3 September 1917 hit Chatham Naval Barracks and killed 136 ratings. Earlier, in May, 97 civilians were killed in Shornecliffe. So Eastchurch and its auxiliaries were very necessary to our safety.

It was run down between the wars, and became an aerial gunnery school. At the start of the Second War it was a Coastal Command Base, under Number 16 Group. Later it hosted fighter squadrons flying cover over Dunkirk; and came to be regarded as a fighter base by the Luftwaffe. They accordingly attacked it with 40 Dorniers on Eagle Day, 13 August 1940, and damaged Blenheims of 35 Squadron, Battles of 12 and 142 Squadrons, and — fortuitously — the Spitfires of 266 Squadron, and six Spitfires of 19 Squadron, all of these last being visitors.

Later, ground attack Spitfire VB.s flew from Eastchurch to support the Dieppe Raid; and then housed squadrons belonging to No. 72 Group Army Co-operation Command. Then, as the war rolled into Europe, Hurri-bombers and Typhoons of 175, 184, 266, 183 and 263 Squadrons made sorties from here in the ground-attack, tank-busting role.

The field died when the war ended, and became an open prison in 1949.

It is sad to think that Amy Johnson cannot have been far from Eastchurch when the Wellington bomber she was ferrying ran out of petrol and let down through a cloud which turned out to be bottomless. I like to think she had a brief glimpse of water before she crashed — not the roofs, pylons, woods she must have been fearing — and that in that glimpse there was hope.

Rochester airfield was founded by Shorts and the Rochester Corporation as a civil airfield in 1933. Soon afterwards, Pobjoys, a Shorts subsidiary, opened its aeroplane factory there; and in 1938 an R.A.F. Reserve Flying Training School was established.

The story of the Stirlings, and of the frequent attempts to raid Rochester and Pobjoys, is an heroic one. My own memory of Pobjoys is more peaceable. At the end of the war I was cycling beside the airport in a gale-force east wind. A Tiger Moth on a training flight was coming in very correctly to land against the wind and moving at an airspeed of possibly 70 knots over Monks Wood from the Medway. This put its ground speed at all of five miles an hour. I dismounted to watch it struggle towards me, still going much too fast to fall out of the sky.

After an eternity it reached me, and hovered like a kite overhead, for a moment stationary. The instructor sat up front with his arm over the side, and the pilot watched me and the airport fence in horrible fascination. Had he been any of the famous women pilots we would have had to fall in love.

Then he began to blow backwards, demanded more work from his engine and began to inch up again, at last passing the perimeter fence. Whereupon, in a panic, with full flap suddenly on, he cut everything, and I jumped on to my bike while he drifted tail-first towards me and squatted earthwards as awkwardly as a crow on to a sheep's back. Later, I served briefly with the Glider Pilots who all trained on Tigers. I told them about it. "It's called luffing," they explained.

The third airfield plum at the centre of things was Gravesend, now a field, a factory and an estate. It was occupied by a number of distinguished squadrons during World War Two, and used as a forward base by Biggin Hill. Before the war it was a sprightly flying club, famous for its big association with Edgar Percival and Sir Alan Cobham.

FRENCHMEN AND OTHER VARLETS

THE TRAMP IN COZENDEN WOOD

Snoozing in nankeen moss among
Unbuttoned mushrooms, his tongue
Untied and his teeth no longer,
His mouth grunting him up

He lay while with other kids
My shadow a long way off
Fitted his snore with acorn,
The peabug from under the stone,

Till the girls and their friends (done
Picking his pockets for leaves)
Drew out from inside its bark
Knothole by knotted inch

His foot and tickled it,
Undoing it stitch and string.
He did not wake, did not live
Did not die; but his sleep

In the wood's black hole
Sucked us inside its giggling forenoon,
Ourselves, and at last the sun.
By night he was gone.

I AM THINKING of all Saint Nicholas' clerks from footpads and dirk-
bellies to foot-landrakers and the long-staff sixpenny-strikers. Had
he been writing today, or even yesterday, Shakespeare would have
included garage-proprietors among his great catalogue of dangers to
the wayfarer. There is no need to cut a man's purse for a shilling or
his throat for a guinea, when you can service his car for £300, and
leave the resulting mechanical catastrophe to do it for you. I do not

exempt Kentish mechanics from the universal charge. At the back of this book you will see a long list of garage proprietors who have paid good money to have their names kept from the text. None of them are Frenchmen.

Why Frenchmen? The Huguenots are honourable among us. They fled from horrible persecution in France in the eighteenth century to lodge in Rochester then build their magnificent mansions. They taught us how to make paper, and, although we already knew, we did not harm them for it. For 200 years in return they have had to listen to the Medway glottal stop — once described as "audible silence" — and they have been subjected, doubtless, to the Strood short laugh (a seismic rather than aural event), especially in their dealings with garage owners.

Every Southern Englishman, whether he is white, brown or yellow, is taught that anyone born north of High Barnet or west of Staines is a wog, or "welisheman" as the *Anglo-Saxon Chronicle* calls him. We Kentish Men are more particular than that. We know there are Welshmen (Old English for barbaric foreigners) no further afoot than London or Tilbury. Indeed, we split Kent itself into two parts, with the civilized Kentish breed keeping to the left of the Medway and the inferior "of Kents" being confined to the right as they face the Pole Star, which they need to do often to tell the time during the hours of winter darkness.

I am reminded that the *Peterborough Chronicle*, resuming the Anglo-Saxon task after a lapse of years, does indeed speak of the French or at least the Normans as "Welshmen", but then the chronicler himself was writing from the north side of the River.

No. This chapter started with my French car which fell into the hands of a Kentish garage proprietor who took it apart before breakfast and said it would take several weeks to put together again, demanding a thousand pounds in advance.

Whereupon I had to take the 122 bus into Gravesend, the old Maidstone and District Brighton-to-Civilization 22, in order to have a swift drink. Gravesend being a riverside town and a port for seagulls has pubs that open early; so exactly at ten o'clock I was downing a pint followed by a rum and shrub served in the Trinity House fashion (extra rum in lieu of shrub).

There were some pleasing fellows in the bar, and in the bar after that. They were all exchanging notes on their profession. Their theme was common. It was Time. One of them asked me when I'd last done any, and I said I'd never been a seafaring man. They said that when they mentioned "Time" they didn't mean the Dog Watch, they meant porridge ("stir", "choky", or "over-the-wall", as it's still called in these parts, whereas up on the Downs the villagers talk of "going on their holiday" or "on her [Her Majesty's] holiday").

I stuck to my story. When they heard I'd never been lagged, they gathered about me and plied me with more shrubless rum to learn the secret of my success. It was then, at last, that the suspended coin fell. While I have been earning a dishonest living (and partly living) writing sentences like this, thousands of God's Gentlemen all about North Kent have made honourable amends by breaking alike into private houses and my father's business empire (four times including an armed robbery and pissing on the floor).

I travelled from Meopham to Victoria, I think by train, with a young probationary officer or social worker. He was going up to town for an interview, *voluntarily seeking to leave Kent*. I asked him whether success would result in promotion. He said no. I asked him why he was leaving. He said he wanted to go from a place where there was more of it to a place where there was less of it. Less poverty, less unemployment, less addiction, less prostitution, less crime. Less "long-staff sixpenny strikers".

No, he said. It wasn't new. North Kent had always been worse, or at least since the Middle Ages, which was as far back as he had studied the matter. He said it felt as if he had been working here since then. He said he was a Welshman.

The Kentish Old Watling Street was always notorious for footpads. It crossed the lonely heaths of Black and Bexley, and there were at least three hills, Shooters, Gads, and the one eastward from the Medway Gap, where a decent traveller would walk his horse. It was always a pack route, as Falstaff's robbers knew, and after Becket's martyrdom it became a pilgrim path as well. Indeed, there were the Celtic shrines before Christ, and earlier migrations, served by the misnamed Pilgrim's Way a few miles south. With the advent of the four-wheeler and the posting inns there were even more places a prudent coachman would ask his passengers to dismount and walk behind to be picked off by highwaymen. If one journeyed alone, there was the beadle with his "stranger's law", though with the town stocks a more likely punishment than the gallows. The Anglo-Saxons were not ones for hanging. The gibbet at a four-went-ways (good Kentish term) was a late Norman innovation for those who robbed wayfarers. Most crossroads had such an ornament at some time or other. Punishment could be local to the crime, and doubtless many a maggoty corpse would greet the traveller as a result, particularly in the seventeenth and eighteenth centuries. But the theory was deterrence, and the County did not catch a footpad every week, still less the borough, so the more likely procedure was to hang the wretch in a public place, then transport his remains in a body-cage of chains or bars to where they could be suspended by something more enduring than the human neck, and exhibited like a stuffed parrot. Some corpses were tarred, to keep out the weather. Some highwaymen paid to have their corpses treated thus to proof them against carrion. There were such gibbets at Black Heath, at the top of Shooters Hill, in Dartford, south of Gravesend where the gap-track from Wrotham crossed the Old Watling Street (just about where the present Toll Gate Motel now stands), in Wrotham north of the Church, at Wrotham Heath, where the road was until recently called Gallow's Hill, at Gadshill, and in Rochester on a site outside the Eastern Wall. Felons were also executed below Rochester Castle at different times. Rochester Bridge — as imposing as any bridge in London — was a good place for the exhibition of heads and corpses.

Gibbets creaked. They were to be avoided on moonlit nights and warm days. There were other apparitions to dodge at the "wents" or junctions, as well as the dead souls forever confined to Middle Earth by reason of their burial at the crossways. Leprosy was rife. Some town-ends boasted a lazar-house. Most did not. A leper would be cast out by the community to live by alms-gathering in a bowl (to prevent clean from touching unclean), or simply by using his or her condition to frighten travellers. The ravaged face would scare like any ghost. There was also the threat of a laying on of hands.

This incidence of leprosy proper in North Kent has been disputed. People have argued for viteligo and for lupus in place of it. But both are scarifying diseases, and produce frightening victims (and extortionists) when they are cast out from human compassion. Lupus (literally *wolf*) is a possible original of "the bogle" or pumpkin-headed land-striker, because it has — hence its name — the unpleasant symptom of rotting away people's noses and leaving a dazzling white scarring, or a shadow, according to light. Viteligo, lupus or leprosy — it scarcely matters. There is hardly a town church dating from the Middle Ages in North Kent that does not display some signs, generally the lintel stones, of a lazar window close enough to the altar to allow "lepers" to stand outside, share in mass or communion, and gaze upon the host. There are such bricked up remains at Milton Parish Church, St John's Meopham, at Stone and possibly at St Peter and St Paul, Shorne, and St Mary Magdalene, Cobham.

The tiny Saxon chapel at Denton is alleged to have a "thrill" or "thirl" for the same purpose. I can see no signs of it, but flint blends easily with flint.

A landscape pinched in by water must expect smugglers, raiders from the sea, and even pirates. Nearly every riverside pub from Erith right round to Wateringbury has its "smugglers' steps" or "pirate tunnel" — in other words places where the publican can hop into a skiff or keep his beer cool. In Gravesend, and more latterly Chatham and Strood, smugglers' inns have been demolished by the acre. I do not know of a gutted beer-shed that is not stuffed with some legend or other. Yarns abound, but facts are harder to come by. I suspect that most of our smuggling heroes were shanty legends, dreamed up in the late nineteenth century to mask the gradual decline of the riverside as a resort and to keep the beer sweet for Londoners. When the fog sets in, the rum gets easier to swallow. So does a tall story. Most of the great smuggling novels come late among sea adventures, and their heroes are generally landsmen, their heroines (is this a clue?) the buxom daughters of innkeepers. They deal with keg-runners and submerged tubs, of pack-saddles and fights with the revenue men; and they leave our bit of Kent alone. The various "gentlemen" of Romney Marsh, and the "Hawkhurst" and "Mayfield" gangs served a specialized bloodline from the continent. They were rustic enough and parochial enough to believe that the excise men came from "up there" and were in consequence foreign. To be a member of a smuggling gang or a wrecker, a man needs to be a singular beast — a countryman who lives close to the sea but has no proper connection with it; no respect for its hierarchies, no concern for its decencies. You can find people like that where the South Downs hang over the water, or in North Devon. Never among us.

There has been piracy in the channel since the Dark Ages. The

French were always active in the Straits, especially once the Norsemen had pillaged among them to breed Normans (we have noticed elsewhere that sea-raiders tend to catch a woman's tongue while capturing her virginity); and the Flemings, and I daresay the Walloons, did filthy things to Britishers off the North Foreland. That's why the Cinque Ports were invented, and why there are nine of them. But here we are river people, and rivers are orderly affairs. They are lined with fortifications. Navies tie up along their walls, and soldiers picnic incessantly beside them. Excise men and police are ever present; and before them kingsmen, comfortable with a flagon and a spying-glass, not to mention informers from among the East Saxons.

There are seventeenth-century records of "men moving lights" at Shoeburyness, and again off Barking Creek. It does not surprise me to discover the Men and Women of Essex as devious as Devonians. In Devon a ship can be lured on to the "anfractuous rocks"—the tradition is still strong and secret there. The doubloons wash ashore, and so do bones, and teeth. The rest is gobbets. But the Essex wreckers could only attract a vessel on to a mudflat or, in the sad case of Barking and the Ingrebourne, a sewage bed. The sailors could, and did, stay snug and lusty enough, albeit with pegs on their noses, to repel all boarders.

Here we are more subtle. Every boatman, every waterman, every sailor, every man and woman who lives within a mile of the river is a villain. But we are not greedy villains. Precious objects fall off the backs of boats quite as easily as they drop from lorries. When spices were specie, they changed hands at Erith and Greenhithe much more simply than they ever did at Rye. Many a drop of cognac has come ashore at Northfleet, Gravesend, Cliffe, Sheerness — you can complete the list yourself. But always in a small, snug fashion.

Chaucer names two rogues with waterish connections. One of them is from Dartmouth (the dirty Devonian). The Aureate Laureate is less precise about the other, but has him fearful of piracy between East Anglia and the Low Countries. He is too sly to make mention of Kent, being Kentish himself by adoption, and anyway responsible for keeping us in order in such matters.

In his time and later, smugglers handled some surprising commodities. One was cloth. Medieval duties stood at seven pounds on a bale of wool so there was a profit in avoiding them. Later there was tea. This was heavily taxed for upwards of two centuries, so heavily that it was a prime cause of the American War of Independence. But whereas

Bostonians took to tipping it into the harbour and giving themselves sleepless nights with coffee, we lads of North Kent simply smuggled it in.

The famous North Kent Gang operated from Thanet and Herne Bay, where the ladings were good and the roads brisk. They had aristocratic patronage and protection, and were a cut above the Hawkhurst mob, who were given to rustic thuggery. They were good lads but not ours.

Our problem was the orderliness of the river. Sailors wear boots or bellbottoms so they can carry things; but it is hard to get more than five pounds of tea in a boot, or a yard of two of calico round calf and thigh, unless one has the advantage of a wooden leg. "I'm waiting for Peg Leg", or "Peg Leg Pete" was a common riverside expression, meaning "I'm expecting something good to turn up", corrupted in meaning to "I'm waiting for pay-day", even "I'm broke", but one-legged smugglers or pirates were always regarded as lucky. Whether because they could carry more is a moot point. A man who could survive the carpenter's saw and the boiling pitch was a lucky card anyway. Then there is the sailors' superstition that it is lucky to touch a wooden leg, unlucky to kick one, exceptionally beneficient (and, for a woman, fertile) to sleep with one. I *think* this lingers on among landsmen in the unseemly urge to add signatures and other graffiti to the plaster casts of people with broken legs. Certainly I have never seen a signed arm or a signed head.

But if we are reduced to smuggling "by Peg Leg Pete", then we are into a small way of business. "I got this from a sailor's boot" is the exact riverside counterpart of "It fell from the back of a lorry", and is invariably answered by "I hope he washes his feet". There is a deal of social anthropology in that exchange.

Not much profit, however. If we spread out a map of the Thames and Medway, and strike off the policed anchorages on the one hand and the mudflats on the other, we are left with a few big towns — unsafe for all but hollow legs and large handbags — and the Hoo Peninsula.

On paper this area seems ideal. There should have been a Cliffe or Cooling Gang as famous as the Hawkhurst Gang, and better because made up of better people. But in the eighteenth century, the Golden Age of Kent smuggling, the Hundreds were sparsely populated, badly drained and malarial. A big operation needed a plentiful supply of recruits, so that rotas could be worked; a populace united against law and order; and roads or paths firm enough to sustain a fast gallop.

The peninsula offered none of these things. On the other hand it was judged secure enough in 1734 for only two Riding Officers, John Tomlin and Francis Rigg, to provide the landguard. One was notoriously lazy, however, and both were probably corrupt; so it was an area where a modest ambition could pay dividends, especially if allied to the sort of local knowledge that inshoremen from the Medway or Swale could be expected to provide.

So it was that Hoo was to be the pivot for some highly profitable smuggling runs, involving men from Rochester, Chatham and Sheerness.

The key figure was one Edward Roots of Rochester. He worked variously with his brother Richard, William Frost and Thomas Wall, all of Rochester, and also John Cage of Chatham, John Jones of Sheerness and several other people, of whom the main entrepreneur was Thomas Prigmore of London, in a variety of boats belonging to John Cage, William Flood and himself. The boats concerned were the "Sloweley" (a disarming title), the "Mermaid", and "John and Mary", as well as a vessel whose name is not recorded. The runs were from Ostend and Flushing, with cargoes of tea, calico and chinaware, but with tea the main and corporate venture. The contraband was put ashore at Otterham Quay, Holyhaven, Chalk Marshes, Cliffe Marshes, Gilling-ham Bridge, and once — by rowboat — at Gravesend. The main buyers were a quartet of London publicans and their women who — peg legs again — carried the tea away under their petticoats.

On several occasions they were chased by Revenue Cutters, and at least twice they were caught by a customs man called Patrick Johnson. This gentleman laid no charges, paid out one of the conspirators in full, and appears to have sold the seized goods himself. The group in all imported two tons of contraband tea, evading duty of nearly £700 and making a profit of nearly £2,000 in just over a year, this at a time when seamen were paid less than £20 a year. Roots did have the "Mermaid" seized, but was able to buy another boat from his profits.

In the seventeenth century, smuggling was more general; and the few people prosecuted were generally the "Customers", or senior Excise officials, for their negligence. Often the duties of Customers were protectionist, rather than fiscal. Kentish "fuller's earth" was important for our own cloth industry, and its export was prohibited.

In the early 1630s the Customer of Rochester was prosecuted in the Star Chamber for allowing 4,000 chaldrons of earth to leave Rochester for the Low Countries since 1627. There were duties, or prohibitions, on most objects of trade, whether coal or wool (Faversham at that time shipped more wool than the other Kent ports put together) or the even more lowly chalk and lime sent from Northfleet. These duties were often evaded, through bad bookkeeping, negligence or a dislike of London. We know of swindles in ordinary accounting worked at Faversham, Rochester, Maidstone and the ports of Milton Creek; so it stands to reason that there must have been evasion of duty on tobacco, spirits, oil, pepper, vinegar, currants, olive and cinnamon, as well as on French and the rarely recorded Spanish wines. As I said, our forebears were villains, but lightly and without the scale that gets into history books.

We know little of pirates proper. The Vikings came to London, but their most famous landings were on either side of the Swale. There is a persistent local tradition (unmentioned in my earlier and more learned tarradiddle on the place; but just as worthy of note) that Sweyne settled at Swanscombe — that is, that he made a brief "setl" there, and that the town was first called Sweynescomb. Van Tromp and de Ruyter surged among us, but Pepys did his best to see that it never happened again; and Dryden sank them with *Annus Mirabilis* in one place and another. They were spicemen themselves, and you will recall how "some were by aromatic splinters slayn" when Dryden's quatrains, if not the English cannonade, finally erupted among them.

Captain Bartholomew Roberts, grandest of West Indian privateers and then pirates, sailed from the Pool, anchored in Gravesend Hope, and then went on to do great things, finally at his rope's end from a yard arm.

William Addams, the Shogun of James Clavell's book, was a Gillingham man, born in Kent and marrying a local girl. What he did in Japan was glorious but bigamous, and his Japanese lines were all sinister. Drake too (if I may call him a pirate) was in essence a Man of Kent, though no Devonian will grant this. The fact is that his father was appointed Vicar of Upchurch in 1560. Earlier, the family lived on a hulk at Gillingham, and young Francis did his first boating on the Medway and Swale. He was Kentish from the age of four.

The Vikings were pirates; but the earlier Jutes, Saxons and such

Angles as settled in Kent were of a different disposition. They did not come to carry off cattle, women and corn; they brought their families with them, and pressed the Romanized Britons aside, by treaty, squabble, and mostly by sheer weight of numbers. We remember them in our confused blood and our tangled place names. Oh, I forgot to mention that North Kent is a-flock with owls (I daren't say a-flutter, for their wings are silent). Every owl in the Hundreds is a hanged pirate flapped free of his gallows. You wouldn't be without knowing that.

Perhaps because of our closeness to Canterbury and Rochester, and sixteen centuries' trampling of warrior Christendom, we have few remnants of "the Old Religion". Witches were scarce among us, and still are. It so happens that I am writing a book about witches in our part of Kent, but to do so I have to interpret the term diffusely. Iberians, Celts, Caesar, Claudius, Anglo-Saxons, Augustine, Vikings, the Normans (quaintly termed Welshmen in the *Anglo-Saxon Chronicle*) have left us too fragmented for the Old Religion to maintain the simplest of covens, let alone hierarchies. Similarly we are short of mumming and traditional morrice, though the latter is being restarted. Possibly there is a geographic factor here. It is hard to dance with Boggart when you are shivering with ague, and downright lunatic to attend a naked sabbat on a saltmarsh. On the Stone, Shorne and Hoo levels God seems a lot more approachable, even in daylight, if you are wearing a topcoat. Not for nothing was one of the earliest deriders of the witch-cult a Kentish man. This was Reginald Scott whose scholarly *The Discoverie of Witches* was published in 1584. He concluded that witches had little power for good or evil, and that charges against so-called witches were largely malicious. Surprisingly, though, he gives two of their recipes for "flying ointment", one of which is frequently quoted by apologists of the cult. Some of its ingredients—henbane and aconite—would induce narcosis, especially if rubbed well in, as he suggests, at wrist, ankle, ear-lobe, groin and the labia of the vagina. He is the first writer to state, at least by inference, that the orgies at the sabbats were not objective happenings but drug-stimulated dreams experienced by overheated solitaries. His reasoned arguments did little to deter the witch-finders and witch-torturers who went on in spite of him to have their seventeenth-century field day.

The recorded North Kentish witches were few, with Sheppey, the Swale settlements and the middle Medway their main breeding grounds. In 1645, for example, Elizabeth Harris of Faversham confessed that she had placed a curse upon John Woodcott's boat because her son had been drowned while sailing on it. Her curse caused the ship to founder. In East Anglia generally (there was a great cloth, coal, lime and earth trade between or through the East Anglian ports and the Swale from 1500 until 1800) it was a common legend that boats could be sucked under by Kentish witches. Certainly, several powerful covens were uncovered at Faversham. In 1645 again Joan Williford spoke of covenanting her soul to the Devil "who promised to be her servant about twenty years, and that the time is almost expired". The Faversham witches, mindful of the Boneless Wind, always feasted with the Devil indoors: "Joan Cariden confessed that Goodwife Hott told her within these two days there was a great meeting at Goodwife Pantery's house, and that Goodwife Dobson was there . . . and the Devil sat at the upper end of the table."

At Maidstone in 1652, Anne Ashby, Anne Martyn, Mary Browne, Anne Wilson, Mildred Wright and Mary Read were sentenced to be hanged at the Common Place of Execution. There was a move to burn them, and a wish among themselves to be burnt, but in the end they were treated as ordinary criminals, though not before their bodies had been searched for "devil's paps". I expect the hangman lifted the poor ladies higher than they had ever been on a broomstick.

I have mentioned the highwaymen of Gad's Hill elsewhere. So have Shakespeare and Harrison Ainsworth, the latter confusingly. In *Rookwood* Ainsworth claims that Dick Turpin robbed a man of Gad's Hill, crossed over by ferry from Lower Higham to East Tilbury, and galloped to York in order to establish an alibi. This feat was in fact achieved by a man called John Williams (or Swift Nick) Nevinson in 1676, or at least a little more than legend says so. The trouble is that Turpin was the member of a gang, and many highwaymen used "Dick Turpin" as an alias. Indeed, highwaymen in general became known as Dick Turpin, even long after he was hanged, much as all vacuum-cleaners are referred to as Hoovers. In my youth, I read a learned and convincing book that asserted that Turpin was a common pickpocket: his highwayman exploits and Black Bess all belonged to Claude Duval. Believe what you will, you will be closer than any sure history.

There seems to have been a murder involved in the Turpin/Duval/Nevinson case, but it is rarely written up, and there is even dispute as to whether it was a man who was stabbed or a woman who was strangled. We never get credit for our murders, and we can and do boast of some jolly ones. Yet not a mention do we get in Colin Wilson's *An Encyclopaedia of Murder, A Casebook of Murder* and *Order of Assassins* or in J. H. H. Gaute's and Robin Odell's *The Murderers' Who's Who*. I shall put that right.

In 1739 a sailor landed in Yantlet Creek, stole to Bene (now Binney) Farm in Allhallows and murdered one of the Boghurst family. He was hanged. At the end of Hitler's war, a young girl was assaulted and strangled near a race-meeting at Brands Hatch. She did not make *An Encyclopaedia of Murder* but her face filled the Sunday papers with innocence, and put us all in mind of a dozen similar cases, equally unsolved. I found her murderer in an extended fiction of mine called *There's a War On*. It is at least as reliable as anything by Harrison Ainsworth.

A few years back, a teenaged boy and girl set out to walk from Gravesend Canal Basin eastwards through Denton and then over the marshes near Shorne Mead. They were met by a man with a knife who molested and killed them in turn. It became a "copybook" murder insofar as a number of sadistic imaginations became heated at the printed accounts of it, and it established a pattern of marshland assaults. As Pip found, our marshes are lonely places, and it is possible to meet worse than Magwitch there.

I write elsewhere in these pages of ritual murders from our druidical past. It is slightly more amusing to notice that before the war there was a poultry-keeper at Harvel who took to raping and strangling his chickens (pullets, not cockerels, you will be comforted to discover). The poor man was discovered after the most exhaustive forensic examinations of the exhumed corpses, and I blundered upon his wickedness only the other day by thumbing through the memoirs of the scientist concerned. At the Exeter Assizes they speak much of sheep. I can only redress the balance by saying that country rumour in our parts is wild with young horses; and remind you that at Upnor in 1914 they dug up an elephant.

SAXON CHRIST AND SOME ANCIENT PARISHES

KING MUD

In a mudflat midnight of sleet
I lie under five forked pins
Watching the stars through water.
The world presses my meat.
A snakeskin knots my neck,
Flax is chocking my tongue
Which sucks on a single stone.

Marsh only partly fills me:
My bowels drop seeds in its mouth.
I utter a foolish breath
And methane popples with wit.
Bring tinder, light my bones;
I burn in the North all night,
I am dragon's kin.

She who must love me lies
Mud-close, with little hair.
My slave shaves her,
Him, or my barber, Rat.

The sun does not need her eye:
Her lids are closed by a fillet
The colour of light through blood —
She worships all Gods in me.

Her gut is set with gruel
More black than the pitch of birth.

Bring her to me in Spring,
Then, stripped to the peat's slime,
Fold knee and then knee to her chin:
Break her to be my twin;
Hung from this Earth's placenta.

Each year she bears my son:
In his belly sixty-four seeds,

In his hand a thorn in its hole

Crushed testicles still in their bag

In his hair, ferret

In his bones, glass

In his mind, Nothing
But a mistletoe prayer for the Sun.

KENT IS A Christian county. True, it is surprisingly rich in the marks of pre-Christian settlement and religion. The palaeolithic finds along the marshes and saltings, the tumuli above the scarp and the megaliths at its foot all testify to the antiquity of man's ordered presence in these parts. Yet the fact is that its real history begins with the christianizing of the kings of Kent, in other words with the coming of the Saxon Christ from Rome, not the Roman Christ, nor yet again the Northumbrian and Mercian Christs who came from Ireland and were Celtic in flavour.

This interests me greatly. In these parts we know little of the Goidels and Brythons, our migrant Iberian forefathers. The Romans and the Romanized Celts left their imprint thick upon the ground, but did little for our traditions, because the legions left and there was a vacancy into which the Saxons came, only to be converted by missionaries rather than the sword, by St Augustine, not his Emperor. Of the Mithraic religion of the legions there is little sign left; still less of Old Taurocephalus or Leontocephalus himself. Their Germanic creeds, their intermittent Christianity, have also vanished without mark. We were the beginnings of the Holy Roman Empire before the Holy Roman Empire was invented. Canterbury, for this reason if no other, is as important to world history as are Rome and Constantinople. It is from these three and accident, rather than dogma and the creative heresies of Mani, Albi, Luther and the Gnoses, that the three world branches of Christianity spring. I am delighted our Christ was not a warrior Christ, was not Eliot's "Christ the tiger"; that he was at most a political Christ, and perhaps not even that. The Saxons were, in any event, gentle—far less terrible in their conduct than the Romans before or the Normans afterwards. I am struck by the fact that the only genuinely capital offence among them was blasphemy coupled with the despoiling of holy places (it would take a highly developed Marxist to claim that this was no more than a primitive instance of the Church protecting its system and its property) and that they manifested an early belief in miracles. The Jutes, too, when they came were quickly converted. We have from them, again in Kent, the delightful Jutish toast wassail: *waes Hael*, be well. We can congratulate ourselves for this. It is as true as any part of Hengist's story; and as one born in the Year of the Horse I shall not question it.

We are not all overtly Christian now, and since the War there are many new cultures and religions among us. Nor must I neglect the prevalence of Non-Conformism in Kent. Wesley was constant here. We bred John Ball, Jack Straw and Jack Cade. My own village houses Baptists and Strict Baptists, as well as the religion of Canterbury. I was myself baptized in the Wycliffe Chapel in Nelson Road, Perry Street, before being converted to orthodoxy by the sword of my mother's tongue when I was five. We have Unitarians, United Reformers, Trinitarians, and of course Methodists. Nor must I forget the Jezreels. We have fine Roman Catholic churches; but I return to the Saxon Christ, whose chapels were frequently rebuilt as Norman churches by later men, and so often stood on prehistoric sites if I am to believe the ley-lines and occasional archaeological or etymological evidence.

The most antique, not necessarily the oldest, of our churches is at Dode. It is still there and signposted, a towerless lump of flint dressed with rag, showing the drop roofline so often associated with late Saxon building. In fact, the nave is supposed to be Norman. I used to cycle there often in my teens. The bullaced lanes around Luddesdown were a great favourite of mine (I met a man in Germany who told me that Luddesdown was the most beautiful place in the world: he was from Essex, so had different standards; but I almost agree with him). The entire congregation of Dode was wiped out by the first visitation of the Black Death in 1349. It has now been visited by the Ordnance Survey, I see. The old 1:60,000 used to show it plain. The new 1:50,000 and even the Second Series 1:25,000 omit it. Of course, the Royal Engineers are active hereabouts. I hope there is no connection.

I have mentioned the fine old churches of Stone, Greenhithe and Swanscombe, all standing close to desolation; but I was so obsessed with the servitude and grandeur of their situation (to borrow from de

Vigny) that I forgot to praise the interior of St Mary's, Stone. There has been nineteenth-century restoration, but tastefully done, and its blend of perpendicular and decorated styles is almost unique in so small a church. So, too, is its sense of light. It really does purify the river sky.

I was once lusty in the choir of St John the Baptist, the parish church at Meopham. In my boyish days, I thought it had a typical Norman tower (the building but not the foundation dates from the thirteenth century). In fact the tower used to have an ugly tapered top, and it was only squared off in the last century. The celebrated ancestor of my poet friend Fairfax stabled his horses in the nave during the Civil War, and either his horses or his troopers chewed the fabric, which was plastered flint. They were good roundheads, nag and gentleman, so I doubt if they were plastered themselves.

I spoke of the Saxon Christ. Queen Ediva owned estates here, held them in close connection with Canterbury, and certainly worshipped in Meopham. This would probably be in whatever holy building occupied this site. John de Meopham went from here in 1327 to become Archbishop of Canterbury.

My two favourite churches in the whole area are at Cobham and Cliffe, though there is a degree of conjecture about the history of the latter. From the eighth century, until somewhere in the tenth, it was supposed to be the meeting place of the Saxon priests and their Kings, and must have played a profound part in the politics, if not the spirituality, of Christianity.

I always find it hard to pass lightly over the faith of some of these monarchs, or of the Saxons in general, hence the thrust of this chapter. My shelves remember the Alfred who wrote *personally* to all of his bishops, commending to them his translation of the *Cura Pastoralis*:

Aefred kyning hateþ gretan Waerferþ
biscep his wordum luflice ond freondlice

Certainly, this interaction of Saxon king and Saxon priest bore enormous fruit, nowhere more strikingly than in Kent. While devotionalists were working in Latin, our priests were writing in pure Kentish, in those Middle Ages when it really did exist:

Þe guode man, midþe rede of his wyve,
yeaf his cou to his preste, þet wes riche . . . and
his zente to þe oþen þet he hedde.

Perhaps Cliffe was *not* the great meeting ground of Saxon culture, but its claims, and the claims of St Helen's Church, are strong.

The present church, in contrasting bands of flint and rag, is an imposing place. Fire ruined much of Cliffe in 1520, and the church was damaged. Its rector's living is totally independent of everyone except the Archbishop of Canterbury attending Cliffe in person. The rector held his own court until the mid-nineteenth century, and was also granted some of the rights of Attorney-at-Law. Two of its rectors became Lord Chancellors; one was made Archbishop of York, one of Canterbury. Fanny Burney's brother, a Greek scholar, was incumbent here. The original rectory, as befitted such an important living, had the scale of a medieval mansion.

I wish I could get further back, at Cliffe, on the Downs, in the saltings. Even our Saxon saints are strangers.

Before the last Ice Age clenched Northern Europe, Kent was joined to the Continent. There were men here before then. They could come on foot, by ox, horse and elephant. The famous Cuxton elephant was prehistoric, and stood some thirteen feet tall. It may have died, been trapped, or been ritually slaughtered. We have no way of knowing whether it was wild or tame. The Swanscombe Skull tells us of the great antiquity of Kentish man, and early Stone Age relics continue to crop up. When the M2 bridge over the Medway was built, (the longest and most modern for this form of cantilever) footing excavations revealed hand-axes belonging to the Acheulian culture of the Palaeolithic or Old Stone Age, dating from roughly 200,000 years BC. We know nothing about these people, little more about those who came to live here after the ice's recession had washed Kent away from the Continent just a few thousand years ago.

These men and women, Goidelic, Brythonic or earlier, left us the seeming dolmens or henges of the Pilgrim's Way, and more particularly the Medway Gap, from the Coldrum Stones at Trottiscliffe to Kit's Coty and its associated megaliths east of the river. Then there are the "sarsens" of Harvel and elsewhere.

The stones seem to be local, but there is no necessary unity of time or purpose in their erection. Some of them may indeed form parts of sun- or moon-clocks, and others altars for equinox or solstice similar to those at Salisbury, Avebury or Castle Rigg in Cumberland. They are mostly open to the south, and to solar inference, even to the "sky-ley" theory or the wilder imaginings of Erich von Däniken. But the Coldrum Stones and Kit's Coty, whatever larger theory they are bullied towards, are pretty certainly the henged entrances of eroded or demolished long-barrows; in other words they are the porches of ritual burial chambers. Why, and in what circumstances, the dead of that not very ancient culture were storeyed together, often several hundred at the time, is not clear. We can only assume that burial in some sort of tribal or regional mausoleum was the common practice, just as we use cemeteries today.

The sarsens are more of a problem. Wherever there is ancient stone, farmers will find a use for it. There are odd monoliths and clusters dotted about the re-entrants north-east of Wrotham that are certainly not all where they were planted, or as many as planted; and which are clearly not glacial deposits. Standing stones may indeed walk, as Shakespeare alleges; but generally some thieving hand has led them on.

In a few square miles south of Northfleet, paleolithic and neolithic shards have been found, and two neolithic potteries; there are Roman chapels, Anglo-Saxon burials towards Betsham, and the entire Roman settlement at Springhead. At little Southfleet, there is ancient Friary Court; and then we play games with place-names, such as Axtane and Coldharbour, both in this same area — a whole patchwork of time, culture and religious observance.

East of Gravesend, a series of Roman burials, possible temples, is intermixed with Bronze- and Iron-Age hoards on the marshes, a medieval priory for Benedictine nuns at sad Church Street; while inland are the ruined Saxon churches of Hill Farm, Shorne; the lost village north of Cobham, and poor plague-stricken Dode Church, that lost its entire congregation in Chaucer's time.

There have also been bog, or rather marsh, burials uncovered in Kent; but they were not all well-recorded, or properly examined. A man in the mud could all too easily be a hulk convict or a sailor, so the larger Jutish question must remain posed but unanswered. Most of the ritual strangulations preserved so extraordinarily well in Jutland peat are about 2,000 years old. The Jutes came to us only 1,600 years ago, long after Tollund and Grauballe Man, or the Winderby Girl. They migrated as farmers, and in Kent they grew some of the grasses and corns found in the bog people's stomachs. So they had the same imperatives for seed sacrifice, save that the weather was better here and Christianity followed hard at heel. We know they kept Celtic slaves at Walmer, or captives at least, but for what purposes we do not know. I am interested enough in the possibilities to include here a poem called *King Mud*. I wrote it when *Bog People* appeared in Sweden, but did not publish it because the same book inspired Seamus Heaney's remarkable sequence with its overwhelming contemporary resonance. My own poem is completely pagan.

The title promised Christ. He was in part residual here — but so was Mithras, ever popular among the legions — part osmotic from the north; but mainly and overwhelmingly He was the outcome of Augustine's great mission to the Kentish Kings.

As he lay dying in Switzerland, James Elroy Flecker had a fine vision of the Saint. I should like to quote the verse from his *The Dying Patriot* in full, in spite of its embarrassing (or magic?) last line. It says a lot for the coming of Christianity to Kent, and is in some ways the better for being penned by such a debauchee.

> Day breaks on England, down the Kentish hills,
> Singing in the silence of the meadow-footing rills,
>> Day of my dreams, O day!
> I saw them march from Dover, long ago,
> With a silver cross before them, singing low,
> Monks of Rome from their home where the blue seas break in foam,
>> Augustine with his feet of snow.

Perhaps saints have cool, clean feet. Becket certainly did not; even his hair shirt was lousy with sanctity. Yet long before the knights journeyed to kill him or Chaucer's pilgrims to pay homage to his remains, there were Saxon parishes at Milton, Cliffe, Allhallows, Shorne, Cuxton, Halling, Cobham, Meopham, Luddesdown, as well as all about the Hundreds, Sheppey and the Swale.

The Medway is an even richer funnel of Saxon settlement and Christian activity. Rochester Cathedral dates in its present form only from the foundations laid by Bishop Gundulf in 1080; but his work replaced the original Saxon cathedral of 604. The Bridge Chapel dates only from the fourteenth century, but probably replaces a Roman, Pagan or Saxon altar to the water-crossing. The churches of St Margaret and St Nicholas are old, but perhaps only Norman-Saxon rather than pure Saxon. Something of the rich patina of Medway's life can be seen in the beautifully restored La Providence, just a few hundred yards from the Cathedral. This was one of the original Huguenot ghettoes in the county, and has now been refurbished for people of Huguenot descent.

St Nicholas', Strood, has similar origins to St Nicholas' and St Margaret's Churches in Rochester — how easy it is to generalize about their combined thousands of years of worship; but odd little Strood offers glimpses of a richer tapestry. On the one hand there is Temple Manor, founded in the thirteenth century by the Knights templar, that odd but glittering order of abstinence, warrior crosses, black magic and buggery. On the other, there are Sikh temples, as at Gravesend, to remind us that rivers ferry a ceaseless migration of minds as well as merchandise.

THE ISLAND OF SHEEP

SUNKEN AMMUNITION TRANSPORT OFF GARRISON POINT

At low tide she's topside clear.
At high tide, deckhouse and derrick;
All weathers her can-opened plates
Scoff sand, dribble oxide, muck.

Reeking, she's sure to blow:
Propellant, wet, is unstable.
Salt chews her fuse by the nose.
She'll ignite if divers unload her.

One day, not quite at once,
Bomb by bomb, hold by hold
She'll stand up out of the tide,
Rip open its legs

And schoolgirls here in this street
Will lie with her rust in their arms.
First the light will come,
Then the sea will come

With the ship in a great glass wall
Full up with seaweed and stones.

SHEPPEY DESERVES A book, though I must say that Richard Church does it proud in his few pages. It is, I think, unique in lowland Britain, more properly an island than Thanet or Grain, less isolate than Wight, though like all of these places shut in on itself. When our territorial regiment supported the "Black Cats", the 101st London Armoured Division, some genius at Warbox decreed that the Sheppey Battery fasten on to the London Irish. At the inauguration of this marriage, their Brigadier said, or our Battery Commander said, or they both said, that Sheppey and Ireland were similars, each of them islands with the souls of continents, and the rest of the world mere adjuncts. It is true. We used to go to Sheppey in dread, timorous to pass its frontiers, not least because it was often hard to get back. The fog would come down like a sheer ness indeed, not an ordinary fog but woven of icicles, and in it some steamer or other would collide with the bridge. To send a truck and six men through Queenborough led inevitably to the filling in of casualty sheets. Gunners used to carry a thermos full of rum, and stop to phone their wives at the last turn-off from the A2. All that is changed now, of course. Sheerness is a ferry terminal.

Sheppey is best understood from a smallish-scale map or a light aeroplane. One does not have to go very high to see it all in plan, and just a few feet of altitude shows the Thames to the north, Medway to the west, and the Swale to the south and east.

It is an odd shape, seeming to spring above Kent in a bunched leap, like a mythical ram in a cave-painting. Or perhaps it reclines on its elbow at ease, a sort of pinheaded Henry Moore woman. Whichever image you prefer the pin head or horn is undoubtedly Sheerness, the fore-leg or elbow is Queenborough, and the rest tapers east. I like my ram image, for there is a spine of slightly higher ground along the north, clearly etched by the road system joining Sheerness, Minster, Eastchurch, Warden and Leysdown. I speak of higher ground, but 200 feet is the maximum. Nonetheless, there is a real ridge, pretty constantly above 50 metres from Warden Point back to Mill Hill above Minster. South-east towards the Swale the island is all woolly underbelly, a wilderness of marsh and drainage cut, almost empty of buildings except for the Ferry Inn in the salt marsh on the Isle of Harty, and one or two farms. Indeed, this southern strip which comprises most of Sheppey, consists of two more islands, Harty and Elmley, separated not only by Windmill Creek and Capel Fleet, but by Eastchurch Marshes.

If it weren't for people, Sheppey would be a paradise. People and their dwellings have marred it and in places spoilt it. That being said, the islanders are special, and their spoiling has been made necessary by isolation. When they have used native brick, stone or timber all has been well. Unfortunately, there is very little of this building material to hand, and there has been a considerable use of concrete slab, rough-cast and uncouth modern brick.

Sheppey is a green place, so it comes as a surprise to see so few stands of timber. It is not a treeless landscape, but in general trees stand in ones

or twos, near churches, farms, older buildings. They appear to be
sitings rather than left-overs. Historically everything except the
northern ridge would have been too wet to grow anything.

This can be checked by walking south or south-east from Sheerness,
Minster or Eastchurch. The green is a wet green, at best the viridian of
marsh turf which holds its light; but southwards there is sedge, reed and
thorn and strange marsh grasses that have a life cycle like rice, damp at
the roots and rusty, then browning off into ochre, madder, strange
oxide hues in high summer, intermixed with thistles.

Elmley Island is surrounded entirely by a riverwall. Harty is not. It
runs its back, and its back fleet or "crick", up against the high ridge.
Nonetheless its inlets, like those on the marsh to its west, are all flanked
by levees grand and little.

Hard to say where Sheppey began. There was a Saxon Queen
Sexburga who built a nunnery here, and Minster, Shurland and Warden
are all ancient places. Minster, as on Thanet, means monastery.
Shurland's old court stems only from the fourteenth century, at
furthest, and now does not look as if it will last through this one; but it
stands on the site of some older fortification. Warden's oldest end,
including the church of St James, has all fallen into the North Sea. The
church, like Ingress at Greenhithe, had been partly reconstructed with
stones from Old London Bridge. This enabled it to assume a gravitas
not its own, like scoring with conkers, but it was antique in its own right
before it sank beneath the waves. The bells, new and old, chime beneath
the water, calling the fish to prayer.

Where I'll begin is Queenborough. It is at the bottom corner, the
forefoot, so to speak; and it is reached by a bridge, formerly a causeway,
and before that the King's Ferry. The Oare Ferry, once crossing to Ferry
Inn, is now disused, and was always a scant affair, so Queenborough
guards the main route to the island.

I mentioned that it was formerly called Binney, until Edward III built
his castle there. Surprisingly there is a Binney Farm near Allhallows,
site of a fine old murder; and another Binney across the Swale at Tonge.
Its origin is not certain, but this prevalence of acknowledged variants of
the same name — compare Yantlet and South Yantlet, High Halstow
and Lower Halstow separated by similar miles of water — suggests a
highly aquatic culture. Men needed boats to settle Sheerness in the first
place.

The castle is now a scant mound, Edward's Queen remembered only in the town name and more properly by a pub called the Queen Philippa. (The beer always tastes good on the island of sheep.) Industry and neglect have done their worst with all that remains of the little town, but there are a few early eighteenth-century houses, and an elegant guildhall of the same period.

Before that, the view up the Swale from the Kingsferry Bridge is worth having. There is a timber-lading hard by for the papermill by Castle Rough on the mainland, a dramatic pylon crossing shore to shore, and an aerial ropeway two miles in length for paper-products on the south bank. On a clear day, that enables the eye or binoculars to pick detail, the Swale is always worth searching along. Sheppey acts as a stopper for Milton, Conyer and Oare creeks and a host of smaller inlets. The walk south-east along the track from the bridge, and then by the river wall from Emley Hills Beacon or below King's Hall Farm, brings these mysteries closer to view. I always find that the marshes call me on if I walk this way, and I'm soon picking my way around, and then back from, Dutchman's Islands. I've now learned to take binoculars, or use my car on the road that runs on the North Ridge. This can be picked up at Queenborough without going into Sheppey, gives one a drink at Eastchurch and another one at The Ferry Inn; then the river wall runs east again for walking beyond Sayes Court.

I seem to have digressed from Queenborough into my favourite wet vistas. I must note that there is another walk south-east from Queenborough either by wall or path across Marshes and Stray Marshes, then a choice of inland bank or track again on to Elmley Island and King's Hill Farm. I promise myself this, or these. I have seen the occasional wayfarer bobbing there a mile to the north as I have walked along by the Swale. I have no guarantee that they have survived; they may even now be planted in salt; but there are some firm banks and blanked walls to guide even a misty foot. In a fog, though, I should return along the main south wall and track, expecting some trouble in the form of doubling about north-west of Sharfleet Creek, where the wall ends on water and one has to retrace a few hundred yards to hit off the alternative track. To walk the bank north-west across Elmley and the Southleas Marshes is a dubious bad-weather retreat, because it conks out in some very damp landscape about a thousand paces short of the not quite aptly named Wallend.

Anyway, these adventures all return one to Queenborough, or at least to Neats Court, Cowstead Farm or Scocles Farm — somewhere in their general direction along the A250. From any of these places one goes to Minster or Sheerness without turning back towards Queenborough, or to either without seeing the other. At the roundabout by Cowstead Farm, the road connects itself to the A249 (its number from Kingsferry Bridge) and becomes less rural. The choice is whether to follow the breeze and pebblesdash round towards Halfway Houses, where the road forks for Sheerness or Minster, or go back to Queenborough and take the Medway Road to Sheerness.

Neither road, to be frank, has the advantage of the other. Halfway Houses is a hideous place, and like certain wents in *Pilgrim's Progress*, or Dante's *Inferno*, it offers no good choices.

No use to pretend there is much deliberate architecture on Sheppey, even on the ridge and along the road. Sheerness and Minster, like Queenborough, have occasional eighteenth-century houses; but these were probably built for newcomers: ships' officers, dock-yard officials, entrepreneurs of the industries of the Swale, with only wood and powder as growth activities until much later in the Industrial Revolution. The churches and town halls had a facelift about then, and the work in Queenborough and Sheerness was good.

Now there are new light industries, and the growing ferry and container-port; but the days for big houses and grandiose town-plans have disappeared. It was too far from London to have big-town ambitions. Once people found themselves here they either left or dug in to survive. Now they can commute across the Swale. In the eighteenth century there was a set style — man, and indeed woman, kept God in his place. Perhaps that is why so little survives here. God keeps on growing. The castles have all gone, the Saxon abbey sunk almost without trace, the best church and its picturesque cottages fallen into the sea. There is a chill keen wind, good for the ague but bad for the bones. Men build not for looks but to keep out this wind. The women used to knit doorsocks and bodgers, adapt old blankets as under-curtains. Now there is double-glazing. There is more double-glazing here than in Hell. I don't mean Roman Hell. I mean the ice-cold Hell of the Angles, Saxons and Norsemen who truly invented it. Hel, the proud Goddess of the Well and the Worm and the Tree, lives under Sheerness in winter.

In Minster the church must be looked at. There are bits of Roman glaze, and an arch from the foundation of St Sexburga (her name is acknowledged in Donald Attwater's *A Dictionary of Saints*, but only as a sister of Ely's St Ethelreda — more famous as a widow, a divorcee and a virgin than our Kentish queen who was only a widow). Clarence, pickled in Malmsey, is supposed to be the stone-armoured knight; and then there is the tomb of Sir Robert Shurland, killed as prophesied by the skullbone of his horse. He had the nag decapitated as soon as he heard the soothsayer, but years afterwards he encountered the severed head and kicked it, piercing his own artery with poisoned bone.

The Shurland estates are interesting. I have already noticed the castle, in occasionally renewed disrepair since the sixteenth century, and visited from Minster by way of the little road from Pigtail Corner. The Shurlands then their new stallions the Cheynes are as restive as the characters in a Shakespearian Chronicle or at least a soap opera; and I believe there is a curse. Henry the Polygamist honeymooned Anne Boleyn here and one of his multiplicity of poxes got into the sheets and then into the plaster. The walls fell a few years after her head and have not kept decent since.

From Shurland the wise foot steps to Eastchurch, or mine always does, whether by road or gas-pedal, seeking the pub by the fifteenth-century church, and the airborne shades of Churchill and Brabazon who both learned to fly here. Rolls crashed and killed himself in the selfsame acres, and left the world to Royce.

Beyond my uplifted glass, Elmley cement works have vanished and so have the dancing druids who circled beneath the magic trees of its name. East are sunken Warden and Leysdown. Leysdown was holiday camps and chalets, some of them on wheels. The holiday trade is uncertain, but since the place is hideous enough as it is, I pray to Saint Sexburga and Ethelreda that it never becomes a ruin.

My prayer will not be answered, but since writing this I have returned from Warden, home in my time of the Mark 24s, most noble of guns. They told me that the post office used to be called "The Smack Aground", a famous smuggling inn, but again in the eighteenth century. The place is not a shack. I am not a Londoner. This is history.

MEDWAY ITSELF

MEDWAY AIR

Upsky
        the storm comes
Smelling of dogs,
Freshening the gutters,
Sweetening drains.

So
        necklaced in rain
The grass-haired girls
Lose their greensick aroma

While under the weir
Fish with flint noses
Sparkle in holes.

I WAS NEVER easy with the Medway Towns. This is no fault of theirs, but of the uses to which my family put them to when I was a child.

Their main function was as a colander through which to sieve my ego. I would be idling at Meopham, trying to understand quadratic equations or enjoying deponent verbs in my Latin Primer, when my mother would scream to me to catch the next train to Chatham and buy dog meat in Strood. The next train would be already due; it would be heard entering the straight mile at Longfield, but I could catch it if I didn't want my ears boxed, my backside tanned or my legs slapped — that is if I could get my gastric ulcer fastened up in time. I always could.

For adults the train ride is a delight. Today I enjoy the swift surge up to Sole Street past the flat fields of Ediva and the early archbishops, then the subterranean wallow through the landfolds south of Cobham.

In those days it was always foggy or raining. I am afraid that I used to pray to Hitler to bomb the railway track in front of the train. Then I would spend the whole day waiting for God to have me arrested as an Undesirable Alien.

Chatham High Street would look dirty but bright, like an East London suburb, the shops all decorated in ways undoubtedly good for trade, but bad for the ideals of a lad brought up to believe that a business emporium should resemble a church, since the Almighty was undoubtedly a shopkeeper. In fact they were clean but old, the bricks black from river-grime and soot. There were a lot of paper posters in the windows, advertising shoes and sausages, mostly shoes. People wore a lot of shoes in the Medway Towns. Then there were tin placards on the walls as if we were still in the railway station. This would disorientate me.

I would run in distress to the dog meat shop, a raw place, open-ended and chilly — a kind of red iceberg. It was supposed to be selling sheep drowned on the marshes. No sheep drowned today. Sheep drown on Tuesday. I had better try Strood. Strood bought its meat from another marsh. It all came back now. My mother had said Strood but she had told me to get off at Chatham instead of Rochester. She had only given me my busfare from Rochester to Strood or from Chatham to Rochester. I took a bus to Rochester. There would be no drowned sheep in Rochester. Rochester was all red meat and ration cards. I should have to walk to Strood.

The walls of the great cathedral city were of very little interest to a ten-, eleven- or twelve-year-old boy hurrying to buy dog meat. I wore short trousers for most of those years, so my knees looked and felt like dog meat anyway. The keen Medway rain made my head look like submerged fleece, and did nothing for the end of my nose. It was immaterial whether I ran along the High Street or walked around the outside of the wall. I didn't know the town and generally abandoned or boarded buses by the cattle-market, which was my only point of reference. By the time I reached the bridge I was in no mood to contemplate its Roman foundations. I always thought the iron span behind it was ugly, and half of any bridge always lies on the far side of the river. Born in Gravesend, I always thought that anywhere on the far side of a river was as remote as Hong Kong.

Strood had the merit of being Kentish. Maps suggest it rises up hills, supporting ridged rooftops, lofty towers and some steeples. My bit of Strood lay in a heap — no, a cross between a mudpat and a rubbish dump at the bottom, in a nasty mixture of clapboard houses, clapboard public houses and hoardings. There must have been some brick somewhere and some slate — brick with clapboard, clapboard with slate. Such architecture looked perfectly fine to me along that other riverside at Gravesend. Here everything was different, even the wharfage, the cranes and the boats. Even the train was different, though it would be perfectly acceptable once it had returned me from Rochester to Meopham or Strood to Gravesend.

Forgive me, Medway. Kindly local people will recognize I was suffering from small-town parochialism laid on Kentish parochialism in graceful patina. I now know that the four towns and their enclosed ancient villages and expanding modern suburbs do not exist solely to sell me drowned carcasses marked "unfit for human consumption" by daubing them with great blotches of radiant green and mauve paint. I knew it then in summertime when I went swimming at, or just east of, Gillingham Strand.

Rochester must be famous for its castle and cathederal, both at my back on that bridge, its superb High Street with fine buildings, some of them preserving excellent timbers, and its coaching inn, tasteful enough, even if owned today by the sellers of steak. Dickens and Pickwick paced here in joy, and that is quite enough for me. (In those days I was forcibly fed Dickens while the bombs fell, so his approbation was less compulsive.)

The castle has England's tallest Norman keep, and the same Gundulf did his work well when he adapted the early Saxon church and the cathedral into his own master plan. There is much of this King's Engineer's intention about the place, and it stands well behind — and above — time's grey enhancements, the old marble, stained battle standards and regimental colours, and new flowers. The cathedral is too early to be intricate, but like Winchester it wears its simplicity well. Saxon stone and Norman common sense suit me better than all that perpendicular stuff we are supposed to admire, let alone the tracery and arcs-boutants. Ely is all very well, and so is Chartres if you press me to it, but they have nothing so atmospheric as Rochester's crypt. It is an austere Roman hole alongside — or inside — ancient mud. Near the cathedral is Jasper's Gatehouse, more properly College Gate. Jasper is Dickens' influence. He stayed here as well as mentioning it in *Edwin Drood*.

Eastgate House is at last properly cared for, even if it has Dickens' chalet rather oddly installed like a botched dental filling. It was built in

1591 by Sir Peter Buck, a paymaster in the Queen's Navy at Chatham Dockyard.

Further along the High Street, away from the tourist end, there are buildings which have so closed ranks down the years that it is possible to miss their variety. They include work from the sixteenth century, sometimes in oddly transported stone or looted brick and, naturally enough, with frames, beams and rafters of ships' timbers. As in the ceilings of North and Central Devon, it is possible to pick out the worm-borings, the bolt marks and scars and scorches from careenings. Here, in the Rochester "Banks", the timber is more comfortable, though. It was got by honest breakerage along the ladings and in the Royal Dockyard, not lured inshore by a murderer's lantern to be sawn up by Hartland rocks.

This end is called "the Banks" because of its raised footways and foundations to ward off pre-nineteenth-century river-flooding.

Then there are the Friars, Langley House and the Old Hall, the Old Vicarage and Milton Cottage around Boley Hill; Southgate, Priors' Gate House and Manor Canon Row. There were many more things, too, of course. That is true of time everywhere; we are all careless of the past until it is in disrepair. I still prefer Rochester to the lofty hub of Lincoln, though, in spite of its squeamish approach to dog meat.

Chatham is Fort Pitt, Naval Barracks, Engineer's Mess, and the historic Dockyard. I used to sweep past all this on bus and bicycle. Now it is all to be changed. The Dockyard has gone up in layers, over more centuries than the history books can uncover, because the tradition was there before the architecture. The Fleet could lie secure here, be built or repaired with Kentish timber, bolted and armed with iron from the Kentish arsenals and foundries. There was powder-making on the Swale, and fine rope, nail and leather in Chatham itself.

I have noticed elsewhere that the Dockyard used to employ very many thousands of men; and its loss is tragic. The naval presence influenced everything in Chatham, its industry, its shops, its architecture.

I have never visited the Dockyard, only entered it — a fair distinction — to call on ships and messes, generally in a drinking capacity, once to escort a silver cup. My overriding impression was of order. The land's edge and the water's beginnings are very rarely tidy, but the Navy ensures that even the waves are laundered. I have been in docks from the Thames to the Tagus and the Lower Hudson, and indeed in other Navy complexes around Portsmouth, but there is nothing quite like Chatham's barracks or Royal Dockyard.

It largely stopped building soon after the arrival of the ironclads, but instead specialized not only in classified repair-work but the development of weaponry and propulsion units. I mention Chatham's predilection for the *avant garde* in my chapter on regiments and fleets, but the Navy — and Royal Engineers — have innovated a great amount here, from diving bells and early submarines, through the fitting and servicing of the Whitehead torpedo, to atomic propulsion and weaponry. I last saw the Navy in Chatham just a short year ago when I overslept on a train from Victoria and arrived in East Kent in company with a very select band of other gentlemen of the hop and grape. One of them was a sailor who shared my taxi back to civilization, and went in very smartly past his guard-room.

Some places, some pieces of architecture, are so mad as to convince me that I am lost inside a nightmare without a map, presumably hunting dog meat. La Sagrada Familia in Barcelona does not strike me that way, nor even does Mont Juic. Archway in North London does, and so did the "Jezreels" in Gillingham.

The "tower" — not so much a tower as a kind of Arding and Hobbs peddling worn-out psychic fantasy instead of modern furniture — used to stand on open ground near the junction of Chatham Hill and Canterbury Street. It was built in the 1870s by a sect called the Jezreels after the assumed name of its founder, James Jershom Jezreel, formerly White. A Christian Jew and highly successful Medway businessman, he gathered other property owners about himself, the tower, and God. He himself had become the Lord's Sixth Messenger, and was spiritual heir to Joanna Southcott. He claimed immortality but died in 1885, presumably at no great age because he had managed to enlist as a soldier at Chatham as recently as 1875. His wife, "Queen" Esther, was autocratic and spiritual in the tradition of many an earlier Kentish Queen, but the building was never finished. It stood there until quite recently, half open to the sky, tinged with weird vibrations though considerably lower than Babel. Nonetheless, it used to terrorize my bus journeys with my grandmother. Writing about it has been therapeutic. I think it coloured my entire feelings about Medway.

LITERARY KENT

ITEM

Morning: I walk through the harps of spiders,
Swallowing kisses.
The fountains
Undo their flies in the sun:
Do the matelots notice?
The long queues of clerks with the wristy flourish?

Item: one crept after nests in the beds of strangers.
Item: one stayed at home, by the light of T.V.:
"If the screen were lower I'd have licked her navel."
"With money you get all the crumpet you want
And find you don't want it."
Take Wellesley, A.,
The first Duke of Double You:
Bought girls by the bustle-load, acre on acre;
Bequeathed Modern Man his prostatic ache . . .'

"There might be a Cosmic Plan:
Continence would thwart it!"
"Fool,
Could we talk thus of our seminal frenzies
Save overhead booms the National Grid?"

FRANK MORLEY IS very bleak about us. Gravesend is not the most important town geographically or historically; yet it is the epicentre of this little book of mine. Mr Morley tells us, on no evidence at all, that Chaucer's pilgrims made a detour to see it, but he does not propose to follow them. W. W. Jacobs lived there, he says, and that is all. Well, well: I wonder how useful his other information in *Literary Britain* may be taken to be.

I have problems enough without him. If I spread the compasses two miles wider on my map I can write about all sorts of interesting

connections: Morris, Rossetti, Marlowe, Dr Johnson, H. G. Wells —
those names just begin the anti-clockwise stroke of my marginally
enlarged circumference; and in some cases the writers actually set foot
or at least toe within our acres. Then, just a few miles further south,
there are Spenser, Sydney, Wyatt and Tennyson. The mind runs mad.

Dickens is over everything, of course. No one can take him away
from us. We have his honeymoon in Chalk, his boyhood in Rochester
and Chatham, his later life and death at Gadshill Place, his multiply
transplanted Chalet back in Rochester via Cobham Park and Crystal
Palace, and a hundred of etceteras. I doubt if there is one of my secret
places he has not visited, urgently, frequently, and on foot. Local
historians have been so busy with him in detail that we now know who
his father bought cakes from in Chatham, who delivered him letters
from Strood, and sold him shoes, groceries and newspapers at Gadshill,
and who painted his walls and hung them with paper.

Yet Dickens, that most public of artists, illustrates the creative
dilemma in a way which explains why literature occupies two chapters
and not one, why I talk about the writers before mentioning their
writing. Dickens used (used up, I almost bleat) our part of Kent in his
novels; and yet we are not sure of many of the locations in his books.
However certain of place David Lean may have seemed to be in his film
of *Great Expectations*, for example, we do not know whether Pip was
seized by Magwitch in Chalk or Higham Churchyard, or in one of the
churchyards in the Hoo Peninsula. Was Joe Gargery's forge in Forge
Lane, at Chalk, or in Cooling, Higham, or somewhere in Shorne? Was
Miss Havisham's house one of that cluster of mellow red-bricks on
Shorne Village or was it Cooling Court? And was Peggoty's house in
David Copperfield—"that most autobiographical of novels"—inspired
by childhood memories of Portsmouth, something at Broadstairs or—
as is frequently asserted—by the house in the upturned boat along the
north side of the canal path beyond the Gravesend basin? My father took
me there often, and I wrote a poem about it. As one of Frank Richards'
characters said somewhere among billions of words while conducting
an auction, "Valuable piece. Once jewelled in every hole. Jewels gone
— holes still there!" With Dickens, the hole is everywhere. The jewels,
as it happens, remain; but we cannot always identify the place he mined
them from.

Algernon Blackwood was born at the Manor House, Crayford.
William Morris for a time lived at — and Dante Gabriel Rossetti

admired — the Red House at Bexley. Chislehurst is full of too many things for me to mention it merely because of Marlowe (or Ted Willis); and Bromley, where H. G. Wells was born and Mrs Samuel Johnson buried, is just beyond my compass.

Sydney Keyes started life in Dartford and finished it in the Western Desert. He is one of the very best poets of the last war, technically far finer than Alun Lewis (or Alan Ross, Roy Fuller or Lawrence Durrell *then*), and visionary in a way that few can aspire towards, including the much more fashionably dead Keith Douglas. Dartford, dominated by marsh, muck and madhouse as it is, formed the substance of Keyes' melancholy, just as family loss generated it. His death when he was twenty removed something from English Literature that shows no signs of being replaced.

One of my prized possessions is an old Poetry London book called *The Glass Tower*, dating back to Tambimuttu's great days, and published in 1944. It has significant early line-and-wash illustrations by Lucien Freud; but the really dazzling element is the poetry — not quite surreal, not quite Apocalypse, all of it absolutely unique. It is written by Nicholas Moore, who has lived for a long time in St Mary Cray, a see-saw (or eyesore?) of a place for such a poet to sit in.

No one who has even an elementary knowledge of Chaucer's handling of his sources can be at all confident that Kent meant much to his poetry. It is easy to see the young Chaucer as the "poet of gardens" and "Kent as his garden"; but this is to play with words, insofar as they are ever separate from ideas. It is truer, but still playing, to say he was "a gardener of dreams" and that "literature was his garden". He knew Boccaccio, Guido, Dante and Statius quite as well as he knew Kent; and when he sent his imaginary pilgrims among us it was probably more important to be right about the star-dating than over-particular about the route. True, he wrote, or assembled, *The Canterbury Tales*, his last and greatest work, while he was living in Kent, and it eventually found a Kentish printer, but none of the dozen and a half early manuscripts are Kentish.

It is popular to regard him as a "realistic", even a "naturalistic" poet of detail, and compared with Gower he is; but no serious critic would push that contention very far. Indeed, to consider fourteenth-century Kent is to sense the limitation of this theory. Kent lay much nearer to tiny London then. It was neither a garden, nor a heath, nor an orchard; though it boasted all three, and all three were central to the poet's imagination. It was a kind of industrial farm, producing and transporting food, fuel, furniture, domestic utensils and architectural materials, for the metropolis as well as for its own settlements.

Chaucer's Shipman, Merchant, Plowman and Country Gentleman exhibit none of this. Nor do his Reeve (who was also a Carpenter) and his Miller. The last two are there as suitable people to tell lewd stories, for which thank God; and his Plowman is included as a brother to the Poor Priest because Langland had already taught that Plowmen and Poor Priests were Christ-like composites. Kent bristled with manufacturing activity. Chaucer mentioned none of it. It buzzed with trade. Chaucer ignores it. It was full of land workers. Chaucer salutes them and Dartford by scoffing at the Peasants' Revolt. He is as Sydney Keyes says he is: a dreamer, "a true planter of the heart's garden". Still, he rode among us, or over us, and he is one of our three or four greatest poets, the father of modern verse and modern English alike.

Poor Gravesend. Only W. W. Jacobs? He was a fine and now neglected story-teller, yet famous in his day, good for more than *The Beast with Five Fingers*: a locational, lively writer of pithy atmospherics. Far better to make a fuss about him than resurrect Algernon Blackwood. I seem to remember that Walter Allen too lived for a time on the Overcliff and he is a novelist and a critic it would be hard to do without. And what of Maurice Bence who taught history and myself for a score of years at the grammar school, lived round the corner from La Luna Restaurant, which is also on the Overcliff, writing strong radio plays and popular novels under the *nom de plume* of David Bruce? His *Valley Under The Cross*, published by Constable, in the first postwar Oberammergau season, was a massive success.

Thom Gunn was born in Gravesend in 1929, and although he was moved early to Hampstead, he came back to live in Snodland for several years, as a teenager. Gunn is one of the major poets of his generation, justly celebrated, though remotely, since he now spends much of his life in the States, where his reputation is high. He won the 1980 W. H. Smith Award for *Selected Poems*. When I was a student we were suspicious of anything that came from Cambridge, mainly because everything did. Nonetheless, we all knew that his Fantasy Press pamphlet, written when he was twenty-one, was a major achievement. I am less fond of his later work but *Fighting Terms, A Sense of Movement*, and *My Sad Captains* seem to me to represent a substantial as well as a totally original talent. Only Ted Hughes and one other poet come within miles of him, and Hughes was born leagues away.

Keats lay dying in a ship off Gravesend. Robert Gittings has now finally wrapped up the old tradition that he wrote his *Bright Star* sonnet while there, but by establishing that the poet "wrote" it several times and to at least two women, I suppose he just leaves open the possibility that he dusted off a syllable or two before skulking round to do dirty things at Poole. The American ladies, with Aileen Ward sternest among them, won't ever allow that Keats did dirty things, so they may let Gravesend retain its Bright Star, as Charles Armitage Brown always said it should.

One or two other matters lie in the field of general hearsay. Thomas Gray visited Milton Church, and stayed at the vicarage. This much is history. Years ago, one of the unconsidered but greedily consumed trifles that came my way was that he scribbled a poem there. The late Reverend Powell, sometime Rector of Milton, told me that this was the nonce poem to a scold which begins: "Go stint thy clack, for sweet St Charity." Ever sceptical, I checked this information and found it to be so. Alas, I cannot again verify the matter, and such information as my own shelves hold all points in another direction. I used to scrump apples from the vicarage garden. I should have a clearer conscience about it now if I could be certain that one of the Rev. Powell's predecessors had a housekeeper who was rude to "one of England's most quoted poets". Where do I get the inverted commas? To be caught between quotation marks is almost as blushful as being found with stolen fruit.

Richard Burns visited Gravesend for two years, fulfilling a distinguished residency at the Victoria Arts Centre. His presence there, the setting up with John Wilson of the Victoria Press and a host of other ventures, acted as a great catalyst. Other local writers declared themselves, and we are beginning to glimpse the burgeoning of a North Kent "School".

The Medway Poets were already active, based, as their name suggests, in the Medway Towns but often visiting Gravesend. A number of them are specially good in performance. Their whole company, by whatever name, seems quite as lively as Edward Lucie-Smith's celebrated gatherings in the 1950s and '60s; and now John Rice has inaugurated his Society of Kent Authors I expect the landscape to buzz. John Rice, busy all over Kent as entrepreneur and publisher, is a fine poet in his own right.

Jane Austen, and John Wesley, had family connections who shipped themselves abroad from Gravesend. I have already mentioned Fanny D'Arblay's connections with Cliffe, to which must be added Squire Ingoldsby's occasional forays across Sheppey. It is not recorded that Shakespeare actually came to Gadshill. To slightly misapply T. S. Eliot: he could gain more information from a book than most men can find in a library. He probably needed no more than the names Gadshill and Rochester. Surely, the Prince, Poins and Falstaff would have found those places altogether too distant for a jaunt from the Boar's Head if their author had actually visited us?

Wyatt, Tennyson and Sassoon all lived a little too far to the south-east to have been more than visitors; but we are again at a point where Dickens is everywhere. Not just in his house, chalet and underground walkway, or his twice weekly jaunts to Gravesend; but in his daily latter-day scouring of the chalk marshes, the landscapes north to Cliffe and Cooling, and south through Cobham to Luddesdown. He walked about Cobham Park by permission of the Darnleys, and was often at the Leather Bottle; his own Mr Pickwick was there twenty years before Dickens was a regular. He was a writer who could haunt a place long after he had given it literary substance on the strength of a youthful acquaintance. Strangely, he was walking in Cobham Park on the day of his fatal stroke.

In Rochester the great man visited Satis House and used it in *Great Expectations*, and Eastgate House which became the nun's house in *Edwin Drood*. The grounds of Eastgate House now house his chalet from Gad's Hill Place. He paced often about the cathedral and its cloisters, of course, again prominent in *Edwin Drood*; but elsewhere history grows dim. His house in Brook Street, Chatham, is falling into disrepair, as is 2 Ordnance Terrace, where he lived briefly as a child. When I was last there, bold schemes were afoot, but I have heard no more of them and dare not return. He haunts me enough as it is.

KENT AS LITERATURE

LOVE FEAST

My dog used to bring me bones from my dustbin,
Bones with my teethmark, bones chewed by him;
The house was always full of nice clean bones,
Bones in new meat, bones in young women,
Bones that only yesterday had strutted on the hoof;
Yet what could I say to him but, Thanks, silly dog. . . .

The dog is now dead and buried near the dustbin:
No one brings his bones, not a dog not a rat
Even when the rainfall makes a map of his skeleton.
I now have a cat who brings my girlfriend spiders
And lets the paw's intelligence escape on the floor.
Me it brings worms, every day worms
And for my girlfriend spiders, knowing our needs
Are for such small morsels, even in our bed
Where once it laid the tail of a sizeable lizard
And next day the lizard in search of its tail.

I always loved the dog in my garden
In spite of its foolishness, in spite of the bones
(The dog found me girlfriends, sniffing at their bones);
And then I loved the cat in my garden
Weightless, inclement, with see-through eyes of grass.

Until I found that cats in the garden, this in my garden,
Meant for ever after I had gardens in my bed.

I DON'T MEAN Kent, do I? I never meant it. I mean our bit of Kent. Kent at large is all England; and our own few acres scarcely less.

Conrad was not here often, perhaps hardly at all, once he had abandoned the sea. His writing was done all over, and when he came to live in Kent his cottage was much further east; but his stories begin about here, in isolated riverside inns like the Ship and Lobster, or in vessels moored in the Gravesend Hope. Even his Secret Agent rushes from Soho to Greenwich as if to be back towards us, and poor Winnie and Comrade Ossipon steam through us on their suicidal trip to Dover.

With Dickens, Conrad has the largest imagination of any English novelist, and perhaps because he started life as a Russian Pole and then carried it on as a French seaman and English ship's officer — what an apprenticeship — his vision is worldwide. He did not learn English until he began this last stage in his early life, and he always said that every sentence he wrote was a linguistic agony for him. How remarkable (but natural and just) that he should choose our river as the central image of his work. *The Heart of Darkness* begins:

The Nellie, a cruising yawl, swung to her anchor without a flutter of the sails, and was at rest. The flood had made, the wind was nearly calm, and being bound down the river, the only thing for it was to come to and wait for the turn of the tide.

The sea-reach of the Thames stretched before us like the beginning of an interminable waterway. In the offing the sea and the sky were welded together without a joint, and in the luminous space the tanned sails of the barges drifting up with the tide seemed to stand still in red clusters of canvas sharply peaked, with gleams of varnished sprits. A haze rested on the low shores that ran out to sea in vanishing flatness. The air was dark above Gravesend, and farther back still seemed condensed into a mournful gloom, brooding motionless over the biggest, and the greatest, town on earth.

The Director of Companies was our captain and our host. We four affectionately watched his back as he stood in the bows looking to seaward. On the whole river there was nothing that looked half so nautical. He resembled a pilot, which to a seaman is trustworthiness personified. It was difficult to realize his work was not out there in the luminous estuary, but behind him, within the brooding gloom.

Between us there was, as I have already said somewhere, the bond of the sea. Besides holding our hearts together through long periods of separation, it had the effect of making us tolerant of each other's yarns — and even convictions. The Lawyer — the best of old fellows — had, because of his many years and many virtues, the only cushion on deck, and was lying on the only rug. The Accountant had brought out already a box of dominoes, and was toying architecturally with the bones. Marlow sat cross-legged right aft, leaning against the mizzenmast. He had sunken cheeks, a yellow complexion, a straight back, an ascetic aspect, and, with his arms dropped, the palms of hands outwards, resembled an idol. The Director, satisfied the anchor had good hold, made his way aft and sat down amongst us. We exchanged a few words lazily. Afterwards there was silence on board the yacht. For some reason or other we did not begin that game of dominoes. We felt meditative, and fit for nothing but placid staring. The day was ending in a serenity of still and exquisite brilliance. The water shone pacifically; the sky, without a speck, was a benign immensity of unstained light; the very mist on the Essex marsh was like a gauzy and radiant fabric, hung from the wooded rises inland, and draping the low shores in diaphanous folds. Only the gloom to the west, brooding over the upper reaches, became more sombre every minute, as if angered by the approach of the sun.

And at last, in its curved and imperceptible fall, the sun sank low, and from glowing white changed to a dull red without rays and without heat, as if about to go out suddenly, stricken to death by the touch of that gloom brooding over a crowd of men.

Forthwith a change came over the waters, and the serenity became less brilliant but more profound. The old river in its broad reach rested unruffled at the decline of day, after ages of good service done to the race that peopled its banks, spread out in the tranquil dignity of a waterway leading to the uttermost ends of the earth. We looked at the venerable stream not in the vivid flush of a short day that comes and departs for ever, but in the august light of abiding memories. And indeed nothing is easier for a man who has, as the phrase goes, "followed the sea" with reverence and affection, than to evoke the great spirit of the past upon the lower reaches of the Thames. The tidal current runs to and fro in its unceasing service, crowded with memories of men and ships it had borne to the rest of home or to the battles of the sea. It had known and served all the men of whom the nation is proud, from Sir Francis Drake to Sir John Franklin, knights all, titled and untitled — the great knights-errant of the sea. It had borne all the ships whose names are like jewels flashing in the night of time, from the *Golden Hind*

returning with her round flanks full of treasure, to be visited by the
Queen's Highness and thus pass out of the gigantic tale, to the
Erebus and *Terror*, bound on other conquests — and that never
returned. It had known the ships and the men. They had sailed from
Deptford, from Greenwich, from Erith — the adventurers and the
settlers; kings' ships and the ships of men on 'Change; captains,
admirals, the dark "interlopers" of the Eastern trade, and the
commissioned "generals" of East Indian fleets. Hunters for gold or
pursuers of fame, they all had gone out on that stream, bearing the
sword, and often the torch, messengers of the might within the
land, bearers of a spark from the sacred fire. What greatness had not
floated on the ebb of that river into the mystery of an unknown
earth. . . . The dreams of men, the seed of commonwealths, the
germs of empires.

The sun set; the dusk fell on the stream, and lights began to
appear along the shore. The Chapman lighthouse, a three-legged
thing erect on a mud-flat, shone strongly. Lights of ships moved in
the fairway — a great stir of lights going up and going down. And
farther west on the upper reaches the place of the monstrous town
was still marked ominously on the sky, a brooding gloom in
sunshine, a lurid glare under the stars.

"And this also," said Marlow suddenly, "has been one of the
dark places of the earth."

I have quoted at length because Conrad has this river in his bones, and
because London dark at his back becomes a palimpsest of the Congo
his story points towards. This incredible novella, which provides the
motif for T. S. Eliot's *Hollow Men*, is also the literary starting point of
Francis Ford Coppola's great mad film *Apocalypse Now*, with its own
modern Mr Kurtz. The passage I have quoted introduces us to
Marlow, Conrad's *alter ego* and necessary narrative device, his means
of being in and apart from his creation. Not for nothing is Chandler's
great ego intrusion called Marlowe — "Marlowe with an *e*", you will
remember him saying. Chandler went to school in Kent before he
lived in California; and like Conrad he could not write until the ego
had been squeezed from his books and then forced back again.

This stretch of the river is implicit in other of Conrad's stories.
Whenever he speaks of picking up or dropping the pilot, in particular
the North Sea Pilot, he does so at Gravesend. A voyage away from

order towards chaos is nearly always begun by leaving the Thames, in *Youth*, for instance, where "We left London in ballast — sand ballast — to load a cargo of coal in a northern port for Bangkok. . . . We worked out of the Thames under canvas, with a North Sea pilot on board. His name was Jermyn, and he dodged all day long about the galley drying his handkerchief before the stove." Jermyn is a stroke of genius if ever there was. Marlow is again the narrator.

The Brute is one of the best, and oddest, of his short stories. It is again a story within a story, but with Marlow the one who listens and repeats it as Conrad, to us, rather than the one who tells it. It begins in the bar, and then the parlour, of the Three Crows, which I take to be the Three Daws by Gravesend pier. Jermyn is there, again drying his handkerchief by the fire. It is a story about a rogue ship, told by a stranger, interrupted by Jermyn, Marlow and a man called Stonor, and again it concerns fateful events on this part of the river:

> The river pilot boarded us just below Gravesend, and the first words I heard him say were: "You may as well take your port anchor inboard at once Mr Mate. . . ."

After the little girl has been crushed by the chain, swept overboard and drowned,

> dusk fell, then a night black as pitch. . . . I heard a low, mournful hail, "Ship ahoy!" Two Gravesend watermen came alongside. They had a lantern in their wherry. . . . I saw in the light a lot of loose, fair hair down there.

Conrad undoubtedly savoured the tombstone associations that could be resonated by the word Gravesend. There is something villainous in the sound of it. That is why Dick Barton came here, and the villains in many a villainous film, and why Sherlock Holmes makes play with it in *The Sign of Four*, and has the *Esmaralda* wait for Jonathan Small there: a letter from Neville St Clair posted at Gravesend in *The Man With the Twisted Lip*. Holmes also telegraphed here for news of the *Lone Star* in *The Five Orange Pips*. He was near Chatham, too, in *The Golden Pince-Nez*, and Beckenham in *The Greek Interpreter*, but I am straying off course.

Captain Marryat took ship at Chatham, and so did his young friend

Edward Howard in 1808, turning his Medway memories to good account in the early chapters of *Rattlin the Reefer*, published in 1836. This is a fine, early nineteenth-century sea story, and it is stuffed with the sort of retchy realism that escapes many of his more famous imitators:

I found the *Eos* all rigged and strong in the breeze, with the not very agreeable aroma of dock-yard paint. The ship's company was not, however, on board of her. They were hulked on board of the *Pegasus*. A very brief introduction to the officers of the watch, and I was shown down, with my sea-chest, my shore-going trunk, and quadrant, cocked hat etc., to the midshipmen's berth in the hulk. One of the after-guard performed for me the office of gentleman usher. It was a gloomy, foggy, chilly day, and the damp of the atmosphere was mingled with the reeking, dank, animal effluvia that came up, thick and almost tangible, from the filthy receptacle of crowded hundreds.

As I descended into darkness, and nearly felt overpowered by the compound of villainous smells, I was something more than sick at heart. My pioneer, at length, lifted up the corner of a piece of dirty canvas, that screened off a space of about six feet square from the rest of the ship's company. This I was given to understand was the *young gentlemen's* quarters, their dining-room and their drawing-room combined. Even I, who had not yet attained my full growth, could not stand erect in this saloon of elegance. I am stating nothing but literal facts. On an oaken table, still more greasy than the greasy decks over which I had slipped in my passage to this den, stood a flickering, spluttering, intensely yellow candle, of very slender dimensions, inserted in a black quart bottle. Beside it was placed a battered breadbasket, containing some broken biscuit; and a piece of villainously-scented cheese, distinguished by the name of purser's, lay near it, in company with an old, blood-stained, worn-out tooth-brush, and a shallow pewter wash-hand basin, filled with horridly dirty water. For seats round this table there were no other substitutes than various chests of various dimensions.

It is at Chatham that Rattlin meets the beautiful Jemima and receives a love gift from her. By the time he has dropped down river to Sheerness, he finds that she has merely passed him a present given to her by one of his shipmates. At the fight's end he concludes, "whatever a tailor might be, a sailor is no match for a tailor's daughter, born and bred up at Chatham".

Chaucer's pilgrims must have skirted Chatham, crossing the Medway at Rochester. The usual first-night halt on an equestrian pilgrimage was Dartford, the second night always at Rochester, the third generally at Ospringe. Chaucer tells us nothing of this, and Kent does not really get into the narrative at all. Certainly our bit does not, for all Frank Morley's wild words. The stories that the pilgrims tell reach all over the place. The nineteen "links" should, one feels, give us precise glimpses of roadside halts, leafy ways, travelling inns. They do not. For Chaucer, North Kent is a straight line drawn between Southwark and Canterbury. Nearly all of his sharpest natural — as distinct from human — description is an elegant translation, some-times with gloss, of his analogues.

Shakespeare scarcely serves us better. In *King Lear* he has Gloucester wander across us to Dover, solely because Shakespeare knows there is a cliff there. Nothing else, except perhaps Cordelia's invasion can be plotted on any map, let alone ours. It would be flattering but pointless to imagine that one of the mad heath scenes is ours. In fact, I think Charles Lamb is right when he suggests the entire play happens inside some infinite skull.

With *Henry IV Part One* we are on more familiar ground. The fine inn-yard scene at Rochester scarcely does us credit, though:

> 2ND CARRIER: Peas and beans are as dank here as a dog . . . I think this be the most villainous house in all London Road for fleas. I am stung like a tench.
> 1ST CARRIER: Like a tench! By the mass, there's ne'er a King christen could be better bit than I have been since the first cock!
> 2ND CARRIER: Why, they will allow us ne'er a jordan, and then we leak in the chimney, and your chamber-lye breeds fleas like a loach.

Shakespeare's invention, and it is only invention, gives us lousy inns, serving bad food and too mean to provide their guests with chamber pots, with the most disastrous consequences to the chimney. When the action moves up to Gad's Hill he treats us to some of his most striking comic invention, however, though Gad's Hill is no more than a name to him, a place where a highwayman may hold up travellers.

The fickleness of his brilliance (if the phrase is allowable) can be seen in the fact that one of the characters also becomes called Gadshill. The bard's contact with us is as opportunist as Chaucer's, even if he really did base Falstaff upon Sir John Oldcastle of Cooling.

So we must be thankful for Harrison Ainsworth, Bram Stoker, and Charles Dickens. In *David Copperfield*, *Edwin Drood*, and above all the marvellous opening chapters of *Great Expectations*, our own man does us proud. Mr Pickwick studies benign matters among us, too; and whenever the master mentions the river, we must remember, *always*, that it is *our* river. *Our Mutual Friend* begins where our own journey began in Chapter Two. I nearly said we travel in good company, until I remember the third traveller in the boat . . .

a rotten stain there which bore some resemblance to the outline of a muffled human form, coloured . . . as though with diluted blood.

Our Mutual Friend was Dickens' fourteenth and last completed full-length novel, and much of it was written at Gad's Hill Place, amidst the ghosts of murderers and highwaymen, and men from the hulks. Something of his own fascinated unease with the squalor of the London Thames is shown in the exchange between Lizzie and her father:

"It's my belief you hate the sight of the very river."
"I — I do not like it, Father."
"As if it wasn't your living! As if it wasn't meat and drink to you!"

Dickens was a workaholic. The whole drab but exciting world was meat and drink to him, and he died of it here at Gad's Hill just a few years later.

Of my own books, *Grandad with Snails* shifts between Northfleet, Gravesend, Hawkhurst and Meopham; and *A World of Men* begins on the Denton and Cliffe Marshes. *In Step With A Goat* deals with local territorial experience, but ranges far in the way of soldiering. Only *There's A War On* is entirely local, a community novel that wrestles with the folkscape of Gravesend, Northfleet, Thong, Bradditch and the fields around Nurstead and the Tollgate. As it happens, I never finished with Austin Gorman, Sonny Drisedale or the Stacks, and with

Sylvia Gorman least of all. Their publisher reminded me of this only the other day. Before he died, the great local writer, Maurice Bence, complained of a long loose end. I must tidy it up before my next tutorial with him.

I don't think much of my poetry could have happened without a few local acres. In a B.B.C. book called *Writers on Themselves*, I see I broadcast a talk called *Killing The Lightning*:

> At some stage in our life a whole landscape sows itself in our mind, so that when we close our eyes that is the landscape we return to. In it we scrump apples, pedal bicycle-races, smell bonfires, make love, see death. . . . Well, the landscape that sowed itself in my head, the world that was to become my inner life for ever, was the small area that had been walked on by lightning for me that afternoon.

I was talking about the area around Nurstead Church. I have made a second space in France since, but my mind is in Nurstead often.

SELECT BIBLIOGRAPHY

Astbury, A. K.: *Estuary*, Carnforth Press, 1980

Bennet, A. S.: *Us Bargemen*, Meresborough Books, 1980

Bignell, Alan: *Kent Villages*, Hale, 1975

Chalklin, C. W.: *Seventeenth-Century Kent*, John Hallewell, 1978

Church, Richard: *Kent*, Hale, 1948

Clout, Norman: *Medway Memories*, Meresborough Books, 1980

Coombe, Derek: *The Bawleymen*, Pennant Books, 1979

Devereux, Paul and Thomson, Ian: *The Ley Hunter's Companion*, Thames and Hudson, 1979

Dickens, Charles: *Dicken's Dictionary of the Thames*, London, 1892, reprinted Taurus Press, 1972

Fearnside, W. G.: *Thames and Medway*, London, 1830

Finch, William Coles: *Watermills and Windmills*, Arthur Cassell, 1976

Graves, Tom (ed.): *Dowsing and Archaeology*, Turnstone Books, 1980

Guy, John: *Kent Castles*, Meresborough Books, 1980

Hall, S. C. and S. M.: *The Book of the Thames*, London 1859; new edition: Charlotte James, 1976

Harker, Sydney: *The Book of Gravesham*, Barracuda Books, 1979

Jessup, Frank W., *A History of Kent*, Phillimore, 1978

K.A.H.R.S.: *Kent Airfields in the Battle of Britain*

Kightly, Charles: *Strongholds of the Realm*, Thames and Hudson, 1979

Major, Alan: *A New Dictionary of Kent Dialect*, Meresborough Books, 1981 *et seq.*

Pratt Boorman, H. R.: *Kent Our Country*, Kent Messenger, 1979

Rootes, Andrew: *Front Line County*, Hale, 1980

Shrapnel, Norman: *A View of the Thames*, Collins, 1977

Smithers, D. W. *Castles in Kent*, John Hallewell, 1980

Turnor, Reginald. *Kent in the Fifties*, John Hallewell, 1978

Webb, William: *Kent's Historic Buildings*, Hale, 1977

West, Jenny: *The Windmills of Kent*, Skilton and Shaw, 1979

Wright, Nicholas: *The Bump*, R.A.F. Biggin Hill, 1980

INDEX